D0420276

Better business writing

HF
5726
B68

Better business writing

WILLIAM H. BONNER, Ph.D.

Professor and Chairman
Department of Business Education and Office Management
Tennessee Technological University

 1974

75184

RICHARD D. IRWIN, INC.   *Homewood, Illinois   60430*
Irwin-Dorsey International, London, England   WC2H 9NJ
Irwin-Dorsey Limited, Georgetown, Ontario   L7G 4B3

© RICHARD D. IRWIN, INC., 1974

All rights reserved. No part of this publication may be
reproduced, stored in a retrieval system, or transmitted,
in any form or by any means, electronic, mechanical,
photocopying, recording, or otherwise, without the prior
written permission of the publisher.

First Printing, February 1974

ISBN 0-256-01545-7
Library of Congress Catalog Card No. 73–89107
Printed in the United States of America

To
Martha Sue

Preface

THE ABILITY to communicate effectively is so important that everyone should strive constantly to improve his communication skills. Because no two people react exactly alike to any given situation and because no person reacts exactly the same way to similar situations that arise at different times, you cannot expect to communicate *perfectly*. You can, though, improve your skills so that you communicate effectively. A significant portion of today's business communication is through the medium of writing. One of your goals, therefore, should be to raise the quality of your writing to the highest level possible. This book has been written to help you reach that goal.

The information in this book has been carefully arranged to allow you to begin writing business letters after studying only *four* chapters that introduce basic principles, format, and appropriate writing style. The principles are reviewed, applied, and illustrated through the text of the other chapters and through the review exercises that follow each chapter.

So that maximum time can be devoted to composing letters and reports, only one format has been included in the text. That format is widely used and is as good as any other. For you who wish to vary the physical presentation of your messages, additional formats are presented in the reference section of this book. The reference section also contains other helpful writing aids such as address forms for special people (churchmen, government officials, and others) and a review of mechanics (punctuation, expression of numbers, word choices, and so on).

This book is organized so that you begin with some of the easiest-to-write letters (favorable replies to inquiries) in Chapter 5 and progress steadily through more challenging types. In Chapter 9 you reach those that are perhaps the most difficult to write (the letters that contain such disappointing news as refusing an important request). Chapter 10 presents a review of the basic types of letters that are discussed in Chapters 5 through 9. Additional review is provided by the special exercises on writing style at the end of each chapter and by the problems that follow the chapters on form letters and dictating.

The problems at the ends of the chapters are the types that you—a college student—will have adequate background for handling, and they require the application of the basic principles that you can use later when writing letters to solve actual problems.

Because internal messages comprise such a large portion of the communications for any group, they are treated in various sections of the book. Internal messages are *emphasized* in the chapters that pertain to personnel administration, informal reports, and formal reports. The fundamentals in Chapters 1 through 4 apply equally to internal and external communications. The information on public relations messages in Chapter 6 is just as important for communicating with persons within the group as with those outside. Some sections of the chapters on form letters and oral communication are especially geared to internal communications.

Letters about employment are extremely important, and they are perhaps the first actual business letters that some college students will write. The chapter on securing employment contains information on not only application letters and résumés but also other letters relating to employment. Among these are letters confirming interviews, following up interviews, accepting offers, declining offers, and resigning.

The ability to dictate well is a requirement for success in an executive position. To help you meet this requirement, suggestions for dictating effectively are presented *after* the final chapter on writing letters. As you must first know how to compose a letter before you dictate, this sequence of chapters is the logical arrangement.

Chapter 11 contains helpful information on producing multiple copies of high-quality messages in a minimum of time and at a reasonable cost. These factors have contributed to the great amount of attention that executives are giving to the popular *word-processing* concept.

This entire book is designed to help you appreciate the fundamentals of communication and thus to enhance the quality of your business writing.

I am very grateful for all of the help that I have received in writing this book. I am indebted to the two reviewers of the manuscript—Professors Carolyn Allen, Pasco-Hernando Community College, and Earl A. Dvorak, Indiana University—for their constructive criticisms.

I express appreciation to my secretary, Dorothy B. Frizzell, whose ability to typewrite the manuscript expertly while at the same time deciphering my longhand scribbling and rough draft typewriting helped make the writing of this book a pleasure.

I give a very special note of gratitude to my wife, Martha Sue, for her encouragement throughout this writing project and for the helpful suggestions she made as she read parts of the text and examined the illustrations.

January 1974   WILLIAM H. BONNER

Contents

1

The communicating process

COMMUNICATING may be defined as "sharing information or an emotion." This "sharing" is a two-way process. Causing another person to understand the information that you transmit or the way you feel about a particular situation is only one part. His letting you know that he understands the information or the feeling that you have transmitted completes the two-way process.

Sometimes communication is accomplished easily, yet at other times the process is difficult to complete. And sometimes when the process has been completed, some question exists in the mind of the sender or of the receiver of the message (and possibly in the minds of both) that communication has actually taken place.

Mediums

Communicating can be done through various mediums. A wink, a smile, or a handshake may very well convey the information or the emotion that is to be "shared." For example, a smile or a wink can, under certain circumstances, tell a person that you approve of what he is doing. A handshake may express a congratulatory feeling better than words do.

Suppose that you are watching a tennis match and the competition is very keen. The person you are "rooting" for wins. Your rushing onto the court and firmly shaking the winner's hand tells him clearly that you are happy about his success. Such a handshake may convey your feeling of happiness much better than would the word *congratulations* or any other oral expression. The winner's smile, no matter how modest, may be the best medium or vehicle that he can use to let you know he understands your feeling of elation. Thus, the two of you have communicated. The two–way process has been completed.

A grief-stricken person seldom derives much consolation from any word that is spoken or written, regardless of the great degree of sincerity that is felt by the person who attempts to console. The person in distress does, however, receive some degree of consolation from knowing that some friend sympathizes with him because of his unfortunate circumstances. A "warm" handshake or some other simple gesture such as placing a hand firmly on the person's shoulder may do more than words (spoken or written) could do to express sympathy or to provide some consolation.

A person who is making a speech or an oral report may have his confidence reinforced by some listener who smiles, winks, or nods his head in such a way that indicates he approves the manner in which the oral presentation is being made. Such a gesture is especially helpful to the speaker if he believes that the person making the gesture is competent to judge the quality of the oral presentation. Using *words* as a medium of expressing approval would not be appropriate in an instance such as this, yet these other mediums can be used and are quite effective. The speaker may complete his part of the two–way communicating process by relaxing or by exhibiting greater self–confidence or enthusiasm. He can exhibit these characteristics through a change in the tone of his voice or a change in his posture.

The mediums or vehicles that are used in communicating are so numerous that an attempt to mention all of them would be a mammoth task indeed, even if completing such a task were possible. An awareness that various mediums are used in a large variety of ways to complete a communicating process is, however, important.

The need to communicate

Everyone must communicate; a person cannot survive as an isolated individual. A normal human desire and genuine need is to "share" joys, successes, failures, and frustrations. Business people have occasions for "sharing" feelings of almost all classifications. While perhaps only a minor portion of the business situations are as dramatic as those mentioned in the preceding paragraphs, some of the frequently encountered business situations do cause some of the people involved to become rather highly emotional. Errors that are made through oversights or negligence that create disappointments, major inconveniences, and great financial losses cause irate tempers and other displays of emotions that require the use of the very best communication skills to restore goodwill.

Fortunately, a high percentage of business communications concern conditions that are pleasant. Some of the business situations create highly elated feelings; most of them, however, are on an even–tempered level. Some may be classified as *routine* in nature.

A successful business enterprise must be staffed by adequately trained personnel. These workers must obtain materials for producing, handling, or selling the products or services the enterprise provides. Only through effective communication can the necessary personnel be employed, and only through effective communication can they perform the duties necessary to make the enterprise survive.

Any consumer, whether he is employed, retired, disabled, or wealthy enough to live a life of leisure, must engage in some business communication in order to exist.

Business executives have known for many years that the ability to communicate effectively is indispensable in business activities. They know that job competency, even with the proper attitude, is of limited value if the worker cannot demonstrate his competency and proper attitude through the various communicating mediums, which include gestures, speaking, listening, reading, and *writing*.

Gestures—winks, smiles, slaps on the back, and so on—do

much to portray goodwill and help stimulate people to perform at a level that is near their potential capabilities. Conversely, frowns, pounding on desk tops, and other displays of negative attitudes destroy goodwill and affect the morale of workers to such an extent that business transactions are delayed and productive activity is reduced below the level that is financially profitable.

Requirements for communicating effectively

To communicate effectively, you must have the right attitude. The person transmitting a message must remember that at least two people are always involved. The transmitter must also remember that the receiver of his message is the most important person in the world—so far as that person is concerned. The receiver of your message—regardless of his social status, financial condition, political affiliation, or level of intelligence—is a human being who deserves to be treated with human dignity. No matter how modest he may be, he wants to be respected. You must never intentionally embarrass him by speaking or writing caustic or accusing remarks or by making statements that he cannot readily understand.

To be an effective communicator, you must be fair minded.

A reasonable command of the language you speak is essential to good communication processes. Complete mastery of the English language is impossible; but the ability to write, to speak, to listen, and to read proficiently is within the grasp of the users of this book. You can enhance the quality of your business writing by studying the following chapters and the reference section of this book. You may, of course, get further help by referring to any one of many grammar books or handbooks for office workers.

To be a good communicator, you must have an adequate vocabulary. You must be familiar with the terms that are used in connection with the business transactions you handle so that you can transmit your ideas in a manner that is appropriate for the receiver of your message and so that you can interpret properly the ideas you receive by listening or by reading. Strive always to increase your knowledge of words, especially those that pertain to your field of work.

A thorough knowledge of the background of the problem or situation that leads to the necessity for communicating is essential for effective communication. This knowledge enables you to understand or to interpret properly the statements that are made about the particular situation. Because a sender of actual business messages usually has an opportunity to become well acquainted with the facts involving the transaction, he can prepare those messages much more easily than he can prepare good messages for simulated cases. A good imagination is, nevertheless, a valuable asset to the communicator in any situation—real or simulated.

Good communication requires open–mindedness of all the people involved—the senders and the receivers. You must be willing to see other people's points of view in order to get them to understand your feelings. Thorough mastery of the mechanics of communication, regardless of how important they are, is useless to the person who has closed his mind to any set of circumstances.

To communicate well, you must be adaptable and eager to break bad habits. Everyone picks up bad habits from other people. The tendency to imitate to some extent seems to be a natural characteristic of human beings. People learn to talk by imitating. Because talking is learned in this manner, accents, pronunciations, word choices, and idiomatic expressions are developed to coincide with those that are used by other people within the same environment. As you associate with more and more people, you become aware of many of the bad habits you have acquired by the natural inclination to imitate. You do not become aware of some of your bad habits, however, unless another person calls your attention to them. Many habits of using certain expressions and of organizing oral and written messages need to be revised.

When breaking a habit of any kind, you must go through three stages: (1) You must become aware that the habit exists and that there is a need for change. (2) You must *want* to break the habit. (3) You must put forth the effort required to break the habit.

Time, diligence, and patience are required to break habits that affect your manner of communicating (speaking, *writing*, listening, and reading) .

Business messages

Business personnel, as well as all other people, use combinations of communication mediums—words, facial expressions, voice inflections, and other gestures—to convey ideas and to acknowledge ideas from other people. An awareness of the uses that are made of these various mediums is essential to effective communication.

Perhaps the communication mediums that can elicit immediate responses are more effective than words that are spoken or written. Because of the current large volume of business and the great geographic area over which transactions must be made, a major portion of business communications must be completed by only one medium—*words* (spoken or written) . Words that are spoken by communicators in a face-to-face setting are accompanied with the previously mentioned mediums (gestures, facial expressions, and so on) and afford immediate responses. Because of the support of these mediums, less care is required in choosing the words that are used in face-to-face conversation than those that are transmitted by some vehicle such as a telephone or a television. The words transmitted by telephone can be chosen with less care than can those that are transmitted by television, because the response in telephone communication is much quicker than in television. The longer the delay in response to a spoken word, the greater care the speaker should exercise in selecting the words that he uses. Carefully chosen words that are spoken clearly and in the proper tone are usually quite effective in communicating.

The *written word* is perhaps the medium or vehicle that is most difficult to use in communication. There are two reasons that the *written word* is more difficult to use than any other medium: (1) It has no support, such as gestures and tone of voice; it alone conveys the emotion of the sender. (2) The delay in response to a written word is greater than is the response to any other communication vehicle.

The use of the written word will, nevertheless, continue to play a vital role in business communication. Even if the time and cost would permit the use of the spoken word for all business communications, many messages would be transmitted in writing so that an accurate record of those messages could be maintained in the files of the senders and of the receivers. Written messages are organic parts of the records of individual citizens, businesses, industries, and governments. The ability to communicate effectively by writing is, therefore, essential for the success of anyone in business. This ability increases in importance with the increasing volume of necessary letters, memorandums, and reports.

The volume of written business messages has reached such proportions that it has given rise to the new *word-processing* concept, which is a widely supported effort to speed up the production of these messages, to enhance their effectiveness, and to minimize costs.

Opportunities for those who communicate well

To be successful, you must have a thorough understanding of your job. You must understand the methods and procedures to be followed to perform the functions for which you are responsible, and you must understand the relationships that exist between the functions you perform and those of the entire organization by whom you are employed.

While an understanding of your job and the factors affecting it is necessary, such understanding is not enough. To succeed, you *must be able to communicate well* with your associates in order to utilize your knowledge and that of other people.

Many opportunities exist for the people who excel in communicating—receiving (listening and reading) and transmitting (speaking and writing). The people who can comprehend what they hear and what they read and can follow directions are much more productive workers than those people who are not good receivers of the messages that are transmitted to them. The good listeners and readers are, therefore, given more responsibilities and, of course, remuneration commensurate with their responsibility and productivity.

The people who excel in *transmitting* messages have many opportunities that are not available to those who transmit less ably. The workers who can organize their thoughts well and can present them well orally by choosing words carefully, enunciating clearly, and speaking in proper tone of voice with appropriate gestures are the ones who are chosen for supervisory or management-level jobs. They can give instructions that can be followed accurately, and they help maintain the proper attitudes and the high level of morale essential for satisfactory working conditions among all of the employees.

The supervisory and management-level employees who can present informative speeches in an interesting manner can do much to sell themselves and to strengthen public relations for their organizations. These people, therefore, have especially good opportunities to advance to higher–level, higher–paying jobs within their present organizations; and they are in demand for better jobs that become available in other organizations. Good speakers are genuine assets to their communities and to their professions in general as well as to the organizations that employ them.

Strive constantly to improve your ability to convey your thoughts and feelings to individuals and to groups.

Because a major portion of business information is transmitted through the medium of written words, the people who can convey their ideas and feelings well by writing have distinct advantages over those who do not excel in this phase of communication. Thousands of business letters, memorandums, and reports must be written every day. These messages must be written well in order to achieve the purposes for which they are used.

Business messages must be written accurately, and they must be written in the proper tone. They must also be written at the most appropriate times. So that the writer can perform his other duties at the designated times, he must be able to write good business letters, memorandums, and reports in a minimum of time.

The job candidates who can write well are preferred by employers, and the employees who write well are given preference over others for promotions to higher–level jobs. The ability to write well and to write rapidly is so important that you can justify spending a great deal of time improving your writing skills.

Meeting the challenges of writing

Because written messages play a vital role in today's business transactions and because the ability to write well is essential for business success, you should be enthusiastic about the challenge to enhance the quality of your business writing. Regardless of how well you write now, you can improve your writing ability. To help you meet that challenge, suggestions, principles, and illustrations are presented in the chapters that follow. You can adapt these suggestions and principles to your own writing without altering your basic style. You do want your writing to reflect *your* personality.

Perhaps no such thing as a *perfect message* exists. This statement is true partially because no two persons react exactly alike in any given set of circumstances and because no person reacts in the same manner day after day. Always write your letters, memorandums, and reports so that they will be as nearly perfect as you can make them. As you write, you can, of course, logically assume that your reader has normal intelligence and can interpret well the information and the emotions that you do a good job of presenting.

The information in the following chapters pertains to the *transmitting* phase of communicating. A major portion of the material in this book pertains to the writing of business letters as letters are used to transmit a large percentage of business messages. Considerable attention is also given in Chapters 13 through 17 to communicating orally and to writing memorandums and reports.

Questions for discussion

1. How can silence coupled with the absence of gestures and facial expressions be a medium of communication?

2. What are some of the communication mediums that were not mentioned in this chapter?

3. What are the chief hindrances to effective listening?

4. What steps can a person take to improve his ability to communicate?

5. What are some of the fastest ways of transmitting written messages?

2

Some principles of letter writing

COMMUNICATING can be easy when the process is limited to such simple symbols and vehicles as smiles, frowns, handshakes, and pats on the back which achieve immediate responses. The process becomes rather complex, though, when the communicating procedures are confined to written words with delays of several days in the response or feedback.

Modern–day business transactions involve such vast geographic areas that a very large proportion of business communication must be done by written words. As a business employee, you will have to decide whether or not a message should be written. Often this decision will be easy to make; for example, you may receive a letter that asks for a reply. The reply will seem appropriate to you; therefore, your decision to write a letter will be extremely easy to make. Other decisions that will be equally easy to make will involve such matters as ordering merchandise and inquiring about some product, as well as numerous similar situations.

The letters you will write in these cases can be written easily and rapidly.

Letters that are written because of some delicate problem in human relations require a high degree of skill and finesse. No formula can be devised for writing these letters. A skillful letter writer does, however, have guiding principles that he can use by adapting them to the specific situations with which he is working.

He realizes that *the perfect* letter has not yet been written; but he knows that by applying sound principles to solving the problem he faces, he can more nearly "approximate" the ideal letter than he could by using a "hit-or-miss" method of communicating. A skillful letter writer, when approaching a letter–writing task, is fully cognizant of the fact that he is writing to a *live* human being who is sensitive (but, hopefully, not hypersensitive) and who uses his thinking powers in much the same general way as does the writer.

To help you enhance the quality of your business letters, these 15 principles are introduced in this chapter:

1. Write promptly.
2. Determine the purpose of the letter.
3. Keep your reader in mind and anticipate his mood.
4. Make decisions before you write.
5. Begin with good news.
6. When you cannot do what the reader would like you to do, tell him *first* what you *can* do.
7. Economize on words.
8. Write as you talk.
9. Make your letters interesting.
10. Omit obvious statements.
11. When you must tell the reader something he already knows, subordinate the "telling."
12. Remember that your letter represents you.
13. Say "thank you" only *after* something has been done.
14. End with something pleasant and specific.
15. Make sure that the reader knows the next step that is to be taken.

The principles on this list, which is by no means exhaustive, will be repeated and discussed as they apply to numerous circumstances that appear in this textbook.

1. WRITE PROMPTLY. Promptness in writing letters is essential. Because your letters represent you and are a significant factor in helping you create a good impression, you must write promptly those letters needed for some particular situation. People want to transact business with others who are alert and energetic. Project a good image by writing promptly.

Ordinarily a letter that calls for a reply should be replied to within twenty-four hours from the time of its receipt. Obviously, such prompt replies are not always feasible. For example, the information needed for a reply may not be available for three days. In most such instances waiting three days to reply would be the appropriate thing to do. If, though, the information needed for your reply will not be available for a longer time (perhaps two weeks), a short letter should be written stating that another letter containing the desired information will be mailed on a specified date.

A thorough understanding and appreciation of the principles discussed in this chapter will help you improve your letter-writing ability so that you can write effective letters promptly.

2. DETERMINE THE PURPOSE OF THE LETTER. So that you can write clearly, concisely, and interestingly, ask yourself, "Why am I writing this letter?" When you are writing to *thank* someone for something that he has done, begin your letter with that note of gratitude. Such expressions as these may be used:

> I thank you for writing to me about the special sale that will begin on October 18.

> Thank you for inviting me to speak to your group on Friday, August 22.

> Your mailing the pencils so promptly is very much appreciated.

When you are requesting information, determine the specific questions that you wish to have answered. Many letters have more than one purpose. Before you begin to write a letter of this type, you must decide the order in which you will arrange the contents of your letter. Perhaps the item that will be of greatest interest to the reader should be written first. Other considerations will also have to be made. Additional factors are presented later in this chapter.

By all means, know the *reason* you are writing before you attempt to write a letter of any type.

3. KEEP YOUR READER IN MIND AND ANTICIPATE HIS MOOD. The reader of your letter is the *most important person in the world—* so far as he is concerned. This statement is true regardless of the

reader's social position, family background, employment status, political standing, or educational background. Your reader is human. As a human being, he deserves to be treated fairly and tactfully.

The better you know your reader, the easier it is for you to write to him. When you know a good deal about his background, you can judge rather well the vocabulary that will be appropriate for him. Knowing something of the experiences he has had concerning the situation about which you are writing will help guide you in determining the tone you should use. If you know that he has a special liking for a particular letter style, you may conceivably have your letter typed in that style.

Perhaps one of the best things you can do to evaluate your letter is to ask yourself before placing it into the envelope, "How would *I* feel if *I* received this letter?"

4. MAKE DECISIONS BEFORE YOU WRITE.   From time to time you will realize that a letter must be written, but you will not know what to write because you must first "ponder the situation." In such cases refrain from writing anything until you have done all the "pondering" you wish to do.

When you grant a request, grant it cheerfully. Decline any request that you cannot grant cheerfully. When you must decline, do so firmly yet courteously.

Suppose that you have been asked to supply some information that you may hesitate to release at this particular time. Study the situation as thoroughly as you need to before you decide whether you will grant the request or whether you will decline it. If you decide to grant the request, you have an easy letter to write. If you decide to decline, however, you must use a little more finesse in writing the letter. You must be thoroughly aware of the possible consequences of your decision and be ready to accept them before you start to write.

Always decide the course of action you will take *before* you begin to write a letter.

5. BEGIN WITH GOOD NEWS.   When you can tell the reader something that he wants to know, begin your letter with the good news. There is no better way to begin. If you are replying to a letter, the reader, when he sees the envelope, will think about the type of information he hopes to read. By starting your letter with that information—provided the information is pleasant news—

the reader will be pleased and will read the remainder of the letter with a receptive attitude.

Never waste words in getting started. Participial beginnings and the prepositional phrase beginnings are too slow and wordy. You should never use a beginning such as the examples that follow:

Referring to your letter . . .

Concerning our agreement . . .

Pursuant to your request . . .

In reply to your letter . . .

In reference to your inquiry . . .

In regard to your . . .

The frequently used beginning "Thank you for . . ." is ineffective in most letters. "Thank you . . ." is an appropriate beginning only for those letters that are written for the primary purpose of *thanking* the reader for a favor.

The *beginning* of your letter is the most important part.

6. WHEN YOU CANNOT DO WHAT THE READER WOULD LIKE YOU TO DO, TELL HIM FIRST WHAT YOU CAN DO. Sometimes the letter writer must say NO. Always catering to the whims of individuals cannot be expected. When you must say NO, you should begin by mentioning what you *can* do for the reader. The thing that you can do will, of course, depend on the situation about which you are writing. You may offer to send a substitute, you may offer to provide a service at some time other than the date for which the service is requested, or you may recommend another source for the desired product or service.

Somewhere in your letter, you should explain the reason for not complying with the request; but by your preceding that explanation with a cordial offer to do something else appropriate for the reader, he will more readily accept your explanation without the loss of goodwill.

Telling the reader *first* what you *can* do is extremely important. References to this principle are made frequently throughout this textbook.

7. ECONOMIZE ON WORDS. A letter should be long enough to be courteous, to cover the topic adequately, and to be written in an

interesting style. A well–written, concise letter might very well be longer than one full page; but any word that does not enhance the quality of the letter should be omitted. *Length* is not a good criterion for judging the quality of a letter.

The use of excess words not only detracts from the effectiveness of a letter; it also wastes time for the dictator, the transcriber, and the reader. Redundant expressions and "wordy" phraseology must, therefore, be excluded from good letters. Some examples of redundant and "wordy" phraseology with suggestions for improvement follow:

Say	*Instead of saying*
a long time *or* a long period	a long period of time
to select *or* for selecting	for the purpose of selecting
is on page 6	can be found on page 6
a $5 check *or* a check for $5	a check in the amount of $5
because	due to the fact that
please send	I should like to order
for October	for the month of October
we can	we are able
as *or* because	inasmuch as

More is said about word economy in Chapter 4, "Writing Style," and in the discussion of other principles presented in this chapter.

8. WRITE AS YOU TALK. With a few minor exceptions, the wording of your letter should be the same as that of your oral message if you had an opportunity to talk with the receiver of your letter. The tone, the vocabulary, and the organization of your letter should parallel that of your oral comments.

Here are a few minor exceptions to this principle of writing as you talk:

a. You have an opportunity to edit what you write. Your sentences will, therefore, probably be of a slightly higher level of accuracy than your oral statements. Good grammar is needed for oral communication, but a major portion of a very intelligent conversation is carried on with sentence fragments. Because the writer has an opportunity to edit his letter, the written message should not contain a sentence fragment or a construction that is not grammatical.

b. Because of tradition, most letters contain a salutation and a complimentary close. These parts of the letter are perhaps equivalent to, but are different from, the usual oral greeting and parting remarks.

A person who would use such a remark as "Dear Mr. Hayes" instead of the usual remarks such as "Good morning" or "How do you do?" when initiating an oral conversation would be classified as *odd* or *eccentric*. A person would seem to be equally odd who would use "Sincerely yours" or some other familiar letter ending instead of "Goodbye," or "So long," "See you later," or some other frequently used parting remark when leaving the presence of another person.

Just as tradition binds us to some degree in fashions for the clothing we wear and the automobiles we drive, tradition governs to some extent the mechanics of up–to–date business letters.

c. When communicating orally, you have gestures, tone of voice, facial expressions, and immediate feedback to help guide you in transmitting ideas. Because words form your only vehicle in written communication, you must be somewhat more careful in choosing words and in constructing sentences and paragraphs than is necessary in oral communication.

9. MAKE YOUR LETTERS INTERESTING.   Frequently, letters are written to people who are not obligated to read them. Many recipients will, as a matter of courtesy or curiosity, read letters that are clear even though the content is of no interest to them. Other readers, though, will not read letters that do not directly concern their welfare unless the letters are written in an interesting style.

To help insure that your letters will be read and to help you make a good impression on your reader, write as interestingly as you can. Applying the principles presented in this chapter will help you make your letters interesting to the reader. A thorough study of Chapter 4, "Writing Style," will provide further help in making your letters interesting.

10. OMIT OBVIOUS STATEMENTS. Omit such expressions as "I have received your letter," "You will find the enclosed copy of the brochure you requested," "Please find the enclosed check for $28," or "I should like to take this opportunity to write you about our high–speed drill."

When your reply to a letter is well written, the reader will know that you have received his letter. Not only is such an expression as "I have received your letter" ridiculous, it is also a time-wasting element for the dictator, the transcriber, and the reader. A person who is intelligent enough to read your letter is also intelligent enough to find any enclosure that is enclosed properly. Do not risk embarrassing yourself and insulting your reader by asking him to "Please find the enclosed. . . ." When you are writing about a high-speed drill or any other product or idea, you are obviously taking that opportunity.

Obvious statements should be omitted.

11. WHEN YOU MUST TELL THE READER SOMETHING HE ALREADY KNOWS, SUBORDINATE THE "TELLING." Busy people make many assignments and requests to many different people through many different mediums on many different dates. They cannot be expected to remember the exact details—dates, mediums of requesting or assigning, persons to whom requests or assignments were made, or the procedures used in making the request or assignment. The person complying with the request or completing the assignment will do the receiver of his letter a favor by referring to the pertinent details. These references, however, must be subordinated.

Instead of writing "You wrote to me on October 16 and asked me to make a list of the professional journals in our company library," you may write "Here is the list of professional journals in our company library that you asked me to make when you wrote to me on October 16" or "The list of professional journals that you asked me to make in your letter of October 16 is enclosed." Such statements as these are courteous, businesslike ways of giving the reader the assignment details that he needs to be reminded of.

Although busy people cannot be expected to remember all

details of assignments and requests, some do remember them. The people who do remember almost all details take great pride in remembering them. They would dislike intensely being told (unless the "telling" is subordinated) the details that they remember. Those people who remember almost all details occasionally forget some specific item. They would be very much disturbed if the details they had forgotten were not included in your letter. Do, therefore, include all pertinent details in your letter; but *when you tell the reader something he already knows, subordinate the "telling."*

12. REMEMBER THAT YOUR LETTER REPRESENTS YOU. Although letters are sometimes written purely for the sake of providing a written record of a message, more often they are written as the sole means of transmitting a message. These letters represent you. Through your letter you make an impression—good or bad.

The appearance of a letter almost always parallels the appearance of the person sending the letter. The close relationship between the appearance of a letter and the appearance of the writer of that letter is discussed further in the next chapter.

The tone, the vocabulary, and the style of expression you use in a letter should reflect your personality. This principle is discussed further in Chapter 4, "Writing Style."

13. SAY "THANK YOU" ONLY AFTER SOMETHING HAS BEEN DONE. "Thank you" is a courteous expression that can be used generously in business letters, but it must be used only at appropriate times. Thank a person *after* he has done something; NEVER thank a person *before* he does something. Many well–intentioned letter writers request that certain products be shipped or that certain things be done and end their order letters or request letters with "Thank you." The person who does this is being presumptuous. He is presuming that his request will be granted—yet it may not be granted.

To let the reader of your letter know that you will appreciate his complying with your request, you may end your letter with some such statement as "Your sending the package by railway express before June 30 will be appreciated," "I shall greatly appreciate your writing to me about the schedule," or "I shall be grateful for your help in determining the cause of the deterioration of the roof." Numerous other possible statements can be used to let the reader of your letter know that you would appreciate his complying with your request. Do use such statements that will help promote goodwill.

People do not like to be taken for granted. You must never, therefore, use the expression "thank you" before your request is granted.

14. END WITH SOMETHING PLEASANT AND SPECIFIC. The *ending* is the second most important part of a letter. (The *beginning* is the most important part.)

The letter ending should be clear, pleasant, and specific. Almost always any action that is requested in a letter is mentioned— either the first time or as a repetition—at the end of the letter. The letter ending should contain a note of goodwill.

Do not use the trite ending "If I can be of further assistance to you, please do not hesitate to contact me." This sentence is wordy, negative, overused, and almost always meaningless. When you would honestly like to give additional help to the reader, a better version would be "When I can help you again, please write me." *When* is positive, whereas *if* is negative. Choose whatever *specific* word is appropriate for the occasion to substitute for *contact*. Other improvements in the suggested version should be obvious.

A few people, mostly older people who have little formal education, still end letters with a sentence fragment such as "Looking forward to hearing from you, I am. . . ." Do not use an ending of this type; instead, end with a contemporary, meaningful statement.

15. MAKE SURE THAT THE READER KNOWS THE NEXT STEP THAT IS TO BE TAKEN. An effective letter *must be* so well organized from the beginning to the end that when the receiver finishes reading it, he knows the next step that is to be taken. If he is to write a letter, he knows who the recipient of his letter is to be. He knows when he is to write, and he knows the type of information that his letter is to contain. If some other step is to be taken by another person, the reader of the effective business letter knows who is to take the other step and what that step is to be. If no further action is to be taken, the effective letter makes that fact clear to the reader.

As a test of the probable effectiveness of any letter that you write, ask yourself before you mail it, "If I were the receiver of this letter, would I know what action is to be taken, where it is to be taken and by whom, *or* that no further action is called for?"

Questions for discussion

1. Which principles are adhered to and which ones are violated in these *opening* sentences for business letters? Explain.
    a. Yes, you may use our mowing machine free of charge for a period of month's time.
    b. Unfortunately, our supply of the four–ply tires you ordered is exhausted.
    c. This letter is in reply to your request of October 6 for a copy of our catalog.
    d. I should like to tell you that I will gladly send the information that you requested in your letter of June 17.
    e. Although we cannot send you a copy of the report that you requested, we would be very glad to have you read the report when you come to our office next month.
    f. You said that you need a secretary who can take dictation at a high rate of speed.
2. Which principles are violated in these *closing* sentences for business letters?
    a. In closing, I should like to apologize again for failing to send the materials so that they would reach you by the date you specified.
    b. I sincerely regret that I cannot accept your invitation to speak to your group on October 11.
    c. I am sorry that we cannot supply the stationery you ordered.
3. Which principles are adhered to and which ones are violated in these eight letters?

September 3, 1973

Mrs. Mary B. Flanders
509 North Peachtree Street
Columbus, OH 43211

Dear Mrs. Flanders:

Mr. Ramsey received your inquiry of August 20. He asked me to tell you that the merchandise you ordered will be available in the near future. You may wish to wait until we receive a supply of these materials, or you may wish to order from another supplier.

We are always deeply grateful for your business.

Cordially yours,

***

September 26, 1973

Mr. Harry B. Brown
Box 1183, Tennessee Tech
Cookeville, TN 38501

Dear Mr. Brown:

Thank you for your letter of September 24. The two pamphlets you requested were mailed to you by parcel post this morning. Please accept them with our compliments.

The chart on page 3 of the pamphlet entitled "Financial Management" contains some figures that should be especially helpful in writing your term paper. You have our permission to reproduce any of the charts in these two publications.

If I can be of further assistance to you, please do not hesitate to contact me.

Cordially yours,

***

September 29, 1973

Miss Mary Bramblett
P. O. Box 411
Sheffield, AL 35660

Dear Miss Bramblett:

I mailed to you by parcel post this morning the two books you requested in your letter of August 1. I believe these books contain a good deal of information that will help you with the term paper you are writing.

Will you please return the two books as soon as you have completed your term paper? We expect to receive other requests for them before the end of the month.

Thanking you in advance, I remain,

Sincerely yours,

* * *

October 1, 1973

Dr. Milton O. Haney
Director of Admissions
Temple Community College
Roanoke, Virginia

Dear Dr. Haney:

In compliance with your request of September 30, I am sorry to tell you that the catalogs for 1973–1974 will not be available until the first of December. I am, though, submitting herewith a copy of the booklet entitled "Earn While You Learn." You stated that you would like to use the information in this booklet when counseling students who are making plans to enroll in a senior college next term.

In the event that any of the students in your school would like to secure further information in regard to this subject, please so inform them that they should get in touch with the placement office at our school.

If I can be of further assistance to you in the future, please do not hesitate to contact me.

Cordially yours,

* * *

July 31, 1973

Mrs. Robert E. Holland
187 Greeze Street
Billington, VT 05042

Dear Mrs. Holland:

I mailed to you by parcel post this morning the three No. 6 calendar bases that you ordered on July 29. As the color of these bases is the same as the pencil holders you ordered last month, they will match perfectly.

An up-to-date copy of our catalog of office supplies is enclosed.

Cordially yours,

***

December 8, 1973

Mr. Clement H. Wainwright
P. O. Box 347
Mason, MT 59469

Dear Mr. Wainwright:

Pursuant to your request of November 28, I am more than happy to comply. You asked me to recommend three good books pertaining to the subject of letter writing. The names of the books that I would like to recommend follow. The names of the authors and the publishers are also given.

Writing for Business by Hall T. Marcrum, Webster Publishing Co., 1817 Ridgeway Road, Laurel, TX 76785

Principles of Letter Writing by Mary Davis and Mark L. Fowler, Standard Publishers, Inc., 1827 Park Avenue, Macy, NY 12145

Letter Writing Simplified by Bradley O. Romine, Hastings Publishing Corporation, P. O. Box 247, Conley, OR 97016

I hope this is the information you need.

Sincerely yours,

***

August 1, 1973

Whitfield Office Supply Company
1148 Market Street
Wheeling, DE 19775

Gentlemen:

I should like to place an order for the following three items:

Model No. 3 electric stapling machine, Catalog No. 42207 $4.87
Tan paper clip dispenser, Catalog No. 38706   1.19
Desk blotter, 15 x 20 inches, Catalog No. 25813   2.89

Total $8.95

Please charge this merchandise to my account (No. 38743) and ship it by parcel post to reach me by August 11.

Thank you.

Cordially yours,

***

April 26, 1973

Miss Carolyn Wisner
Route 3
Marblehead, MD 21101

Dear Miss Wisner:

I am sorry that I cannot send the seventy-five ballpoint pens that you requested for favors for the secretaries who will attend your meeting on May 19. Our stock of that item has been depleted. I can, however, send you seventy-five attractive paper weights that I believe your meeting attendants would like to have.

I hope that you will have a very enjoyable, worthwhile meeting.

Sincerely yours,

3

Physical presentation

Your letter represents you. If you could go to distant places to discuss each business transaction, you might conceivably do that unlimited traveling. But obviously the time and the cost involved in making trips (short or long) to order merchandise, congratulate someone, make an inquiry of some type, ask for an adjustment, or transact any other type of business prohibit such extensive traveling. You must, therefore, write business letters.

When you go to a businessman's office to discuss business matters, you dress neatly and appropriately for the occasion. You will have had a bath, your hair will have been brushed, your nails will be clean, and your clothes will be clean and neatly pressed. Your clothing will be up–to–date in fashion and appropriate for the occasion. You will wear a business suit or dress rather than formal attire, a swimsuit, or an athletic uniform.

Because your letter represents you, it must be as neat, as much up–to–date, and as appropriate in style as your personal appearance would be. The appearance of a person's letter usually parallels his personal appearance. A person who is neat, clean, and dressed in fashionable, well–kept clothing is careful in presenting his typewritten message. His letter is spaced well on the page and is typed with a typewriter that has clean keys and a dark ribbon. Even stroking is used so that all letters are the same shade of darkness because some light and some dark letters would detract from the appearance of the message. Erasures are made so neatly that they can be detected only through *close* inspection.

Conversely, a person who would attempt to transact business with dirty fingernails would also mail a letter that was typed on a typewriter that had dirty keys. The person who would wear clothes that do not fit properly would not be careful about the placement of his letter on the page. The letter might very likely be too high or too low, or it might have one margin that is significantly wider than the other. Other characteristics of his letter would probably parallel other poor qualities of his personal appearance.

A business employee chooses clothing of good quality. He avoids quality that is ostentatious, and he avoids a cheap or skimpy quality. Likewise, he should choose stationery that is appropriate for his particular organization.

Many styles of business suits or dresses are appropriate for business wear. Also, many styles of letters are appropriate for business use. As the primary purpose of the material in this book is to help you improve the *content* of your letters, only one style of physical presentation of business letters is considered in this chapter. Various other styles of letters and of stationery are discussed in the reference section. Anyone who prefers a letter style different from the one discussed in this chapter can consult the reference section. The letter style and the stationery qualities discussed in this chapter are popular among outstanding businessmen and are easy to use. They are as good as any others that are described anywhere else.

Choosing the stationery

White 20–pound bond paper of 25 percent rag content is the most popular type of paper for business letters. Paper of these specifications is appropriate for plain paper and envelopes that are to be used by individuals writing personal business letters. Paper of this quality is recommended for envelopes, letterheads, and additional pages of letters that are longer than one page.

Thinner paper, perhaps 7–pound weight, should be used for the carbon copies of letters.

LETTERHEADS

The most popular size of paper is the standard 8½ by 11 inches. This size is used for letterheads, second pages of two–page letters, plain sheets on which personal business letters are written, and for the thin paper that is used for making carbon copies of letters.

Virtually all businesses use printed letterhead stationery. The letterhead, which ordinarily extends less than two inches from the top of the paper, contains the name and the address of the organization and something to indicate the nature of the business. Quite often the name of the organization indicates its nature. Other types of information that frequently appears in the letterhead are mentioned in the reference section of this textbook.

ENVELOPES

The name and the address of the organization are printed on the upper left–hand corner of the front of the envelope. This information is printed in the same style and color as appear on the letterhead sheets, but frequently the print is smaller on the envelope.

Envelopes are of two standard sizes. The No. 10, which measures 4⅛ by 9½ inches, is used for most business letters. This size is always recommended for one–page letters that transmit small enclosures and for two–page letters that do or do not transmit one or more small enclosures. Many people prefer to use only one size (the No. 10) envelope in the office, except of course for the letters that accompany enclosures that are too large for envelopes of this size. In such cases the large manila envelopes are used.

Typewriting the message

Once you have obtained the stationery and have decided just what you wish to write to your addressee, you are ready to typewrite the message. Pay careful attention to the appearance of the envelope and the letter.

ENVELOPE

The envelope, the wrapper for your message, is obviously the first thing that is seen when the message reaches its destination. It must, therefore, present a good appearance. Regardless of the size of envelope you use, the address will contain whatever information is needed to enable the postman to deliver the letter to the addressee. Usually, business letters are written on letterhead stationery and are mailed in envelopes that have the return address printed in the upper left-hand corner of the front. When such envelopes are used, the name and the address of your intended recipient is all that has to be typed on the envelope.

Now that optical scanners (one of the many types of electronic computers in use today) are used in some post offices, the envelope address should be arranged so that the optical scanner can read the address. This process speeds the sorting of mail in the post offices that have installed optical scanners. These machines are being installed in more and more post offices.

Single space all envelope addresses. When you use a No. 10 envelope, begin the first line of the address on the 14th line from the top of the envelope. The address should begin approximately 4 inches from the left edge. When you use a typewriter that has elite type (12 spaces to a horizontal inch), insert the envelope against the paper guide, which should be set at 0, and begin typing at 50.

When you use a No. 6¾ envelope, begin the first line of the address on the 12th line from the top of the envelope. The address should begin approximately 3 inches from the left edge. When you use a typewriter that has elite type (12 spaces to a horizontal inch), insert the envelope against the paper guide, which should be set at 0, and begin typing at 30.

Always include a courtesy title (Mr., Miss, Mrs., Ms., Dr., Professor, or other) for the person to whom you are addressing the envelope. Omitting a courtesy title would be a breach of business etiquette.

Letters can be delivered without a ZIP number. Using a ZIP number does, though, speed up the delivery. The time saved by using the ZIP number is significant, especially when an optical scanner is used for sorting the mail. When you use a ZIP number, you should use the two–letter state abbreviations that were devised by the postal service. The ZIP number should be placed 2 or 3 spaces to the right of the state abbreviation.

A list of the new two–letter state abbreviations is in the reference section (see page 429).

When you use a plain envelope that has no return address printed in the upper left-hand corner, type your return address in that position. Frequently, one of many possible things happens that prevents the postman's delivering the letter to the addressee. The addressee may have moved without leaving a forwarding address; there may be an error in the address typed on the envelope; or the envelope may have become defaced so that the address cannot be read. In such cases the letter can be returned to you if your return address is in the upper left-hand corner.

Be sure to type your name and address in the upper left-hand corner of the envelope. A woman may use a courtesy title (Miss, Mrs., Ms., Dr., or other) when typing her name in the return address position. A man NEVER gives himself a courtesy title (Mr., Dr., or other) in the return address position.

Because the optical scanner reads from the bottom to the top of the envelope, any special notation such as an attention line, REGISTERED MAIL, SPECIAL DELIVERY, and AIRMAIL must be typed above the envelope address.

Study the envelope arrangements on the next two pages.

LETTER

Your letter must be arranged attractively on the letterhead that you have chosen or on a plain sheet of paper. These seven standard parts of a business letter should be included:

1.   return address
2.   date
3.   inside address
4.   salutation
5.   body
6.   complimentary close
7.   signature

These seven standard parts are illustrated in the letters on pages 33 and 34.

RETURN ADDRESS. As the letterhead contains the name and the address of the organization, no return address is to be typed when a letter is written on letterhead stationery. When plain paper is used for writing a business letter, you MUST type your return address; otherwise, the recipient of your letter may not be able to reply. In most business offices the mail is opened by a clerk who throws the envelope away when she removes the letter.

The return address on plain paper should begin on the fourteenth line from the top of the page and should begin at the hozizontal center (at 50 for elite type and at 42 for pica type).

The return address should include all the information, except your name, that is necessary for the recipient to use when addressing an envelope to you. Your name is typed at the bottom of the letter. Repetition may be properly used for emphasis in the

```
TENNESSEE TECHNOLOGICAL UNIVERSITY
    SCHOOL OF BUSINESS ADMINISTRATION
DEPARTMENT OF BUSINESS EDUCATION AND OFFICE MANAGEMENT
       COOKEVILLE, TENNESSEE 38501


    CERTIFIED MAIL



                    Dr. Ronald T. Moss, Chairman
                    Department of Business Education
                       and Office Management
                    Capital University
                    Columbus, OH  43211
```

```
TENNESSEE TECHNOLOGICAL UNIVERSITY
    SCHOOL OF BUSINESS ADMINISTRATION
DEPARTMENT OF BUSINESS EDUCATION AND OFFICE MANAGEMENT
       COOKEVILLE, TENNESSEE 38501



Attention Adjustment Manager


                    Harrison's Department Store
                    129 South Main Street
                    Minneapolis, MN  57216
```

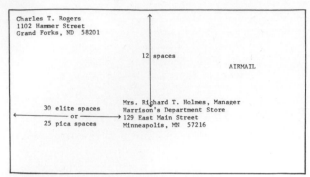

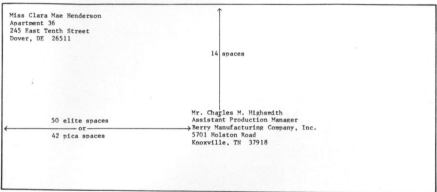

body of the letter. As the content of the letter (rather than your name) is to be emphasized, your name should appear at only one place on the letter—below the complimentary close.

Ordinarily, the information needed for the recipient to reply to your letter includes your house or apartment number; street, avenue, and so forth; city; state; and ZIP number.

DATE. The date (month, day, and year) should be typed below the city and state in the return address. When you use a letterhead, type the date at least 2 spaces below the city and state. Fourteen spaces from the top of the page is good for most letters. The horizontal position for the date may be determined by the letterhead style. In almost all instances, however, the date may begin at the horizontal center of the page (at 50 for elite type and at 42 for pica type).

When you are using plain paper for your letter, you should type the date on the line immediately following the city and state.

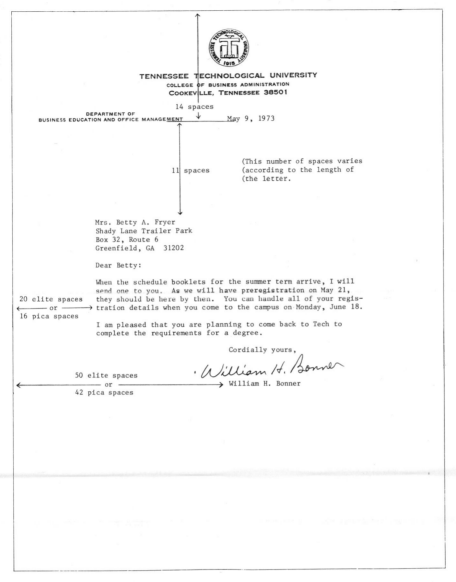

INSIDE ADDRESS. The inside address, which should be identical to the address on the envelope, must contain whatever information is needed to enable the postman to deliver the envelope to the addressee. If the letter is to go to an individual at his home, the address usually includes the name of the person who is to re-

```
                                    129 Pine Street
                                    Hattisburg, IL  61842
                                    October 3, 1973




          Mr. Richard T. Holmes, Manager
          Harrison's Department Store
          129 Main Street
          McMinnville, IL  60909

          Dear Mr. Holmes:

          I am very much interested in the Electromatic vacuum cleaner
          that you advertised in yesterday's McMinnville Sentinel.  Will
          you please send a representative to my home within the next
          three weeks to demonstrate that machine?

          As I work from 8 a.m. until 5 p.m. each weekday, evenings or
          Saturday mornings would be the most convenient times for me.
          Could you let me know when he can give this demonstration so
          that I will be at home when he arrives?

                                    Sincerely yours,

                                    Mary M. Taylor
                                    Mrs. Mary M. Taylor
```

ceive the letter; his house number and street, avenue, rural route number, box number; and the city, state, and ZIP number.

Good business etiquette and common courtesy dictate that you use a courtesy title (Mr., Mrs., Miss, Dr., Professor, or other) before the person's name in the inside address.

The number of vertical spaces between the date and the first line of the inside address will depend on the length of the letter. You must leave at least 3 vertical spaces between the date and the first line of the address. Three lines would be sufficient for a long letter. In most cases, though, more than 3 spaces will be required for the letter to be spaced so that it appears to be centered on the page.

Perhaps 6 to 10 lines would be the right number of spaces between the date and the inside address for a large majority of business letters.

SALUTATION. The salutation should always be 2 spaces below the last line of the inside address.

When you address your letter to a person rather than an organization, you should in most instances use a three-word salutation (Dear + courtesy title + surname). When you use a person's first name in conversations with him, you may use a two-word salutation (Dear + first name) in your letter. You should be careful about using the first-name salutation. You must not use the first-name salutation if doing so may lead to possible embarrassment to you or the addressee when another reader may feel that you are using political influence to gain unfair advantage.

"Dear Sir" is an outdated salutation and should NEVER be used when writing a letter to a businessman or to a private citizen.

When you write to an organization (a group of any kind) that employs at least one man, you use the one-word salutation "Gentlemen." When you write to a group that is made up exclusively of women, you should use the one-word salutation "Mesdames."

Without exception choose a salutation that is appropriate for the *first line* of the inside address. Study the following examples of inside addresses and salutations:

Miss Harriette M. King
126 Central Avenue
Birmingham, AL 35660
Dear Miss King:

Mr. Ralph J. Albright
Route 2
Hot Springs, AK 36666
Dear Ralph:
(or Dear Mr. Albright)

Mr. George W. Matthews
President, Land and Co.
1109 Main Street
Fargo, ND 58222
Dear Mr. Matthews:

Mrs. Lucille J. Armstrong
Assistant Claims Manager
Walker's Department Store
Columbus, OH 43211
Dear Lucille:
  (or Dear Mrs. Armstrong)

Dr. L. M. Holt, Dean
College of Commerce
University of Wyoming
Laramie, WY 35333
Dear Dr. Holt:

Ralston Furniture Company
1905 East Broad Street
Nashville, TN 37777
Gentlemen:

Business and Professional Women's Club
Cookeville, TN 38501
Mesdames:

Mississippi State College for Women
Columbus, MS 36666
Gentlemen:

Kelley Manufacturing Company, Inc.
1109 Market Street
Dover, DE 21888

Attention Mr. James M. Hargrove

Gentlemen:

Always use a colon after the salutation if you use a comma after the complimentary close.

BODY. The body of the letter, which may be one short paragraph or several paragraphs (even enough to require typing on a second page), should always begin two spaces below the salutation. Single space the paragraphs and double space between the paragraphs. Each paragraph begins flush with the left margin in the letter style presented in this chapter. For some of the letter styles described in the reference section, the first line of each paragraph is indented.

The body of the letter should be centered horizontally as well as vertically. A 5–inch writing line (60 spaces for elite type and 50 spaces for pica type) is appropriate for a large majority of business letters. A longer line should be used, of course, for very long letters. Certainly, a line longer than 5 inches would be required for a two-page letter.

Here are four reasons for using a 5–inch line for most business letters: (1) Most business letters are of such length that this spacing easily leads to proper centering on the page. (2) This line length helps to make the right margin appear to be fairly straight. Longer lines, which cause the margins to be narrow, emphasize the "raggedness" of the right margin. Shorter lines also emphasize the "raggedness" of the right margin. (3) The 5–inch line can be read easily. (4) Because this length is so popular, readers are accustomed to seeing it and tend to like the appearance it creates.

The *effect* of the 5–inch line is more important than the exact length. There is nothing magic about 60 elite type spaces or 50 pica type spaces. You may very well vary the line length 2 to 4 spaces if doing so will help you place your letter more attractively on the page.

COMPLIMENTARY CLOSE. The complimentary close should always be 2 spaces below the last line of the body of the letter. For the letter style discussed in this chapter, the complimentary close should begin at the horizontal center of the page (50 for elite type and 42 for pica type).

The modern letter writer usually uses some combination of two or three of these words for a complimentary close: *sincerely, cordially, very,* and *yours.* "Sincerely yours" and "Cordially yours" are perhaps the most popular combinations for a complimentary close. For any complimentary close, only the first word is capitalized.

Always use a comma after the complimentary close if you use a colon after the salutation.

SIGNATURE. The letter writer's name should be typed four spaces below the complimentary close and should begin at the horizontal center (50 for elite type and 42 for pica type). A man NEVER gives himself a courtesy title (Mr., Dr., or other). A woman may use a courtesy title. If she does use a courtesy title when typing her name in the signature line, she does not repeat the courtesy title in her pen-written signature.

Always sign each letter with a pen in the space between the complimentary close and the typed signature line. A pen-written signature is extremely IMPORTANT. Such a signature may possibly mean the difference between having the letter accepted as a legal document, which is sometimes the case, and not having the letter accepted as a legal document.

Even when no legal point is to be considered, the pen-written signature indicates that the letter writer is thorough and careful in handling his business transactions. Usually, the pen-written signature is the same as the typewritten signature line; though these two exceptions are sometimes made: (1) The writer who uses a first name for a salutation usually writes only his first name in ink immediately above the typewritten signature line, which is always (except for the courtesy title) the same as the recipient would use when replying to the letter. (2) As was mentioned previously, the courtesy title for a woman is used only once.

Study the examples that follow (see opposite page) :

In addition to the seven standard parts of a business letter that are described in the preceding paragraphs and are illustrated on pages 33 and 34, some special parts are frequently needed for some letters. These special parts include such notations as:

1. title of position
2. reference initials
3. enclosure notation
4. attention line
5. special mailing notation
6. other

These five special parts are illustrated in the letter on page 40.

TITLE OF POSITION. When you use a letterhead and write as a representative of the organization for which the letterhead was designed, you should type the title of your position on the line immediately below your typewritten signature.

REFERENCE INITIALS. Reference initials are used to identify the person who typed the letter. When you type your own letter, you do not need to include these initials. When reference initials are

Sincerely yours,

Kenneth M. Pratt
Kenneth M. Pratt

Sincerely yours,

Betty Welch
Miss Betty Welch

Cordially yours,

Miss Rebecca L. Wheeler
Rebecca L. Wheeler

Cordially yours,

David
David T. Hobbs

Very sincerely yours,

Christine
Miss Christine Wiley

Very cordially yours,

Keith M. Latham
Keith M. Latham

Very cordially yours,

Melinda J. Harris
Mrs. Melinda T. Harris

Sincerely yours,

Mrs. Hilda L. Watts
Hilda L. Watts

used, they should be typed flush with the left margin and usually one or two spaces lower than the typewritten signature or title of the position.

ENCLOSURE NOTATION. When some item is placed inside the envelope with the letter, the word *Enclosure* should be typed flush with the left margin and one or two spaces below the reference initials. When reference initials are not used, however, the word *Enclosure* is typed in the reference initials position.

When more than one enclosure accompanies the letter, the word *Enclosures* should be used and should be followed by the number of enclosures (see page 133). Some people like to itemize the enclosures. Itemizing them is desirable when the enclosures

A REGION OF THE

Southern Business Education Association

May 17, 1973

Harrison Printing Company
P. O. Box 157
Nashville, TN   37202

Attention Mr. Harry M. Stewart

Gentlemen:

The advertising copy for the program booklets for our upcoming
convention is enclosed. I will send you the photographs of the
speakers by Thursday, July 17.

When the booklets are completed, I will come by your office to
get a copy for each advertiser. August 15 will be early enough
for you to ship the other copies to me.

Cordially yours,

William H. Bonner
President

dbf

Enclosure

CERTIFIED MAIL

President . . . . William H. Bonner, Tennessee Technological University, Cookeville, TN 38501
President-Elect . . . . Lois Frazier, Meredith College, Raleigh, NC 27602
Vice-President . . . . Margarett Huggins, Belhaven College, Jackson, MS 39202
Secretary . . . . Juanita B. Parker, West Virginia Wesleyan College, Buckhannon, WV 26201
Treasurer . . . . Basil O. Sweatt, Southeastern Louisiana College, Hammond, LA 70401
Membership Director . . . . Nancy Langley, Ahrens Trade High School, Louisville, KY 40202
Editor . . . . Max R. Carrington, Florence State University, Florence, AL 35630
Past-President . . . . Wilson Ashby, University of Alabama, University, AL 35486

Officers

are very important or when you believe that the person opening
the envelope may overlook one or more of the items enclosed.

ATTENTION LINE.   When you address a letter to an organization
but wish to direct the letter to the attention of a particular person
within that organization, you should type an attention line be-

tween the last line of the inside address and the salutation. The attention line may begin at the left margin.

Note that even though an attention line is used, the salutation is still the one word (*Gentlemen* or *Mesdames*) that would be appropriate for the *first line of the inside address*.

SPECIAL MAILING NOTATIONS.   When you wish to send your letter by any method other than regular first–class mail, you should type the notation for the special handling (REGIS-TERED, CERTIFIED, and so on) either above the inside address or below any other parts of the letter. Although the post-man will not use this notation, it will provide a record for the receiver so that he will know that the letter was sent by a special method. This notation on the carbon copy of the letter will pro-vide a record for you of the method of mailing.

OTHER.   Some other less frequently used special notations are discussed and illustrated in the reference section.

Almost all well-written letters are less than one full page in length. Occasionally, though, longer letters are necessary. The instructions for typing multiple-page letters are in the reference section.

Handwriting the message

Only the smallest businesses do not have a typewriter. An in-creasing number of individuals have access to a typewriter. Most business letters, therefore, are typewritten. Some of the reasons for using a typewriter to prepare letters are these: (1) The letter can be written in less time. (2) The typewritten letter presents a better appearance and is easier to read. (3) Carbon copies can be made easily. (4) Most typewritten letters are only one page or less in length.

Even though most business letters are typewritten, some still have to be handwritten. When you have no typewriter available and must write a letter by hand, you should use the same type of stationery that you would use for typewriting the letter; and you should use the same letter parts that are discussed in this chapter. The only variation that is necessary in the letter style discussed in this chapter is indenting the paragraphs for easy reading. Use a

259 East Tenth Street
Moline, Indiana 61376
January 25, 1974

McDonald Publishing Co.
1126 Second Avenue
Columbia, Ohio 42133

Gentlemen:

Please send me a copy of your brochure "Executives Must Communicate." I wish to use some of the information in your publication for a term paper that I am preparing for a business communications course.

As my paper is due on February 28, I shall appreciate your sending the brochure before February 15.

Cordially yours,

James L. Hansard

pen—*never a pencil*—and write legibly so that the reader will focus his attention on your message rather than spend undue time trying to decipher the handwritten words.

When you have to write a letter with a pen, keep the lines straight (perhaps some type of guide would he helpful) and be sure to leave at least *one–inch* top, side, and bottom margins. A letter written with pen is illustrated on page 42.

Folding letters

A successful business executive realizes the importance of good grooming. He knows that the people with whom he communicates will respect his ability to make sound decisions and will admire his ability to direct the work of others if his appearance is appropriate for the job he performs. Among other factors of good grooming, such as personal hygiene and freshly polished shoes, he makes certain that his suit is clean and *well pressed.* Even though his suit is clean, it would not help him to project a favorable impression if the creases in the trousers were improperly placed. A poor job of pressing a suit would cause the effort and the financial expense of cleaning that suit to be a real waste.

Just as the executive pays close attention to the appearance of his clothing, he makes certain that his letters look good enough to command the respect of their readers. The content of a letter represents the writer's thinking, and the appearance of a letter reflects the writer's grooming. A letter must not only be spaced well on the page and typed with a dark ribbon and clean typewriter keys, but it must also be folded properly. The creases in a business letter affect the appearance of that letter as much as the creases in trousers affect the appearance of a business suit.

Continue your attempt to make a favorable impression with your business letter by folding it properly for whatever envelope you choose to use. The two most popular sizes of business envelopes for letters that are written on the standard $8\frac{1}{2}$ by 11–inch stationery are the "long" (No. 10) and the "short" (No. $6\frac{3}{4}$).

Long envelope

Only *two* creases are needed for the proper folding of a letter that is to be mailed in a "long" (No. 10) envelope. *First,* place the letter "face up" on the desk and bring the bottom edge of the letter up toward the top edge so that roughly one third of the page is left uncovered, as in the following illustration.

Crease the letter at this point. *Second,* bring the top edge of the letter down over the bottom one third of the letter that has already been creased. The top edge should come to within *about* one quarter of an inch from the crease you have already made in the letter. Hold the top edge in this position as you make the second and final crease in the letter, as in this illustration.

The folded letter is now slightly smaller than a "long" envelope and can, therefore, be easily placed into the envelope.

Short envelope

Three creases are required for the proper folding of a letter that is to be mailed in a "short" business envelope. *First,* place the letter "face up" on the desk and bring the bottom edge of the letter up toward the top edge of the letter so that the bottom edge is within about one quarter of an inch of the top edge. Crease the letter, as in this illustration.

Second, bring the right edge of the letter over toward the left side so that approximately one third of the width of the letter remains uncovered by the portion that extends from the second crease that you have made, as in this illustration.

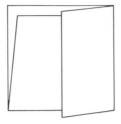

Third, bring the left edge of the letter over toward the right so that the left edge is within about one quarter of an inch from the second crease that you have made, as in this illustration.

The folded letter is now smaller than the "short" envelope and can, therefore, be easily placed into the envelope.

The appearance of a letter that has been folded correctly for either of the two popular sizes of business envelopes will be as good as it was before it was folded. Improper folding would have an adverse effect on the appearance of a well-spaced letter. A letter that has been folded correctly can be opened easily and will fit into the files as it should. Easy handling of correspondence is quite important in large offices where dozens (and possibly hundreds) of letters are opened each day.

Questions for discussion

1. How does the appearance of a letter contribute to the effectiveness of the contents of that letter?

2. What are some advantages in addition to those mentioned in this chapter of using a 60–space line for most business letters?

3. How does proper folding contribute to the appearance of a letter that is mailed in a No. 6¾ or a No. 10 envelope?

4. Even though almost all business letters should be typewritten, what are some of the reasons that some letters should be written in longhand?

5. What are some of the reasons for beginning the date and the closing lines of a letter at the horizontal center of the page?

Problems

1. Assume that you are the student who composed the letter in this problem. Typewrite that letter in proper form on a sheet of plain white 8½ by 11–inch paper.

    Please send me a copy of your brochure entitled "The Executive Must Communicate." I should like to use some of the information in that publication for a term paper I am preparing for a business communications course.

    As my paper is due on May 1, I shall appreciate your sending the brochure before April 15.

    The person to whom you should address this letter is Harold L. Baker. He is the General Manager of the Butler Publishing Company. The address of that company is 1122 Furman Road, Dover, Delaware 40765.

2. Address a No. 6¾ envelope for the letter that was typewritten for Problem 1. Sign the letter for Problem 1, fold it properly, and place it in the envelope.

3. Assume that you are the student who composed the letter in this problem. Typewrite that letter in proper form on a sheet of plain white 8½ by 11–inch paper.

    I am enclosing the brochure "The Executive Must Communicate" that you mailed to me on April 2. Some of the information in that brochure was just what I needed to complete my term paper for a business communications course. I thank you for sending me your only copy.

4. Address a No. 10 envelope for the letter that was typewritten for Problem 3. Sign the letter for Problem 3, fold it properly, and place it in the envelope.

5. Address a No. 10 envelope for each of the following three addresses:

    Mr. Robert F. Jones, Manager, Johnson Manufacturing Company, 1122 Market Street, Florence, Alabama 35630

    Mr. Thomas L. Winningham, Public Relations Director, Wright Finance Corporation, Jackson, Tennessee

    Miss Margaret Ann Hitchcock, Secretary, Office Girls, Inc., First National Bank Building, Lincoln, Nebraska

4

Writing style

THE EXPERT WRITER strives to write so clearly that his message *cannot be misunderstood*. Such accurate expression should be the goal of every writer of business messages, as there is no substitute for clarity.

In a business letter, words are the only symbols or vehicles that can be utilized for effective communication. Smiles, frowns, gestures, and tone of voice are not nearly so apparent in writing as they are in talking. A well–written letter may, however, reveal to some extent such factors as the facial expressions and the tone of voice of the person writing the letter.

Enhance your writing style in every way that you can so that your letters will be as effective as you can make them.

Conversational tone

The principle of writing as you talk is important. When you write to a person, you should use the same first– and second–person pronouns, contractions, idioms, personal references, contemporary expressions, and word choices that you use in oral conversation.

PERSONAL PRONOUNS

When you write a business letter on letterhead stationery, you write as a representative of the organization that is identified in the letterhead. The pronouns *we, us, our,* and *ours* mean the group that makes up the firm, business, or organization the letterhead identifies. You should not use such words or impersonal expressions as *our firm, our company,* and *our organization.*

By no means should you ever resort to the use of such wordy, impersonal, outmoded third–person expressions as "The Smithfield Wholesale Company welcomes the opportunity to supply your packing supplies" when you are writing as an employee representing the Smithfield Wholesale Company. Instead, you should write, *"We* welcome the opportunity to supply your packing supplies."

Second–person pronouns should be used for the reader of your letter. When you write to a person who, as a reader of your letter, represents a particular organization, use such expressions as "We welcome *you* as a customer" instead of stilted expressions as "We welcome your company as a customer" or "We welcome the Wright Manufacturing Company as a customer."

The personal pronoun *I* should be used when it contributes to the conversational tone of your letter. The tone of your letter should reveal your genuine interest in the reader. This interest, frequently referred to as the *you attitude,* can be established much more naturally by using first–person pronouns appropriately than by omitting these pronouns and thus creating a telegraphic style. "Appreciate your writing to me on April 17" contributes less to displaying the *you attitude* than does "I appreciate your writing to me on April 17."

CONTRACTIONS

Contractions, provided they are used discreetly, add to the natural conversational tone of your business letters. Contractions can be used appropriately in such instances as congratulatory letters to a business friend or associate; in sales letters for inexpensive, widely used products; and in some routine letters to people with whom you have corresponded on a somewhat regular basis for a long time. In many business letters that are more formal than these, contractions are good when used sparingly.

You should always use care in choosing contractions. Such contractions as *don't, doesn't,* and *won't* seem natural and in good taste for the types of business letters mentioned in the preceding paragraph. On the other hand, the use of such contractions as *I'd, you'd,* and *they're* may cause many readers to feel that you are not a careful, well-bred business communicator.

In many instances contractions are considered inappropriate. Such letters are those concerning employment; those written to a person whose background is not familiar to you; and those to older, formally well–educated businessmen should probably be written without using contractions.

When deciding whether to use contractions, your best guide is to apply the principle of keeping your reader in mind. If you believe he would like them, use them.

Idioms

Idiomatic expressions that are well known to both the writer and the reader can enhance the conversational tone of the letter. When writing to a businessman whose business is experiencing financial difficulty, such an idiomatic expression as "When you are on your feet again" not only sounds conversational but also it can carry the positive, pleasant feeling that you wish to convey. Countless other similar expressions can, when well chosen, contribute to the tone you wish to use for your message.

Here are two precautions you must take, however, when using idioms:

1. If the reader is not familiar with the idiom you use, he may be confused by your message.

2. If the idiom you use can have different meanings in different contexts, the reader of your letter may misinterpret your expression, thus causing your otherwise well–written letter to convey an idea entirely different from the one you intended.

Be especially careful about using idiomatic expressions in letters involving contracts, topics about which people are especially sensitive, and any other matter in which goodwill may be adversely affected.

PERSONAL REFERENCES

Human beings, the most interesting creatures on earth, communicate on a higher level than do any other living organisms. Write about people, therefore, and refer to them by appropriate, well–chosen nouns and pronouns.   •

Common nouns such as the banker, the president, the secretary, and the assistants can be used liberally. By the same token, the personal pronouns *he, she, they, them, I,* and *you,* can be used to add interest and conversational tone to your letters. You can frequently improve the readability of your letters by including proper names—Mr. Booth, Mary Harris, Miss Robbins, and others.

Obviously, personal references must be used ethically. Use the same ethical standards in writing names that you use in making personal references in business conversations.

Do you often use the name of the person with whom you are conversing? If you do, use your reader's name in your letter in the same manner that you use it when talking with him. Excessive use of a person's name, though (especially a person who is not a close friend), can cause your reader to think that you are insincere—that you are trying to use flattery or possibly even trickery to accomplish a selfish objective.

You should NEVER use your reader's name in the first sentence of your letter when you use a salutation. You can readily recognize the inappropriateness of such a practice by reading aloud this illustration: "Dear Mr. Haney: I congratulate you, Mr. Haney, on the success of your end-of-the-year sale."

If you seldom use a person's name when you talk with him, you should avoid using his name in the body of your letter. To do so would cause your letter to sound unnatural and thus lose the conversational tone.

Whether or not you use a person's name frequently in conversation, DO always use the reader's name in the salutation!

CONTEMPORARY EXPRESSIONS

Some older people hesitate to change their preferences for types of clothing. They become accustomed to wearing certain styles of clothing, and they resist changes that are necessary for them to dress fashionably. Many of the "senior citizens" become "set" in their ways of writing business letters and decline to update their manners of expressing ideas.

Some other writers continue to use outdated writing styles only because they are not aware of better ways of writing.

Young people are usually eager to adopt new clothing fashions. They are alert and energetic, and they want to make a good impression on their associates. These young people are adaptable and are often equally enthusiastic about wearing fashionable clothing and using current writing styles. They know that the impression that they make by writing "fashionable" letters is just as important as the impression that they make by wearing fashionable clothing.

Compare the following two columns (*up-to-date* and *outdated*) of frequently used business expressions. As you can see, the expressions in the *up-to-date* column are more appropriate for conversational tone as they are clear, short, and tactful.

Up-to-date	*Outdated*
Here is	Enclosed herewith
Because *or* as *or* since	Due to the fact that
. . . is enclosed	Enclosed please find . . . .
. . . is attached	Attached you will find . . . .
tell	advise *or* inform
to improve	in order to improve
addressed envelope	self–addressed envelope
to help you	to be of service to you *or* to be of assistance to you
now *or* presently	at the present time
Sincerely yours, *or* Cordially yours,	Respectfully yours, *or* Very truly yours,
is on page 6	can be found on page 6
later	at a later date
soon	in the near future

The *up-to-date* expressions are not only more effective but also they save time for the dictator, the transcriber, and the reader. These lists are by no means exhaustive. They merely represent the many frequently used business expressions that affect the impression that you make on the reader of your letter. What type of impression do you prefer to make?

WORD CHOICE

Your proper choice of words will enable your reader to interpret accurately the ideas, information, opinions, feelings, and judgments you wish to convey and will help you to develop the tone you wish to use in expressing your thoughts. Choose your words carefully by considering the reader's vocabulary, your own personality, preciseness of meanings, and the advantages of using verbs to make your letters as readable and as interesting as you can make them.

READER'S VOCABULARY. Your purpose for writing a letter is to convey one or more ideas, feelings, opinions, judgments, or some specific information. You attempt to write *so clearly that your message cannot be misunderstood,* and you want your reader to be favorably impressed by your letter. Use only those words that you believe he will readily understand. If he has to ponder the meaning of a word or has to consult a dictionary to determine its meaning, he focuses his attention on that particular word rather than on the content of your letter. Avoid using any word that will cause your reader's attention to be distracted from the *content* of your letter.

Good letter writers have good vocabularies. Good letter writers also know how to use their vocabularies to greatest advantage. They know that when writing to a person who has had little formal education they cannot expect that person to have a large vocabulary (even though there are many exceptions). Many people, including Abe Lincoln, who had very limited formal education, possess a tremendous vocabulary and a tremendous command of the English language. Mr. Lincoln, by combining his knowledge and compassion for others with his great command of the English language, wrote many documents that are frequently quoted not only for their content but also for their literary qualities. His letter to Mrs. Bixby and his famous Gettysburg address are two of those documents.

Some people are genuinely well educated and certainly have the ability to learn words that are unfamiliar to them. Using a technical or specialized vocabulary when writing to such persons, however, causes them to spend time interpreting your letter rather than reading it easily and taking quickly the steps you want them to take. Make the very best use of your vocabulary; but when you doubt that your reader knows the meaning of a word you are tempted to use, substitute another word that will be familiar to him and will enable you to communicate effectively.

A truly well–educated person can communicate effectively by using simple words. He can also maintain the respect of his readers—regardless of their educational backgrounds.

In many instances polysyllabic words (including those of a specialized, technical nature) should be used. For example, when a physician writes to another person in the medical profession, he can communicate best by using medical terminology. By doing so, he achieves clarity of expression and maintains the tone of a conversation that the two might have. When a physician writes to someone outside the medical profession, however, he must refrain from using medical terms. He must use words that the reader readily understands. The ideas expressed in this paragraph apply equally to other fields—engineering, mathematics, and so forth.

When you prepare to write a letter, consider your reader. Use specialized terms and other words that will help you and your reader to communicate. Remember, too, that you can use simple words and still maintain the respect of your reader. Big ideas are much more important than big words.

YOUR OWN PERSONALITY.   Even though you have many characteristics that are common to all people, you are different in some respects to all others. No two people look exactly alike. No two people should do or say the same things in the same ways under identical circumstances. When you attempt to communicate through the medium of words—in writing as well as in talking— choose words that best fit *your* personality.

A young man who had driven with his family to New York City from a distant state had an opportunity to participate in a live TV show. In rehearsing for that show, the young man was asked, among other questions, "How was your drive to New York?" He was instructed to answer, "It was *lovely.*" He refused, even after considerable prompting, to say that his trip was *lovely.* He said that he never used this word, that it did not "fit" his personality, and that his friends who would see the show would realize that he was *not being himself.* He was then permitted to choose another adjective to describe his enjoyable drive to New York City.

Use the same vocabulary for writing that you use for talking. Continue building your vocabulary, but study the words that you learn and decide whether or not they can be adapted to your personality. Words that can be used naturally by some people cannot be used effectively by you.

PRECISENESS.   In writing so clearly that your message cannot be misunderstood, you must choose words that express precisely the idea you wish to convey.

Study this example. "The employment procedures for the transportation division *warrant* further study." A reader may interpret this sentence to indicate that the employment procedures are perhaps questionable, or he may interpret it to mean that the employment procedures are good—worthy of additional consideration. By substituting the word *merit* for *warrant,* "The employment procedures for the transportation division *merit* further study," the sentence would probably be interpreted to mean that the employment procedures are good and that further study would perhaps improve a situation that is seemingly leading to conditions that are being sought.

Instead of writing "We look forward to an opportunity to *serve* you again," substitute a word that will state specifically the type of service or product you look forward to supplying. Some examples follow:

> We look forward to an opportunity to provide bi-monthly service for your factory generators.
> We look forward to an opportunity to send you another shipment of building materials.

Writing *"There are* slightly more than 150,000 people in Sioux Falls, South Dakota" is less exacting than "Slightly more than 150,000 people *reside* in Sioux Falls, South Dakota." Incidentally, a sentence that begins with *There* is usually unnecessarily wordy and less precise than if it begins with some other word.

Countless other word substitutions can be made to give the precise meaning that you would like for your written messages to project.

VERBS.   People like action. You like to observe others acting (you like to attend football games and other sports events) and to participate in activities (dance, swim, or pursue at least one hobby). People also enjoy reading about action. You should, therefore, make ample use of verbs to add to the zest and interest of your letters.

A verb is a word that expresses action or a state of being. The verbs that express action are the stronger, but very often the verbs that express a state of being best serve the purpose you are striving to accomplish. Verbs in active voice (the subject of the sentence does the acting) are preferred in most instances over the passive voice (the subject of the sentence receives the action). Not only are the sentences that are written in active voice more interesting, but they are also shorter in most cases. Study these examples:

> The personnel manager dictated the three letters.
>   (active voice—seven words)
> The three letters were dictated by the personnel manager.
>   (passive voice—nine words)

> The committee accepted the suggestions.
>   (active voice—five words)
> The suggestions were accepted by the committee.
>   (passive voice—seven words)

Pay special attention to words ending with *tion*. Very often verb forms can be substituted effectively for these words, as in the following examples:

> One hour will be required for the *completion* of this exercise.
> One hour will be required for completing this exercise.
> One hour will be required to complete this exercise.
> The exercise can be completed in one hour.
>
> Installation of the heating system can be accomplished in one hour.

Installing the heating system can be accomplished in one hour.
The heating system can be installed in one hour.
We can install the heating system in one hour.

Using verbs not only adds strength to the sentence but it also shortens the sentence. Short sentences are superior to long sentences when they are as nearly complete, are as accurate, and are as interesting and courteous as the longer ones.

Use verbs to eliminate such weak, overused expressions as these:

as soon as possible
at your earliest convenience

Instead of using either of these two wornout expressions, you may write, "as soon as you can." By substituting the phrase "as soon as you can," you can improve your letters in four ways:

1. You eliminate the trite expression.
2. You use a verb *(can)*.
3. You use the pronoun *you,* which *may help* you show the "you attitude."
4. You use a shorter expression—more words than "as soon as possible" but a shorter space for the improved "as soon as you can."

Study other possibilities for improving the effectiveness of your letters by using verbs.

Specific and positive statements

A good letter writer knows that specific, positive statements enhance the effectiveness of his business letters.

SPECIFIC

If you have thought about your letter–writing task sufficiently to determine the real purpose of the letter you are getting ready to write, you should be able to use words and statements that are specific. Vagueness or rambling detracts from the effectiveness of your business letter almost as much as does poor grammar. Specificity helps to make a good impression on the reader of your letter. He knows that only those people who can think clearly can write specifically. Conversely, he knows that vague or indefinite words or expressions in a business letter indicate that the writer was poorly prepared to write that particular letter. Study the examples in the two following columns:

Specific	*Vague or indefinite*
your letter of April 17	your recent letter
I appreciate your writing me *or* I appreciate your calling me	I appreciate your contacting me
Thank you for your inquiry	Thank you for your letter
by October 8	as soon as possible
by parcel post	under separate cover
before May 26	in the near future

Numerous other examples could be included. Memorizing is not, however, the purpose of discussing the importance of using *specific* words or statements. These examples are given for study in applying the principle of writing specifically. Apply that principle when writing your business messages.

When you want your reader to do something within a short time, you should in many instances specify the date by which you would like him to do it. Stating that a particular thing is to be done within two weeks' time is better than saying that it is to be done "as soon as possible" or "at your earliest convenience." Because the reader may not know whether you mean two weeks from the date of your letter or two weeks from the date he receives it, an even better approach would be to specify the date such as "by November 14."

Keep these points in mind as you specify a date on which something should be done:

1. If you specify a date that is too far in the future, the reader may lay your request aside with the thought that he has plenty of time and thus become so involved with other jobs that he will forget to comply with your request.

2.   If you specify a date that is too close at hand, the reader may not have an opportunity to comply by that particular time and will therefore erase your request from his mind. He may very likely be out of town when your request arrives and therefore would not be aware of your request until after the date you specified.

On some occasions specifying a date is impossible, or at least it is not feasible. In these cases a statement such as "as soon as you can" is as specific a statement as you can use.

Just as negative words or statements are occasionally superior to positive words or statements, generalities are occasionally better than specifics. Some occasions for which generalities may be recommended are discussed in Chapter 7.

Learn to use specifics almost always.

POSITIVE

The power of positive thinking is great indeed. Most people think positively and are more favorably impressed by positive comments than by negative words or comments. When a good rapport exists between two persons, one has a tendency to do what the other suggests. A letter writer who wishes to call attention to a specific item in a catalog, pamphlet, or any other publication may profitably write "Turn to page 4 and read the description of the. . . ." The reader is much more likely to read the description than if the writer used the weak, wornout phraseology "A description of the . . . can be found on page 4."

Find and *found* are good words, but they are frequently used inappropriately. Such expressions as "can be found" and "you will find" are seldom appropriate for effective communication. A person who is intelligent enough to comprehend the message you are transmitting is intelligent enough to *find* whatever you call his attention to, provided it is in its proper location.

Just as the positive suggestion "Turn to page. . . ." tends to cause the reader to turn to that page, the phrase *why not* tends to cause the reader to think of reasons for not doing whatever is suggested. Avoid, therefore, using *why not* when suggesting that your reader take positive action. Also, avoid using negative expressions or words such as *sorry, regret,* and *unfortunately.* As is true with other negatives, though, occasionally (but seldom) there are times when these words can be used advantageously.

Positive expressions are usually shorter than negative expressions. They can be understood more easily, and they have greater appeal to the reader. Compare the expressions in the two columns that follow:

Positive	*Negative*
remember the meeting	do not forget the meeting
come in to see us	why not come in to see us
please write us	please do not hesitate to write us

Like the other examples that are included in this textbook, this list is representative rather than exhaustive.

Use positive words and statements in almost all instances. An occasional negative expression may, however, attract the desired attention or provide the change of pace that is needed to enhance the interest quality of your messages.

Study your letters carefully to eliminate most negative words and expressions.

Courtesy expressions

Courtesy is essential in any successful business endeavor. Gestures, facial expressions, tone of voice, and choice of words help you portray courtesy when communicating orally. Because the written word is the only medium through which courtesy can be expressed in a business letter, you must choose your words carefully and use them in the proper contexts.

"Thank you," "please," "grateful," and "appreciate" are courtesy expressions that are used frequently in business letters. Even when ordering an item that you know the supplier is eager to sell, "Please send. . . ." seems considerably more courteous than does "Send. . . ." Men in prestigious positions know the value of using "courtesy words," and they use them freely. They know, however, that excessive use of such expressions causes the reader to believe that the writer is insincere—that he is using flattery or perhaps trickery or is "talking down" to the reader. A reader who suspects that the writer has used courtesy expressions for any of these three purposes looks askance at the letter. The effectiveness of such a letter is nil.

Excessive use of courtesy expressions can also cause the reader to think that the writer is a weak-kneed individual who possesses limited self-respect or backbone. You must give due consideration to other people, *and* you must give equal consideration to yourself. No one thinks more highly of you than you think of yourself. The egotistical person fails in business; so does the weak-kneed person who cannot take a firm stand on an issue in which he believes. The person who can be firm yet tactful, diplomatic, and openminded possesses the strong character that wins friends and commands respect.

Use courtesy expressions liberally, though not excessively, in your business letters to portray strength of character rather than weakness. Such usage wins the reader's confidence.

Many well-intentioned, though poor, writers spoil what would otherwise be a good business letter by inappropriate usage of "courtesy remarks." Some of these writers append a terse "Thank you" to the ends of their letters. This ending for a letter is *poor*. When something has been done that deserves a note of appreciation, you should specify the item for which you are thanking the person. The ending "Thank you" is often used for a letter asking a favor. Such usage is a major violation of good letter-writing principles. You should never *thank* a person before he has granted the favor you are asking.

A poorer ending than "Thank you" that is used frequently is "Thank you in advance." One of the poorest possible endings is the following sentence fragment or some variation of it: "Thanking you in advance, I am." This poorest-of-all ending violates these four basic rules for writing a good business letter:

1. Write complete sentences.
2. Never thank a person for doing something before he does it.
3. Do not end a letter with a sentence beginning with a participle, except in very rare instances.
4. Eliminate trite expressions.

Appropriate endings that tell the reader you will appreciate his complying with your request are "Your returning the completed form will be appreciated," or "I shall be very grateful for your help in locating the missing manuscript," or some variation that applies to the particular situation about which you are writing. Your personality, your writing style, and other sentences in the letter will help you in choosing an appropriate note of gratitude for the endings of your letters.

CONCISENESS

Conciseness, a desirable characteristic of business letters, differs from brevity. Brevity usually means incomplete. Perhaps only the highlights or the most significant points are included in a letter that is brief. Conciseness means that all essential elements are covered adequately but with no redundant or excessive verbiage. Concise writing is direct and forceful, yet tactful.

To write specifically and tactfully, you will sometimes need to use more words than are absolutely necessary to transmit the vital information in your letters. In these situations, however, using the extra words to create the impression you want to create is worthwhile. Study the contrasting examples in the two following columns:

Specific and tactful	*Weak*
I thank you for writing to me on October 18.	Thank you for your recent letter.
We are glad to have an opportunity to ship the No. 10 envelopes to you.	We are glad to have an opportunity to serve you.
We appreciate the opportunity to clean and adjust the machines in your factory.	We are glad to have an opportunity to serve you.
Please write to me when you sponsor another fund–raising campaign.	Please write to me when I can be of service to you again.
We will ship the merchandise the day we receive your order.	We will ship your order promptly.
We shipped two Model 8 electric typewriters to you by railway express this morning.	We shipped your order today.

Words that add to the smoothness or readability of your sentences can be justified, too. For example, a sentence can be read more smoothly when a date is preceded by an adverb or a preposition. Either "The group met last Tuesday" or "The group met on Tuesday" is preferred over the shorter "The group met Tuesday."

The telegraphic style of writing exemplified in the following list must not be used in business letters:

> Received casters from factory today. Shipping same tomorrow.
>
> Will attend meeting in Boston January 18.
>
> Received goods today. Package was damaged in transit.

Using the words *former* and *latter* is false economy of words. Sometimes the use of one of these words saves time for the writer, but it requires unnecessary time for the reader. He almost always has to reread at least one sentence and often a whole paragraph, to recall the ideas to which the word *former* or *latter* refers. A similar waste of time is caused by beginning sentences with indefinite pronouns such as *this, these, such, that,* and *those.* These words can be used quite well as adjectives. Using them as pronouns, though, sometimes necessitates the reader's rereading the preceding sentence to identify the "specifics" being referred to by the indefinite pronoun.

Beginning a sentence with the indefinite pronoun *it* is poor. The same reference to a preceding sentence is required for this sentence beginning as is required by the sentence beginnings *this, these, such, that,* and *those.* Beginning some sentences with the indefinite pronoun *it* adds unnecessary length. "It is the purpose of this meeting to elect officers for next year" is longer and less effective than "The purpose of this meeting is to elect officers for next year."

The principles to which the examples in this section pertain are worthy of a great deal of study. Apply the principle of word economy, but do not hesitate to add length when an addition improves the quality of your letter.

Sentences

Even though much intelligent conversation—personal and business—consists of sentence fragments, complete sentences are used when communicating in writing. Your sentences must be well constructed.

"Variety is the spice of life." Variety in sentence structure—length and style—adds much to the interest and readability of your business messages.

LENGTH

Sentence length depends somewhat on the personality or the writing style of the writer. Some people write rather long sentences that are clear and easy to read, while other people tend to write shorter sentences. Length alone cannot be used as a good criterion for judging the quality of a sentence. Variety in sentence length contributes to the interest, readability, and overall effectiveness of a letter. Some short, some medium, and some rather long sentences are desirable in many letters. The average of the sentence lengths should be perhaps between thirteen and nineteen words. Certainly some sentences should be shorter than average, and others should be longer. Restricting sentence lengths to within the thirteen-to-nineteen range would be as senseless as placing a well-adjusted executive in a straitjacket when he enters his office each day.

A letter writer, when considering "average" sentence length, may be wise to remember the little old lady who could not swim, but thought she could safely wade across a river. She was 5 feet 4 inches tall, and the river had an average depth of only 4 feet. She drowned.

As a river has some shallow areas and some deep areas, most well-written business letters will have some short sentences and some long ones.

Not only should the writer's personality be considered in writing style, but the reader's background should also be considered. When you write to a poorly educated person, you would do well to write shorter sentences than when writing to a person who is well educated on the particular subject about which you are writing. Regardless of who the reader is or what his background for the subject matter is, sentence length can be used to emphasize any specific point. In some letters, especially those that have several long sentences, a very short sentence can be used well to emphasize a point. In other letters a longer-than-average sentence may be used advantageously in emphasizing an idea or thought.

Vary the *lengths* as well as the *styles* of your sentences.

STYLE

A variety of styles is just as important as a variety of lengths for the sentences in your business letters. For some letters only one sentence is needed. In other letters the number of sentences required for an effective letter is so limited that little opportunity exists for variety in sentence style or length. In such short letters as these, very little variety is needed. A high percentage of business letters are sufficiently long to merit your wise use of variety of sentence styles (simple, compound, complex, and compound–complex) to make your letters readable, interesting, and effective.

SIMPLE. Simple sentences are easiest to construct and to punctuate. Perhaps you should use more simple sentences than any other style, but do not bore your reader by using simple sentences so extensively that your letters are dull and ineffective.

COMPOUND. Use some compound sentences. Be sure that the ideas you express in a compound sentence are appropriately related and that the two principal ideas are joined by the appropriate conjunction or a semicolon. When the two independent clauses of a compound sentence are parallel in content, use one of the coordinate conjunctions *or* or *and*. Your choice between these two conjunctions should be determined by the context of the sentences. When the two independent clauses present possible alternatives, use the conjunction *or,* as in these examples:

> The sales manager will attend the meeting in St. Louis, or he will ask his assistant to go.
>
> The two–page report will be mailed this afternoon, or it will be delivered by the salesman tomorrow morning.

The conjunction *and* is used to connect the two independent clauses that express parallel positive ideas, as in the examples that follow:

> The secretary took dictation from two executives this morning, and she transcribed all of her notes before she left the office at four o'clock.

Mr. Green talks rather slowly, and he dictates slowly and carefully.

Use the conjunction *but* in a compound sentence in which contrasting ideas are expressed by the two independent clauses, as in the following examples:

The personnel director dictates very slowly, but he expects his secretary to be able to write very rapidly.

Electronic computers are very expensive, but they do a great deal of work rapidly and accurately.

Some compound sentences can be written without the use of a conjunction to join the two independent clauses; a semicolon is used instead. In such cases the two main ideas in the two clauses must be very closely related, and both clauses must be written in the same voice—active or passive. The following sentences are examples:

Mr. Gray received the requisition for display cases on Thursday morning; he ordered them on Friday afternoon.

The books were ordered on Tuesday; they were received on Friday.

When the independent clauses of a compound sentence are joined by a semicolon instead of a conjunction, the independent clauses should be short.

Another way of providing variety with compound sentences is to use some compound sentences without stating the subject in the second clause, as in the sentences that follow:

Mr. Miller received the letter on October 28 and answered it on October 29.

The envelope was placed in my mailbox and was opened by my secretary.

Yet another type of compound sentence utilizes conjunctive adverbs for joining the independent clauses. Some examples follow:

Our store will remain open until 7 P.M. each weekday until Christmas; consequently, we must employ additional salesclerks for this period.

The assembly lines will close temporarily on April 16; therefore, the specifications for your automobiles must reach us before April 5.

COMPLEX. The use of some complex sentences adds to the effectiveness of much business writing. Complex sentences may begin with the subordinate clause, or they may end with the subordinate clause. The following sentences are examples:

When you learn to write several types of sentences, you will write letters that are interesting.

You should write good letters after you study this textbook.

COMPOUND–COMPLEX. In some business letters, especially the longer ones, compound–complex sentences can be used. Here are some examples:

If you will return the card before October 8, I will send you a copy of our current catalog; and I will ask our representative for your area to stop by your office before the first of November.

I have shipped the four electric drills that you ordered on May 6; and because you are one of our preferred customers, I have instructed our mailing department to place your name on our mailing list to receive copies of all illustrated brochures that we produce.

Use variety in the types as well as in the lengths of the sentences you write in business messages. Use the types of sentences that best express the specific ideas you wish to convey.

Paragraphs

Paragraphing is important. Just as words must be properly organized to form good sentences, sentences must be properly organized to form good paragraphs. The principle of grouping closely related ideas into one paragraph or making separate paragraphs for ideas that are not so closely related must be adhered to. The adept writer can, nevertheless, usually organize his thoughts so that he can logically write paragraphs of varying lengths. As short paragraphs can be read more easily than long ones, *most* paragraphs should be short. Excessive use of short, one–sentence paragraphs, however, tends to cause the reader to think that the letter was written by a person who is poorly educated or who gave insufficient thought to organizing the letter.

Exceedingly long paragraphs are not only difficult to read, but they also have a bad psychological effect on the reader. They frequently reflect poor organization and lack of thorough preparation for letter writing. Paragraphs should be from one to about eight lines. The average length may very well be four or five lines. As is the case with sentences, some short paragraphs are effective for emphasizing some particular ideas expressed in a letter. In other instances longer paragraphs are especially effective for emphasizing ideas.

Because the beginning of a letter is the most important part and the ending is the second most important part, the writer should *usually* strive to write short first and last paragraphs of multiple–paragraph messages. Varying the lengths of paragraphs helps to create interest and to improve the readability of business letters.

Mechanics

The principles presented in Chapter 2 and the suggestions for enhancing your writing style that are presented in this chapter can be used effectively only when the mechanical details of your writing are correct. Correct spelling, punctuation, word choice, and sentence structure are essential to achieving competency in writing business letters. A dictionary, a thesaurus, and a good English handbook should be used often by anyone who is to write letters of good quality.

Some of the mechanical details—spelling, punctuation, expression of numbers, and so on—are presented in the reference section of this textbook. Refer to that section for special help.

Questions for discussion

1. How can you improve your vocabulary?
2. What is meant by "contemporary expressions"?

3. What are some of the idiomatic expressions that you hear frequently?

4. What are some of the exceptions to the principle of "write as you talk"?

5. What are some of the words that could be used appropriately to describe women but should not be used to describe men?

Exercises

Improve the following sentences that were taken from business letters:

1. Our organization will be glad to make the adjustment you requested in your recent letter.

2. We shall be happy to supply your company with automotive parts.

3. Am grateful for your help in the completion of the writing project.

4. Will you please give our representative an opportunity to give you a demonstration of our company's sanding machine?

5. A description of the motor can be found on page 4 of our catalog.

6. Due to the fact that the form must be returned before October 16, I am enclosing herewith a self–addressed envelope for your use.

7. In order to be of further assistance to you, I will come to your office in the near future.

8. Enclosed you will find a set of special instructions.

9. We look forward to an opportunity to be of service to you.

10. There are 227,000 people in Louisville.

11. The sale was made by the representative.

12. Organization of the group can be accomplished during the month of October.

13. I shall appreciate your sending the merchandise as soon as possible.

14. The book you ordered has been mailed under separate cover.

15. Your order was shipped this morning.

16. You can complete this assignment in a short period of time.

17. Why not visit our store during our special sale, which begins on October 21.

18.   Please do not hesitate to get in touch with me.

19.   It is a pleasure to visit you again.

20.   Twenty–five people were in attendance at the meeting.

Problems

1.   Rewrite the following letter:

Mr. Hugh M. Stults, Manager, Hayes Manufacturing Company, 1142 Bethlehem Road, Wyndotte, PA 00632

Dear Mr. Stults: Enclosed is a copy of our operations report for the month of July. You asked, when you telephoned me last week, that this report be sent to you before Monday of next week. This report, which is thirty–four pages in length, was written by Edith Downs and Wayne E. Combs.

I believe that you will be especially interested in reading a description of the results we obtained by instituting the new procedures for handling the materials in the warehouse. You will find those results described on page 17.

It is my opinion that Miss Downs and Mr. Combs have done a fine job of the preparation of this report. If, however, you have any questions concerning the contents of this report, please do not hesitate to contact me. Cordially yours, H. S. Camp, Production Manager, Enclosure

2.   Rewrite the following letter:

Mrs. Ada M. Hatfield, 1221 Stoneview Road, Vinona, WI 54876

Dear Mrs. Hatfield: I want to take this opportunity to thank you for calling my attention to the defect in the carrying case for the portable typewriter that we sent to you last Monday. You should receive a replacement for it in the near future. We wrote to our supplier under the date of May 8 and requested that a new case be mailed to you as soon as possible to replace the defective case that you received.

Ordinarily, we would have another case in stock; but due to the fact that this particular typewriter has been so popular, our supply is depleted at the present time.

We hope that you will be pleased with your portable typewriter. Cordially yours, Niles F. Williams, Order Department Manager

5

Good news letters

SOME LETTERS are difficult to write because the writer cannot foresee the reader's reaction to the letter. He does not know whether the reader will feel that a letter should have been written; and even if the reader does feel that it should have been written, the writer does not know which approach would appeal most to the reader.

The types of letters discussed in this chapter have one common characteristic: They contain information that almost anyone would appreciate receiving under the circumstances that are described. They are, therefore, easy to write.

The three types of letters discussed in this chapter pertain to:

1. Complying with requests.
2. Showing gratitude.
3. Ordering.

Promptness in writing these letters is important.

Complying with requests

Of all the types of letters that are written in business, the letters that are written to comply with requests are perhaps the easiest to write. You know that when the person who made the request receives an envelope with your return address printed in letterhead form or typewritten in the upper left-hand corner, he will hope that the letter contains a compliance with his request. You know, therefore, how to begin. You know what he wants to read, and you are prepared to give him that information. *Begin* your letter by telling the reader that you *are* complying or that you *have already* complied with his request. Do this cheerfully. No other beginning would be better for this type of letter.

The following sentence illustrates one of the many possible appropriate first sentences of a reply to a reader who requested a copy of a brochure you published:

> A complimentary copy of the brochure "Shortcuts for Sales Managers" is enclosed.

One of the many possible appropriate opening sentences for a reply to a letter requesting an adjustment of $5 because of an overcharge follows:

> Here is a check for $5 to adjust the overcharge on your purchase of a fishing tackle box on April 6.

When replying to a request for permission to take a vacation earlier than the usual time, you may begin with this sentence:

> Yes, you may take your vacation from June 14 through June 27.

When you enclose materials or state in your letter the information your reader asked for, he can readily see that you *have already* complied with his request. Frequently, though, you must send the requested merchandise or other materials in a separate mailing or shipment. Everyone realizes that from time to time he cannot do the things he intends to do. Even though you honestly intend to send some item at some specific time and you have good reasons to believe that you can follow through with your good intentions, circumstances can—and they frequently *do*—prevent your sending it as scheduled. You should, therefore, mail or ship whatever materials you cannot send with the letter and *then* write a letter saying that you *have* sent them.

Be specific in telling the reader about the action you have taken. Do NOT use the trite phrase "under separate cover." DO tell him the method (parcel post, railway freight, first–class mail, or others) you used to send the materials.

The following opening sentence of a business letter is a good illustration:

> The two 3–ring notebook binders you ordered on January 26 were sent to you by parcel post this morning.

No one is expected to do everything he is requested to do. Some requests are unreasonable; and others, though reasonable and quite ordinary, cannot be granted because of existing circumstances. Only those requests that *are to be granted* are discussed in this chapter.

The requests that must be declined are discussed in Chapter 10.

When you are requested to do something, you should do it *cheerfully* or not at all. By beginning your letter with a cheerful granting of the request, you promote goodwill, you make a good impression, and you put your reader in a good frame of mind for reading the remainder of your letter.

The *beginning* is the most important part of a business letter; but even though the beginning is good, the tone of the letter can seem to be somewhat curt unless there is some follow-up that helps the reader realize that your compliance is done with a cheerful attitude. Some possible follow-up sentences for the letter beginnings that have just been presented follow:

> A complimentary copy of the brochure "Shortcuts for Sales Managers" is enclosed. The four points discussed on page 14 apply specifically to the term paper you are writing.

> I wish you much success in completing that assignment.

* * *

> Here is a check for $5 to adjust the overcharge on your purchase of a fishing tackle box on April 6. I appreciate very much your writing to me so that we can adjust the overcharge that we would not have otherwise discovered.

> A copy of the latest edition of our catalog of sporting goods is enclosed. We can ship any of these items the day we receive your order.

* * *

Yes, you may take your vacation from June 14 through June 27.

The work on the assembly line can be adjusted easily so that production will not be affected during that time. In fact, that adjustment can be made much more easily now than later in the summer.

Drive carefully and enjoy the Colorado scenery.

* * *

The two 3–ring notebook binders you ordered on January 26 were sent to you by parcel post this morning.

Because so many other people have placed repeat orders for this particular binder, I believe you will be especially well pleased with it. Orange is the most popular color for all styles of the loose-leaf folders.

I am enclosing five order forms for your use when ordering more office supplies.

None of the preceding four letters is very long, but each one contains enough information to let the reader know that he has been given courteous consideration. In each letter the request was granted in the first sentence, and sincere concern for the reader is shown in the rest of the letter.

When someone applies to you for credit, he wants to read that you have approved his request. He realizes, of course, that your complying with his request will make it possible for him to transact business with you conveniently; and he will feel complimented by knowing that you have made a routine investigation of his credit standing and are favorably impressed by the information you received. Beginning your reply by telling him that you have approved his request is the best way you can begin the letter.

Having read this excellent first sentence, he is receptive to any sales talk you may wish to include so long as the sales talk is of high calibre. High-pressure tactics, however, could drive him away from you. Do follow up your compliance with his request by letting him know that you are genuinely interested in transacting business with him. Let him know that you provide prompt, reliable, and courteous service as well as merchandise that he will want to purchase.

In the letter shown next, the writer granted credit to the customer; and he stated the amount of credit in a positive manner. Note that instead of saying, "Your credit purchases must be limited to $600 a month," he said, "You may charge purchases up to $600 a month." Such positive wording tends to cause the reader to feel that he is being complimented.

DELTA DEPARTMENT STORE

Jacksboro, Mississippi

May 17, 1973

Mrs. Steven L. Hampton
259 Riderwood Road
Mason, AR 72180

Dear Mrs. Hampton:

All you have to do to charge a purchase at our store is to present the enclosed charge card to the salesclerk and sign the sales slip. We look forward to having you visit our store again soon.

We are very happy to have you as a credit customer. You may charge purchases up to $600 a month. The people whose names you gave as references for our routine credit investigation paid you compliments that you must be proud of.

When you wish to shop by mail, please include your account number (A-26734) in your letter so that the sales clerk can process your order speedily. The merchandise you request will be shipped within twenty-four hours after we receive your order.

Cordially yours,

John Reed

John Reed, Manager
Credit Department

mmc

Enclosure

More details are required for a letter accepting an invitation to speak to a group. In such a letter the time, the date, and the place of the meeting should be specified in addition to a definite acceptance of the invitation. The person who invites a speaker likes to know that these details are clear to the person who accepts the invitation. *Verify the date carefully;* for example, make sure that May 26 is *Friday* rather than Thursday or Saturday. An error of this nature can cause anxiety, and it usually necessitates additional correspondence or a telephone call. Mentioning the length and the topic of your speech is also helpful. The time you expect to arrive at the meeting place and your mode of travel—especially when tight scheduling is involved—should also be mentioned in your reply. You should also tell the reader the special facilities (screen, overhead projector, tape recorder, and so on) that you will need for your speech.

A letter illustrating some of these points is on page 77.

When you reply to some types of requests, you may sometimes have additional information, publications, or sample merchandise that you think would be helpful to the reader of your letter. Send such items in addition to those requested. You will, of course, refer to these additional items. Any item that is enclosed with a letter should be mentioned in the letter.

Resist the temptation to end any letter with the trite *"If I can be of any further assistance to you, please do not hesitate to contact me."* Many otherwise good letters have been *spoiled* by such an ending as this. When you feel that you have done as much as you should do for the reader, do not suggest that he ask for more assistance. When you do feel, however, that it is probable that you *can* help the reader in the future and you would *like* to help him, refer in a positive manner to your offer to help him again. Some examples of positive statements of offers to help follow:

Just let me know when I can help you again.

* * *

When I can help you again, please write me.

* * *

We will be glad to send you copies of our other publications if you should need them for another term paper.

FLORIDA PUBLISHING COMPANY

Lakeview, Florida

February 15, 1973

Mr. Randy M. Thomas, Jr.
President, Marketing Club
Lakeland University
Sheffield, GA 30306

Dear Mr. Thomas:

I shall be very glad to speak to your group at 6 p.m. (EST)
on Tuesday, March 31. Thank you for inviting me.

Will you please have a small screen and an overhead projector ready for me? I shall use some transparencies to introduce the subtopics of my speech, which is entitled "Sales
Talk for The Twentieth Century."

As my plane (Delta Flight No. 685) is scheduled to arrive in
Sheffield at 3:35 p.m., I should have ample time to get to
your administration building before the meeting begins.

I look forward to seeing you on March 31.

Cordially yours,

Glen E. Bradford
Glen E. Bradford
Sales Manager

bhw

The most important thing to keep in mind is that you should
provide whatever assistance you feel you should provide in complying with a request and that this compliance is almost always
enough to offer. Sometimes an offer to give further help if re-

quested to do so can detract from the help you have already given. Such an offer can cause the reader to believe that you may be withholding some assistance that you should provide.

Sales talk such as that in the letter adjusting the $5 overcharge and the letter stating that the notebook binders have been sent is appropriate when writing to customers. You should be very discreet, however, in including sales talk when writing to people who do not buy from you. Including sales talk in a letter complying with a request from a person who is not one of your customers can detract greatly from the courtesy you are showing him by complying with his request. He may very well be led to believe that your primary motive in granting his request was to try to sell your merchandise or services rather than to assist him with his endeavor.

When you have reason to believe that some sales information would be appreciated by the recipient of your letter, you may add his name to your list to receive sales talk later. You should be careful that you never cause a person to feel obligated to patronize you because of your complying with a request that he has made.

Try to reply to a letter within twenty-four hours from the time you receive it. In some instances, though, such quick responses are not feasible. For example, you may have to wait three or four days to receive the information or the materials that you were requested to send. In such cases delaying your reply until you can comply with the request may be your best course of action. If, however, you must wait somewhat longer (perhaps three or four weeks) to supply the requested items, you should reply within twenty-four hours by specifying the date on which you can comply with the request.

Replying *promptly* makes a favorable impression on your reader.

Showing gratitude

Everyone is called upon from time to time to help someone else. Also, everyone must be assisted by others occasionally. Sometimes assistance will be given to you voluntarily. At other times you must ask for it. No one is completely self-sufficient. Certainly, you should use your own resourcefulness and ingenuity to accomplish your objectives; but when you realize that you need advice, direction, or tangible materials from someone else, ask for the help confidently and courteously.

When you help someone, do you appreciate his acknowledging your help and his expressing gratitude to you? Of course you do, even though you were glad to help him and you did not want him to feel obligated to you. Other people feel the same way. When someone grants you a favor, therefore, express your sincere appreciation promptly.

Frequently, an oral "thank you" or "I appreciate your helping me" is sufficient expression of your gratitude. When you cannot make such an oral comment promptly or occasionally when the favor you have received is somewhat out of the ordinary—or a big one, so to speak—you should write a letter. Such a letter is easy to write. You know the purpose for writing, and you know that the addressee will be pleased to receive the letter. Begin immediately with a statement of appreciation for the *specific* favor.

The following sentences illustrate some of the appropriate ways of beginning this letter:

> Thank you for lending me your copy of *Executive Decision Making*.

> I appreciate your helping me solve the records storage problem in our office.

In some instances one sentence may be all that is needed. Often, though, additional comments enhance the effectiveness of the letter. The person who granted you the favor obviously has some special interest in you or in the particular matter with which he helped you; therefore, some comment about the *specific* ways you were benefited, the present status of the project, or the expectations may reveal your sincere appreciation and convince him that his assistance was beneficial.

Expressing your desire to reciprocate is sometimes appropriate for inclusion in this type of letter.

Study these examples of letters that were written to express appreciation.

> Thank you for lending me your copy of *Executive Decision Making*. I shall use information from some of the charts in Chapter

6 when I speak to the management professors of our state university next month.

I mailed the book to you by parcel post today.

*   *   *

I appreciate your helping me solve the records storage problem in our office. The transfer cases you suggested are much superior to any others that we have used.

Please come by to see us when you come to Athens next month. I should like to show you our new offices.

Keeping your reader in mind, getting off to a good start, writing as you talk, beginning with good news, and economizing on words are among the principles that apply specifically to letters showing gratitude. Some people, unfortunately, waste words and still never actually say what they mean because they begin with such wordiness as "I wish to thank you . . . ," "I should like to thank you for . . . ," and "I should like to take this opportunity to thank you for. . . ." Simplicity, directness, and sincerity are desired qualities of a letter expressing appreciation.

Letters have several advantages over oral communications. Repeated oral expressions of gratitude can become boring to the listener, and excessive repetition can cause the listener to believe that the person talking is insincere or is insecure. Chances are good that the recipient of a letter of appreciation will read that letter several times. Although the letter may not be filed, the addressee will probably keep it on his desk until after he has read it several times. Repetitious reading will have a desirable effect on him because he will read it voluntarily and only when he is in the proper mood to read it.

Letters that express appreciation promote goodwill. Write them when you sincerely feel grateful and when you feel that the reader will not think that you are attempting to "apple polish" him.

Ordering

A supplier of any type of merchandise is obviously pleased to receive an order. Generally speaking, the more merchandise that is ordered from him, the greater are his profits. Some suppliers provide order forms to simplify the ordering process for both the customer and the supplier. When such an order form is available, no letter is necessary. Simply fill out the form *accurately* and mail it. Quite often, however, no order form is available. You must, therefore, write a letter to obtain the desired merchandise.

The four items of information that are essential in an order letter are: (1) identification of the merchandise desired, (2) cost, (3) delivery instructions, and (4) method of payment.

IDENTIFICATION

The types of information necessary to identify the merchandise you desire vary from situation to situation. When a *catalog number* is available, specify that number in your letter. State the name of the item, the desired size, color, style, weight, and any other variable characteristic of the items you are ordering. Also, include the desired quantity.

Special features such as monograms should be clearly stated in your letter.

COST

Specify the cost of each item in your order. This information is important even when the cost does not fluctuate because of different grades, sizes, styles, and similar reasons.

DELIVERY

Tell the supplier the method—parcel post, railway express, railway freight, air express, or other—he should use in sending your merchandise. If you wish to have the package insured, include these instructions in your order letter. Generally, the person ordering the merchandise pays the delivery costs. Include this amount in your check when you send payment with the order letter.

If items you are ordering are to be delivered to different destinations, give the name and complete address to which each item is to be sent. When merchandise is needed by a specific date, be sure to mention the date and possibly the occasion; for example, ". . . for our annual spring sale, which begins on April 7."

PAYMENT

Tell the supplier *how* you will pay for the merchandise. You may wish to enclose a check, a money order, or a bank draft for the payment. Refer to the exact amount of the payment you are enclosing so that the supplier can readily see that you have sent the correct amount. If you have an account with him, you can say that the entire amount for the merchandise and the delivery expenses are to be charged to your account.

Any enclosure should be referred to in a letter. Be sure to refer specifically to the check, money order, or other type of payment that you are enclosing.

Use a *format* that will make your letter easy to read. When you are ordering several items, try to tabulate the information. Tabulating is sometimes impractical, however. In such instances you may prefer to space all information pertaining to one item of merchandise in paragraph form and number the paragraphs. Two appropriate formats are illustrated in the following letters.

Spacing the contents of your order letter in such a manner that the prices are in a column on the right–hand side of the letter will enable the supplier to verify quickly the total amount for the merchandise and the delivery charges. Show this total clearly in your letter.

Regardless of the format you choose, arrange the information so that it can be read easily and accurately. Such an arrangement will help the supplier to fill your order with the greatest expediency and will help insure that you receive all the merchandise you ordered.

Remember that the addressee will be pleased to receive your letter. You can, therefore, begin immediately with a courteous request that the merchandise be sent. Bear in mind that the principles of good letter writing apply to *all* letters. End your letter with a note of goodwill. A courteous, positive reference to your belief that the supplier will fill your order promptly can be a very good ending.

Mayfield Handicrafts, Inc.

Mayfield, Indiana

April 26, 1973

Miller Office Supply Company
1181 Broad Street
Athens, Ohio

Gentlemen:

Please send me the following merchandise by parcel post:

Quantity	Description	Price	Total
4 reams	Onionskin, 8½ by 11, 7-lb.	$ 3.30	$13.20
3 reams	Bond paper, 8½ by 11, 20-lb., white	6.50	19.50
2 boxes	Envelopes, No. 10, white	5.40	10.80
2 dozen	Pencils, No. 2, black lead	1.20	2.40
1 dozen	Typewriter ribbons, black, cotton for Royal manuals	18.00	18.00
	Postage		3.60
	Total		$67.50

A check for $67.50 is enclosed.

Cordially yours,

Max M. Perkins

Max M. Perkins
Chief Accountant

/bac

Enclosure

THE FARM AND GARDEN SHOP
Livingston, AL   35470

June 2, 1973

Pick-Wick Wholesalers, Inc.
1226 First Avenue North
Birmingham, AL   35200

Gentlemen:

Please send us the three following items and charge the total
for them and the shipping cost to our account--No. 386670:

     Harvey 25" Riding Mower, No. 3-4604, 5 H.P., B & S
     4-cycle engine, 25" cut, 3 speeds forward and reverse
     parking brake $574

     Robin Tiller, 5 H.P., Cobb and Rainey engine, recoil
     start $188

     Steel wheelbarrow, 3 cubic feet $9

I shall appreciate your sending these items by motor freight to
arrive at our store before June 8.

               Cordially yours,

               Michael L. Denton

               Michael L. Denton
               Manager

/twf

Questions for discussion

1. What are some of the steps you can take to help the receiver of
    your order letter to send each item to the proper address when you
    ask that items be sent to different addresses?

2. What are some appropriate sentences that you may use as good-will endings for your order letters?

3. What are some appropriate sentences that you may use as first sentences for letters that you write to acknowledge orders?

4. Why is format more important for order letters than for some other types of business letters?

5. Why should you thank a person for calling your attention to an error that you have made?

Exercises

Improve the following sentences that were taken from business letters.

1. I should like to take this opportunity to thank you for sending the catalog that I requested October 6.

2. Enclosed you will find a check in the amount of $5.00.

3. You will find a description of Model No. 634 on page 8.

4. The pamphlet you mentioned in your inquiry of October 8 will not be off the press until November 15.

5. Due to the fact that prices are rising, some items will have to be eliminated.

6. The installation of the machine is a simple job.

7. In the event that we have rain on Saturday, the sale will be postponed.

8. It is a pleasure to assist you in making the changes.

9. The document was issued under the date of July 17.

10. The contract is effective for a period of one year.

Problems

1. Which letter writing principles are adhered to and which ones are violated in the following letter?

   Enclosed you will find two copies of the report entitled "Your Future in Advertising" that you requested in your recent letter.

   Although this report usually sells for 75 cents a copy, we are glad to send two copies to you without charge. On page 17 you will find a list of the companies for whom we have prepared advertising copy within the past three years. I believe you will enjoy reading this unusual report.

If I can be of further assistance to you, please do not hesitate to contact me.

Rewrite the letter. Add any specific information you wish to without changing any of the facts that are presented in the letter. Supply the inside address and other necessary parts.

2. In what ways can the following letter be improved?

Miller Office Supply Co.
1181 Broad Street
Athens, Ohio

Attention Mr. James L. Miller

Dear Mr. Miller:

I am interested in obtaining several items of merchandise for use in a class that I shall begin teaching soon. If you carry these items in stock, will you please send them as soon as possible.

I will need 4 packages of onionskin, 3 packages of bond paper, 2 dozen pencils, 100 plain envelopes, and 2 dozen typewriter ribbons.

If you need additional information to ship this order, please do not hesitate to get in touch with me.

Cordially yours,

3. What are some of the good characteristics of the letter that follows?
What are the trite or wordy expressions that should be revised?
What letter writing principles are violated?

Please send me two flashlights (catalog No. 30455) and two boxes of No. 2 pencils with red lead (catalog No. 3096). My check in the amount of $14.00 to cover the cost of this merchandise and the postage is enclosed herewith.

Please send the above items as soon as possible.

Thank you.

4. You are the professor who conducted a short correspondence workshop last Saturday morning for the Tuscaloosa chapter of

the National Secretaries Association, International. As you have taught business communications courses for several years, you have a large, up–to–date library. Recommending a book on letter writing will, therefore, be an easy task for you.

Reply to the following letter that you received this morning. Recommend a book and send Miss Long the information she will need to obtain a copy. Do *not* send her a book. Include any comments that would be appropriate for this letter.

T. L. PATRICK AGENCY
FIRST NATIONAL BANK BUILDING
624 Market Street
Tuscaloosa, Alabama   37402

October 5, 1973

Dr. William W. Mosley
Department of Business Administration
Foothills University
Gatlinburg, Tennessee

Dear Dr. Mosley:

Enjoyed your correspondence workshop so very much at the Secretarial Institute this past Saturday at the YMCA, and feel that I gained from it.

I am wondering if you have the time to give me the name of a good book on letter writing and if you could, I would appreciate it so very much.

Very truly yours,

(Miss) Annette Long

5. Today you received the pamphlet "Making Ends Meet" that you ordered from the McDonald Publishing Company, P. O. Box 1862, Maysville, Illinois. The letter accompanying that publication was signed by Nancy Polhill, publications manager.

   Write to her and let her know that you are grateful for her help.

6. Order four of the following items from the Smithfield Sporting Goods Store, 5104 Carlton Pike, Ridgeway, Connecticut:

    a   Ragsdale Golf Cart, deluxe bag brackets, 10½″ cast wheels $19.98.

    b   Roomy vinyl golf bag, $8.44, colors: green, black, beige.

    c   Men's suede golf shoes, $11.96, colors: olive, tan, gray, sizes 6–12.

    d   "Bobby Sampson" golf clubs (starter set—3 woods, 4 irons, putter) $72.88 (men's).

    e   "Under Par" golf balls, $3.96 a dozen.

7.   Order these two items from the Charleston Discount House, P. O. Box 872, Billington, Vermont: 1 doz. bottles Prim Shampoo at 67 cents a dozen and ¼″ Gray and Smiley electric drill, $12.88, with extra long electric cord.

    The drill is for your brother, whose address is 1151 Walton Road, Brotherton, Massachusetts. Ask that the drill be mailed to him.

8.   You are the assistant manager of Fairview Office Supply Company, 124 Main Street, Littleton, IA 50153. Today you received from Frank R. Scofield an order for an Oliver portable electric typewriter and a Swingway 500 stapling machine. You can ship these items immediately. This order is the first one you have received from Mr. Scofield, whose address is Route 8, Lincoln, IA 50652. Write to him. In your letter let him know that you are glad to have him as a customer.

9.   When you applied for a part–time job on your college campus, you gave as one of your references the name of your high school principal. You were offered the job for which you applied and were told that the principal had given you an excellent recommendation, which was a strong factor in the decision to hire you.

    Write a letter to your high school principal and thank him for helping you get the job.

10.   Your son's room is being redecorated, and you found just the perfect sheets and bedspread in the Spangle catalog. Order this colorful "Roadrunner" ensemble today.

    2 Twin Flat Sheets 63 × 104 inches—69Z122M $3.97, 2 for $7.54.

    2 Twin Fitted Sheets fits 39 × 76-inch bed—69Z123M $3.97, 2 for $7.54.

    2 Twin Spreads 78 × 110 inches—69Z125M $9.97.

Two of your friends, Mr. and Mrs. Joseph T. Johnson, 579 Pine Street, Rock Creek, Wyoming 84039, became the parents of a baby girl last week. You want to order a Raggedy Ann Nursery lamp to be sent to them. The catalog number is 69B123A, and the lamp sells for $9.98.

Since you have a charge account with Spangle, have these items charged to your account and mailed by parcel post. The address is Spangle, Inc., 1442 High Street, Lakeview, MI 48650.

6

Public relations messages

PEOPLE like to be remembered. Letting them know that you think about them by writing to them can be very rewarding for them and for you. Casual as well as intimate friendships, both personal and business, are strengthened by good public relations experiences.

Any letter—whether it is an order, an inquiry, a compliance with a request, a refusal of a request, or any other type of letter —should contain some characteristic of goodwill. Each letter should be written in such a manner that it establishes, maintains, promotes, or possibly reestablishes goodwill in addition to serving some other possible purpose. Some messages are mailed for the sole purpose of goodwill or good public relations. Messages of that type are discussed in this chapter.

Sincerity is the key to good public relations. Any message that is sent solely for public relations purposes, therefore, must be sent only when the sender is honest and sincere about his professed interest in the person to whom his message is addressed. True enough, the sender may have the ulterior motive of increasing his business or achieving some other benefit for himself; but an intelligent, fair-minded person realizes that he cannot continue to succeed when he achieves a measure of success at the expense of someone else. When an experience is mutually beneficial, the two communicators can reap genuine rewards.

Everybody appreciates compliments, and people of average intelligence can sense the difference between compliments and flattery. Do not, therefore, insult your own intelligence or the intelligence of the person with whom you are communicating by attempting to flatter him.

The message you send should be in keeping with the characteristics of the people involved and the occasion which prompts you to send it. Your message may be presented in a handwritten or a typewritten letter, or it may be presented by means of a printed greeting card.

Printed cards and letters may be mailed on numerous special occasions. Birthdays, Christmas, anniversaries, special programs, sales, and the time of moving into a new location or into a new business venture are among the many occasions on which special public relations messages may be mailed.

Whether you send public relations messages as an individual or as an officer of some organization, you should pay very careful attention to the content, vocabulary, and mechanics of these messages. Always *sign with ink* any message that you mail as a goodwill gesture. A personal signature contributes a great deal to the warmth and effectiveness of such a message—whether it is in handwritten, typewritten, or printed form.

Greeting cards

The number of people or groups to whom you wish to send special greetings may be so great as to prohibit your sending individual letters. In such instances you may choose to send a printed card. In still some other situations the printed card may seem to be more appropriate than a letter.

While the sender has a great deal of freedom in choosing the message and the card design, the greeting card selection should be made on the bases of the relationship that exists between the sender and the receiver, the nature of the organization from which the card is sent, and the personal characteristics of the recipient. The message to a client, customer, or other business associate should not be so personal as the one you would send to a relative or a personal friend; but it should let the recipient know you are thinking of him as a person and not just as a name in an accounts file or on some other such list.

Because a printed message will be mailed to many individuals, the anticipated recipients must be categorized so that one message will apply to every member of the group. This grouping forces the sender to make some generalizations when selecting greeting cards. The more homogeneous the group to which greeting cards are to be mailed, the easier it is to select a card that is appropriate for the recipient. For example, a card that would appeal to adults may not appeal to children. Obviously, the greater the degree of heterogeneity of the group, the more general the nature of the message must be.

Such businesses as stationers and printers would perhaps be expected to send a card of high-quality printing on equally high-quality paper. Other types of businesses, especially the smaller organizations and the nonprofit organizations, may prefer to send less expensive greeting cards. Banks and other similar institutions may very likely choose to send a card that is of a somewhat conservative nature, whereas an organization such as a resort hotel or restaurant may be best represented by a more elaborate greeting card. A novelty shop could appropriately send an unusual or novel form of greetings.

Designs, emblems, or pictures that represent the organization sending the message or pictures of the geographical region in which the organization operates may very well be incorporated in the layout of the card.

A greeting card may be signed by one person only, or it may be signed by several persons. The owner, the officers, or all of the employees of an organization—provided the total number is small —may sign the card. The signatures may be in random order, in alphabetical order, in rank order of the offices held, or in still some other order. Quite likely, each person who signs the card will use his own pen; and he may even use a color of ink different from the others. Such variety can contribute to the "personal touch" of the message. The signatures do not have to be carefully aligned, but a large number of signatures in a "scrambled" arrangement may make it too difficult for the recipient to locate some particular name he wishes to see.

Some examples can be found on page 94.

BIRTHDAYS

An appropriate message is usually a welcome piece of mail on a person's birthday. Greeting cards are especially appreciated by youngsters and elderly people. Your choice of a letter or a printed card may be governed by many possible factors. If you are sending birthday messages to a large number of customers or other business associates during the year, for example, you may be compelled to choose a printed card. Handwriting or typewriting such a large number of letters may be prohibitive, and you certainly would not want to send a form letter.

Be especially careful that your message makes no reference to the age of the recipient unless you are certain that he is quite happy to publicize his age. Youngsters and elderly persons often fit into this category.

When you send a birthday greeting to a business or professional acquaintance, limit the message to the birthday greeting only; do *not* make any reference to a business transaction of any nature. The inclusion of such an item as advertising literature or an announcement of a sale would spoil an otherwise *good* public relations gesture. A printed greeting card of any type should be mailed in an envelope that bears a handwritten address and, of course, the personal signature of the sender. If the volume of such correspondence prohibits the amount of handwriting necessary for these mailings, do not mail birthday messages.

The birthday card that is illustrated on page 94 was designed to be used for any customer of the department store for which the card was prepared. Any greeting card should be used only once for any one recipient. You will need to maintain some type of record to indicate which cards have been used for each customer.

CHRISTMAS

Some business or professional men and women send greeting cards to their clients, customers, or other business associates dur-

The front of this greeting card has a picture of the store front—a scene that is familiar to all persons who receive a copy of the card.

The front of this greeting card has a picture of a scene from the local ski lodge.

The front of this greeting card has a picture of a sleigh.

ing the Christmas season. Under certain circumstances this practice can be quite good. While no one objects to receiving such a piece of correspondence, most people receive so many greeting cards at that particular time that they pay little attention to cards, except the ones from their relatives and personal friends. Unless you have some special reason to believe that clients or customers would be especially pleased to receive a greeting card at Christmas time, perhaps you should choose some other occasion for sending them a special greeting.

For business or professional relationships that do not ordinarily afford an occasion on which you can appropriately send a special message, you may wish to send a Christmas greeting card.

Christmas greeting cards addressed to people of the Christian religion may or may not bear a message of a religious nature. Ordinarily, a Christmas card bearing a message of a religious nature would not be appreciated by a person whose religion is non-Christian.

The first Christmas card on page 94 was mailed by the manager of a ski club; it was signed by the manager and his two office assistants. The second Christmas card was mailed by the owner of an automobile agency and was signed by the owner, his two office assistants, and his three salesmen.

ANNIVERSARIES

Some businesses such as jewelry stores and department stores may keep a record of wedding anniversaries of their customers and send greeting cards on that occasion. Such a practice is, however, not practical for all such stores. When the list of regular customers is quite large, the store may send greetings for only the special anniversaries such as the silver or the golden anniversary. Anniversary cards can be chosen easily, as a message that would be appropriate for one person would also be appropriate for another who is celebrating the same occasion.

The greeting card on page 96 was mailed from a jewelry store.

Some organizations prefer to send messages to their clients or customers on the anniversary of their becoming associated with the organization. While cards may be used for such an event,

The front of this greeting card, which is in silver finish, contains this wording: "Your Silver Anniversary."

letters are often more desirable. Letters that may be written at such times are discussed later in this chapter.

PROGRAMS

From time to time organizations sponsor a special program for which they issue invitations to a large group of people. Among these programs may be appliance or equipment shows or demonstrations by manufacturers or distributors, fashion shows by department stores, and parties or concerts by schools or other groups. Engraved or printed invitations are usually mailed for these programs.

The invitation should include information concerning the type or nature of the event, the time and date, the exact location, and a specific invitation to attend. If it is desirable, but not absolutely necessary, that you know the approximate number of people who expect to attend, you should request a reply. In some instances simply adding the letters R.S.V.P. in the bottom left-hand corner of the invitation will serve adequately to get the needed replies. Chances are good that a few of the people on your long list to receive an invitation will be lax in handling their correspondence and will not reply as promptly as perhaps they should; and of course, now and then some of the most careful handlers of correspondence will for one reason or another not reply as they should. To make the task of replying easier for the recipient of your invitation and, incidentally, to make it easier for you to process the replies, you may choose to enclose a card that is to be returned as the reply. The practice of enclosing a reply card is especially appropriate when you feel reasonably certain that as many people would like to attend as can be seated or otherwise accommodated. For such an occasion you may ask that the recipient make a reservation by returning the card by a specified date. Then if some of the cards are not returned by that date, you can invite others to attend the event.

The invitation on this page was engraved for mailing to a list of selected purchasers of high-quality merchandise.

Include whatever information is necessary to let the receiver of the invitation know the name and the address of the person who is to receive a reply. You may need to include directions (a map may be very helpful) on how to reach the site; and under certain circumstances, you may need to instruct the recipient to present the invitation card when he arrives. Still other special information may be desirable.

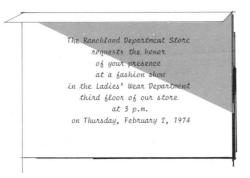

The Ranchland Department Store
requests the honor
of your presence
at a fashion show
in the Ladies' Wear Department
third floor of our store
at 3 p.m.
on Thursday, February 2, 1974

The front of this greeting card contains an engraved silhouette of a woman.

Be sure to follow the principle of writing so clearly that your message *cannot be misunderstood,* and also follow the principle of simplicity of presentation. Always present invitations as tastefully as you can.

SALES

Notifying your customers of special sales in which they may be interested is a courteous, considerate, and smart thing to do. This announcement can be sent on a printed postal card or on a card similar to the other greeting cards discussed in the preceding paragraphs.

Perhaps the postal card would be best for large sales of general merchandise (low-priced, medium-priced, and high-priced items).

For the high-priced exclusive or luxury items, though, perhaps the greeting card style of announcement would be in better taste for a list of *preferred* customers.

Sales announcements are discussed further in Chapter 7.

OTHER

The special occasions (birthdays, Christmas, anniversaries, programs, and sales) mentioned in the preceding paragraphs of this chapter do not comprise an exhaustive list. Numerous other occasions—special as well as holidays—afford an individual or a group opportunities to send greetings to their clients, customers, fellow workers, and other associates.

The principles discussed in this chapter apply to all instances for which you may wish to send greetings for public relations purposes.

Letters

A letter could be written for any of the special occasions that were mentioned in the greeting cards section of this chapter. As was mentioned for those particular instances, though, a greeting card is more practical and usually accomplishes the public relations purpose just as well as a letter would. For some other occasions a letter would be more effective. Letters of that type are discussed in the paragraphs that follow.

Some of the instances for which special letters are usually appropriate are welcoming new residents to the area, welcoming new clients or customers, complimenting customers for prompt payments, showing appreciation for continued patronage, congratulating, and expressing sympathy.

NEW RESIDENTS

New residents of an area may be potential clients or customers of your organization. Cultivate potential business. If a new resident is not yet acquainted with a banker, or a department store, for instance, a person in one of these positions has a golden opportunity to add him to his family of clients or customers. By offering your services, you can help the person who has recently moved into your community; and you can increase your own business. What better conditions could you have than an opportunity to provide a service or a product and thereby benefit both you and another person.

```
                              RALEIGH NATIONAL BANK
                              Raleigh, Virginia  23673



                                    May 26, 1973



        Mr. Barry L. Mabry
        276 Vine Avenue
        Mattson, SC  29065

        Dear Mr. Mabry:

        We welcome you to Raleigh, and we offer you any of the services
        of our all-purpose bank that you wish to use.

        Can we help you locate living accommodations?  We have an exten-
        sive listing of homes that are for sale or for rent inside the
        city as well as those in surburban areas.  Mr. Harry Allen, a
        member of our staff who has helped locate houses for some 87 new
        residents of Raleigh during the past two and a half years, would
        be glad to help you with this task.  Just write to him if you
        would like for him to help you.

        We pay 5½ percent interest on two-year certificates, and we
        have regular and Golden savings accounts.  You may write as
        many checks as you wish each month without charge when the bal-
        ance in your checking account remains above $100.  Our loan
        department will be glad to work with you in any way.

        As I am confident you already realize, Raleigh College plays an
        important role in the lives of our residents.  We appreciate the
        contributions that the college faculty, staff, and students make
        to our city; and we like to become acquainted with each newcomer.
        Please come by the bank for a visit when you arrive later this
        summer.

                              Cordially yours,



                              Nolan L. Mayo, Jr.
                              Public Relations Director


        wsh
```

An officer of one of the four banks in a small college town secures a list of the names and addresses of new faculty members for the college and new employees on the management level for the various manufacturing concerns in the locality. He writes a letter to each of these people before they move into his town. He no doubt uses the same letter, or possibly similar letters, for each person but has it typewritten to each individual as is described in Chapter 11. In this letter the bank official welcomes the newcomer and offers the services of his bank. He mentions only briefly the routine services—checking accounts, savings accounts, loans, and so on—but he stresses special services such as helping the newcomer locate suitable housing for renting or purchasing. He invites the newcomer to come to the bank upon his arrival in the town, and of course he follows up this letter by getting in touch with the newcomer and greeting him personally.

For people who move into the town in the summer or fall, the banker encloses a wallet–size card containing the football game schedule for the local college as he assumes that most people are interested in this type of recreation. He may very well include some other type of information that is of general interest such as a schedule of concerts that have been arranged for that geographical area.

Numerous people have said that this letter caused them to go to that particular bank rather than to one of the other three local banks to open accounts and to make other financial transactions. The letter on page 99 is typical of the type that is mailed to new residents.

NEW CUSTOMERS

Everyone likes to be appreciated, and he likes to be given special consideration within acceptable limits. A new customer for a department store, for example, does not expect to be granted higher discount rates than older customers of that particular store; but he does appreciate the store personnel's letting him know that he is thought of as an individual—not just as a name on a customer list—who can expect the courtesies and the services the other customers receive. Store managers, therefore, should consider carefully the possibility of writing letters welcoming new customers.

Very little needs to be said in a letter welcoming a new customer. The writer should tell the new customer that his business is appreciated, and he should mention any existing discount policies and special sales conditions. He may also outline the procedures for opening a charge account if he believes the customer qualifies for credit. The mere fact that the store employee has enough interest to send an individually typewritten, personally signed letter is often sufficient to cause the new customer to continue to purchase from that particular store rather than from one of the store's competitors unless of course the competing store offers better prices, services, or merchandise.

A form letter that is designed so that minor changes can be made quickly and easily is usually quite effective for this type of communication. Each letter should be typewritten either personally or by use of an automatic typewriter. Such letters can be worded so that they sound as if they were composed especially for the recipient because what a fair-minded store manager would write to one new customer is what he would also write to other new customers. Use a direct, friendly style of writing and avoid any references to what your "records show" concerning the addressee.

Such statements as the following should not be used because they do not cause the recipient to feel that he is getting personal consideration:

> Our records show that you purchased $347.86 worth of merchandise at our store on May 16.
>
> * * *
>
> According to our records, your first purchase at our store was on June 26.
>
> * * *
>
> I was pleased to learn, when glancing through our records, that you have purchased merchandise from us four times since January 1.

The purpose of these goodwill letters would be defeated by such statements. While the new customer realizes that the employees of any large business must refer to records in order to recall all the details of every purchase or for every customer, he is not favorably impressed when a letter writer refers to the records when the purpose for sending the letter is purely good public relations.

RANCHLAND DEPARTMENT STORE
Spring City, Kansas

November 3, 1973

Miss Alice Coleman
Apartment 314
Chandler Towers
2715--22 Street
Billings, Nebraska   68015

Dear Miss Coleman:

Mrs. Geraldine Northcutt enjoyed helping you make some clothing selections when you visited our store last Friday. All of our salesclerks are very much interested in helping customers choose from our large variety of high-quality merchandise.

We have added your name and address to the list of persons who will receive announcements of our special sales. Please remember that the 2 percent discount that you received by paying cash last Friday applies to any purchase that you make from us.

We look forward to your visiting us again soon.

Sincerely yours,

Max Weinstein
Max Weinstein
Manager

glm

The letter welcoming the new customer should be written within a few days (perhaps within one week) after the first purchase is made. This letter, which is comparatively short, can be followed by sales announcements and other sales materials at whatever intervals seem most appropriate for the occasion; but such items should not accompany this letter.

The letter on page 102 was written to a customer four days after her first purchase at a large department store.

COMPLIMENTING CUSTOMERS

Praise is a *positive* motivating device. Use it freely and sincerely to promote goodwill among your associates. Everyone likes to know that his good performance is recognized and appreciated.

Although all customers are expected to pay their accounts on time, your letting them know that you appreciate their fine paying habits can mean a great deal to them. Perhaps you should write them a letter from time to time to compliment them. These letters should be short, direct, and friendly. They should be sincere and should be mailed at *irregular* intervals. Mailing them at obviously scheduled intervals such as every five years would detract from the effectiveness of this thoughtful gesture and would cause the recipient to feel that your mailing is purely mechanical in nature. He would perhaps sense the routine handling of records that prompted you to write the letter.

Too frequent mailing of letters of this nature to any particular individual would also detract from the effectiveness of such correspondence. The frequency of writing to a customer may be determined by the length of time he has transacted business with you, the frequency of his purchases, the size of his purchases, his personality, or by one of several other factors or a combination of factors. Regardless of the system you use to schedule these public relations letters, write in such a manner that the reader will realize that you are genuinely interested in him as an individual. The letter on page 104 has been used for this purpose.

Form paragraphs, as discussed in Chapter 11, can be devised to serve as parts of many of these letters. Special, individually dictated paragraphs can be added to the form paragraphs at the time the letter is typewritten.

RANCHLAND DEPARTMENT STORE
Spring City, Kansas

August 20, 1973

Mr. Burton M. French
1126 Hazelhurst Road
Fleming, Nebraska 68539

Dear Mr. French:

You know, of course, that your bill-paying habits are of the
highest calibre; and we want you to know that we realize that
too.

We surely do appreciate having you as a regular customer. Your
clothing selections represent us well, and we shall continue to
provide high-quality merchandise that will appeal to you.

Because you are one of our "preferred" customers, you can purchase any item that we sell by simply signing the sales slip.

Sincerely yours,

Hal T. Francis, Jr.
Hal T. Francis, Jr.
Credit Manager

cfy

CONTINUED PATRONAGE

Some customers do not have the best habits of paying their
accounts; that is, they do not pay as *promptly* as you would like
for them to—yet they always pay their accounts in full without

your having to prompt them. You value these customers, too. Because they have been buying from you for several years and are satisfied with your products and your services, you want to encourage them to continue to patronize your organization.

A letter similar in nature to the one you mail to compliment

RANCHLAND DEPARTMENT STORE
Spring City, Kansas

March 8, 1974

Mr. Elliot W. Sawyer
267 West Sixth Street
North Plains, Kansas 66651

Dear Mr. Sawyer:

We like transacting business with you and your family. To keep
you as regular customers, we will continue to offer only the
highest-quality merchandise. We will offer it at competitive
prices and provide the same courteous, efficient services that
you have come to expect since you opened your account with us
some six years ago.

Your signature is as good as cash in any department of our store.

Cordially yours,

Hal T. Francis, Jr.
Hal T. Francis, Jr.
Credit Manager

cfy

the customers who always pay promptly can be sent to these valued customers also. You would of course omit any reference to their paying habits, but you would let them know that you appreciate their business. These letters should be short; and they should be written in a direct, sincere, and friendly tone. Read the letter on the preceding page.

Any one of the letters mentioned in this chapter is more appealing to the recipient if it is typewritten than if it is duplicated. The number to be mailed can be so great, however, that you may have to use some form of high-quality duplicating to produce the letters. Chapter 11 contains more information on the mailing of identical or similar letters.

CONGRATULATING

Congratulate is a good word. Any of its derivatives connotes pleasantness. When a person receives some honor or succeeds in some endeavor—is elected to an office, is promoted to a higher–level job, and so forth—he has reason to be happy. Human nature's being what it is, people want to recognize the successes of their friends and associates and to share the thrill of accomplishment. This eagerness to share happiness is very frequently expressed by using some form of the word *congratulate*.

When congratulating a person with whom you are very closely associated, an oral statement is usually the most appropriate way to congratulate him. This statement may be combined with some such gesture as a wink, a firm handshake, or a slap on the back.

When you wish to congratulate someone you do not expect to see within the next few days *or* when the accomplishment is a very unusual one, you should write a letter. Write immediately and make your congratulatory remarks early in the letter.

Such beginnings as these may be used:

I congratulate you on passing the Certified Professional Secretary's examination.

* * *

Congratulations on doing a fine job of writing the article "Dilemmas of the Purchasing Officer" for the October issue of the *Office Executive*.

In almost all situations the letter writer will have enough interest in the accomplishment to write more than just a one–sentence letter. After all, the letter is written because the writer is interested in the reader and wants to make him feel good. As is true with all other letters, the sentences that follow the beginning —the most important part of a letter—must be good. In the sentences that follow the opening, say something *specific* about the accomplishment that will let the reader know that you have given some thought to the matter.

Comments such as these that follow may be appropriate:

I congratulate you on passing the Certified Professional Secretary's examination.

Because less than 3 percent of the people who take that examination pass all six parts on the first attempt, you have justification to be especially proud of your accomplishment. Your hard work in preparing for the examination obviously paid rich dividends.

I wish all of the graduates of our department would set the CPS rating as one of their goals.

* * *

Congratulations on doing a fine job of writing the article "Dilemmas of a Purchasing Officer" for the October issue of the *Office Executive*. I am especially interested in your proposed solution to the human relations problems that arise because bids are mailed after the date announced for opening them.

I look forward to seeing you at the convention in Kansas City in December.

Your superiors are just as much human as you, your peers, and your subordinates. Congratulating them is a fine practice, provided your remarks are sincere and are stated in such a manner that the reader does not think you are "apple polishing." Be especially careful that you do not volunteer *advice* or appear to be trying to direct the activities when writing your congratulatory message. Just about all congratulatory messages should be short.

The following example contains a congratulatory comment, a specific reference to the accomplishment, and an expression of confidence.

> Congratulations! I was pleased to read in the *News-Sentinel* yesterday that you were elected president of the Jackson Chapter of the Rotary Club.
>
> I am confident you will perform the duties of that office in your usual efficient manner.

Repetitious oral statements of congratulations for any one measure of success would soon become boring to the listener, and he would believe that your remarks are insincere. The person who receives a letter congratulating him will, however, read it several times before he discards it. Because the repetitious reading will be voluntary, it will have a good effect on the reader.

Use letters advantageously. By writing sincere congratulatory messages, you boost the morale of the reader, you make yourself feel good, and you make a good impression on the reader. You make this good impression in an ethical manner.

Do not overlook the possibility of writing a congratulatory message when you believe that such a letter will be appreciated.

SYMPATHIZING

Everyone has a tragic experience from time to time. The tragedy, which may affect either directly or indirectly the business or the personal affairs of the individual, is sometimes minor. Sometimes, unfortunately, major tragedies are encountered. Just as the mature, fair–minded person wishes to share the thrill of the accomplishments of his associates, he is also concerned with their misfortunes. When misfortune strikes one of your associates, you should express condolence in some manner—possibly by writing a letter.

In some cases an offer to help in a *specific* way would be an appropriate step. For example, suppose a friend's warehouse is destroyed by fire. If you have space that he could use until he can arrange to rent space or rebuild the structure, your offering that space at a reasonable rate (or possibly without charge for a short period) may help him greatly to overcome a severe hardship. If you do not have space to offer, telling him about space that someone else can provide may be equally helpful. Regardless of whether or not he wishes to use the space you mention, chances are extremely good that he will appreciate your thoughtfulness and your willingness to help.

No one is completely self–sufficient; everyone must be assisted in some way at various times.

When you offer assistance, make your letter sound cheerful and optimistic for the reader. Study the following letter that was written by one businessman to another whose tobacco warehouse was heavily damaged by fire:

The 2000 cubic feet of space that was added this fall to our warehouse on Highway 61 is not being used. We would be very glad for you to use that space on a complimentary basis until March 15, the date Mr. Charles L. Hall's lease will become effective.

I am sorry that the fire damaged your warehouse on Pine Street. No doubt, though, the repairs will be completed before March 15.

Personal tragedies such as the death of a business partner or a member of the family are so great and of such nature that the only assistance you can provide is an expression of sympathy. Sympathy is frequently expressed by making personal visits, sending a representative of your organization when you cannot make a personal visit, sending flowers, mailing printed cards, or contributing to special funds. One never knows exactly which action would be most appropriate. Often, writing a letter is the thing that is appreciated most. In almost all instances, writing a letter is much more appropriate than sending a printed card.

The main idea to bear in mind concerning letters that are written to express sympathy because of a death is that you can accomplish only one objective: let the reader know you are thinking about him. Seldom can you say or write anything that would be especially comforting to him. Do not add to the reader's anguish by reminiscing or by referring to sentimental experiences.

The letter on this page was written with a pen to an associate whose daughter had been killed in an automobile mishap.

627 Market Street
Handley, Virginia
February 5, 1974

Mr. and Mrs. Ray M. Gald
286 Fifth Avenue
Hazel, Montana

Dear Mr. and Mrs. Gald:

I realize that at a time such as this there is little I can say that would be very comforting to you, but I do want you to know that you have my deepest sympathy.

Sincerely;

Kermit M. Hayes

Handwriting is probably preferred over typewriting for letters of this nature.

Simplicity is the key word for letters expressing sympathy.

Questions for discussion

1. What are some of the occasions not mentioned in this chapter that would probably prompt you to write a letter to someone whose name is listed in your file of good customers of long standing?
2. Who are some of the people besides customers, new residents, and others mentioned in this chapter to whom you should probably write public relations letters at some time?
3. What are some of the advantages of sending personally written letters instead of printed cards?
4. You could delegate to your secretary the handling of some public relations messages. What are some of them that she could handle as well as (or perhaps even better than) you could?
5. What are some sources of names and addresses of people whose names are not in your records?

Exercises

Improve the following sentences that were taken from business letters.

1. I hope that you will be able to be in attendance at the meeting on June 6.
2. In reply to your letter of January 26, I am enclosing a copy of the report that was written by our sales manager.
3. I wish to thank you for sending me a copy of the brochure entitled "Your First Adventure in Business."
4. You will find a self–addressed envelope enclosed.
5. Please return the enclosed card as soon as possible.
6. Why not visit our store during our annual sale?
7. We are looking forward to your future orders.
8. We shall be glad to be of service to you.
9. I hope that this schedule will not be inconvenient for you.
10. It is our policy to be prompt and fair to our customers.

Problems

1. You are the manager of a large department store in a city of 300,000 people. Austin M. McAlister's family have been regular customers of your store for almost five years. Mr. McAlister has a wife and four children who apparently buy almost all of their clothing as well as many other types of merchandise from your store. The McAlisters use their charge account for all of their purchases, and they have never been late in paying an account.

   You value their patronage, and you have reason to believe they will continue to be satisfied customers and that they will continue to pay promptly.

   Write a letter to Mr. McAlister. Express your appreciation of his patronage and compliment him on his good paying habits. (Omit any specific reference to your *records*.)

   Mr. McAlister's address is 259 North Elm Street in Franklin, Tennessee.

2. Yesterday you read in the local newspaper that Mike Phillips, a member of your high school graduating class two years ago, has been elected to Who's Who in American Colleges and Universities. You have not seen him since high school days.

   In addition to being a track star, he is editor of his college weekly newspaper and is president of the sophomore class. His major is journalism at Colorado Southern College, Pike Springs, Colorado.

   Write him a letter and congratulate him.

3. You are the manager of a department store in a city of some 100,000 residents. Mr. and Mrs. Harlan J. Cope moved to your city when they were married 25 years ago. Since that time they have been two of your best customers. They buy almost all of their clothing, as well as many other types of merchandise, from you.

   You have had an opportunity to talk with them occasionally. You have learned the exact date of their silver anniversary next month. Write a letter to them and congratulate them.

4. As manager of Independent Wholesale Foods, write a letter of sympathy to one of your regular customers, Big Foods of America, whose basement was flooded during the storm we had last Monday. Although the water did not reach the main floor of the grocery, many food items totaling several thousand dollars that were stored in the basement were destroyed. Mr. David Allen Winston is manager of Big Foods. The store is located in your city.

5. You are the owner and manager of Ramsey's Furniture Store, 57 West Broad Street, Century, CT 06011, which opened two months ago. Your grand opening was a marvelous success, but business has slacked down a little now. You have decided to send letters to all new property owners inviting them to visit your store and buy any furniture they may need to fill their new houses or to replace worn–out pieces they may have.

   Emphasize the fact that your store offers 20 percent off when cash is paid or will establish credit accounts for all qualified customers. Of course, your Drexwell and Thomasburg furniture is nationally known. Delivery is made within two days to anyone within a 100–mile radius of Century.

6. You are the owner and operator of a laundry and dry cleaning establishment in Greenwich, Maryland. The home of one of the Greenwich residents who has been one of your regular customers for several years was destroyed by fire yesterday. You know that Mrs. Louise F. Riddle, whose home was destroyed, had very little insurance on the property.

   Write a letter of sympathy to her. She is a teller in the First National Bank of Greenwich.

7. As public relations director of the Bank of Sterling, Sterling, Montana, write a letter congratulating one of your customers, Mr. Paul Wilson Bryant, on passing the Montana Bar Examination, which was held last June. You read of his achievement in the *Sterling Public Dispatch*.

7

Persuasive letters

THE ABILITY to persuade is essential to business success. Some degree of persuasion is involved in any leadership role. Executives, as well as personnel on the lower levels of the organization chart, know that a great deal more can be accomplished through persuading (convincing—but not begging) people than through attempting to drive them.

A self–confident person "sells" his ideas to his associates, regardless of who they are—superiors, subordinates, prospects, customers, and others. He displays his leadership ability by convincing them that whatever he is trying to "sell" is worthwhile, and he does this diplomatically. Fair minded as the successful businessman is, he thinks of the ways his associates will benefit from "buying" the concept, the service, or the product that he is trying to "sell." He points out these benefits in a simple, specific style; and he omits all attempts at flattery.

A salesclerk in a clothing store may stress, among the other attributes of a garment, the quality of the material of which it is made, the tailoring, and the manner in which that garment enhances the appearance of the prospective purchaser. The salesclerk obviously expects to make a profit for the store when he makes the sale, but he has no reason to mention this anticipated gain. He concentrates on the benefits to be derived by the prospective purchaser; and he mentions these benefits in a sincere, cheerful manner. Obvious flattery in such a sales situation would probably cause the prospective customer to go elsewhere to purchase a similar or identical item.

When convincing a person to accept an assignment (with or without pay), the person who is trying to do the convincing uses the same techniques that he would use to make a sale in a department store or in any other situation.

The same principles that are used for oral procedures in selling are used in persuading through the medium of written words. Letters that require some degree of persuasion are often written to invite, to request, to ask for an adjustment, to solicit, to collect, and to sell products or services.

Inviting

When you invite a person to speak to a group, to serve on a committee, or to submit suggestions or recommendations, you compliment that person because your invitation lets him know that you believe he has the ability to do what you are asking him to do. You can, therefore, extend the invitation in a straightforward manner without the necessity of feeling in any way apologetic. Frequently, though, the person you invite may have to be "sold" on the idea of accepting your invitation. You may have to convince *him* that he has the ability to carry out the assignment you are asking him to accept, or you may have to convince him that his completing the assignment will benefit him or someone else.

You must always write the invitation so clearly that the reader knows exactly *what* you are asking him to do and *when, where,* and *how* he is to do it. Facts are almost always more useful than opinions in persuading someone to accept an invitation. You should, therefore, give one or more reasons for your selecting him as a participant. You may need to convince him that you believe he is the only person or is one of the few persons qualified to accept the assignment that you are asking him to take. You should perhaps state the benefits, which may be monetary, that he can expect to receive; and you may explain how his participation will contribute to the success or welfare of some individual or a group. Write *persuasively,* cordially, and confidently. Use the positive approach. When you believe that the recipient of your invitation will accept that invitation, you can write more convincingly and he is therefore more likely to accept.

ASSOCIATION OF NEVADA BUSINESS TEACHERS
P. O. Box 1126
Desert Sands, Nevada 89301

February 1, 1974

Mr. Wendell W. Robbins, Chairman
Business Education Department
Hastings Community College
Hastings, CO 81041

Dear Mr. Robbins:

The four members of our organization who heard you speak at the Utah Business Education Association convention in Miller last November 22 have recommended you so highly that we would like for you to be the speaker for our dinner meeting on Wednesday, May 12. We will meet at 6 p.m. in the Walnut Room of the Riley Motel. Some 115 business teachers will attend.

Could you give the same speech, "Enthusiastic Teaching," that you gave at the Utah meeting? Our four representatives liked the content of that speech and the manner in which you presented it.

We will pay your expenses and give you an honorarium of $100. I will be glad to reserve a room for you at the Riley Motel, the newest motel in Desert Sands, for the night of May 12.

Please let me know as soon as you can whether you can accept our invitation to speak to our group.

Cordially yours,

Edwin A. Rogers

Edwin A. Rogers, Chairman
Business Education Department

pac

A negative style of writing can cause the addressee to decline an invitation that he would otherwise accept. While you should not make it so easy for him to decline that such an easy task would *suggest* that he decline, you must allow him to make the decision as to whether or not he will accept your invitation.

Never use pressure in an invitation. Remember that persuasion is much more effective than force. Study the letter on the preceding page.

Requesting

Requests—routine and special—make up a part of the normal business operations of our economy. These requests are made by business personnel, housewives, and all other citizens. Many requests are made by writing letters. As is true for all other situations involving letter writing, the writer must remember that he is writing to a *living human being;* and he must apply the basic principles of letter writing that pertain to the particular problem at hand.

ROUTINE REQUESTS

When you request something that is generally available upon request, you have to use very little persuasion. A courteous tone is all that is needed. Courtesy should, of course, be a characteristic of any letter.

In making routine requests, show proper consideration for the reader and at the same time do yourself a favor by making it easy for the reader to understand your letter and easy for him to reply to it. If your request is for a product, provide all the details necessary to identify the specific item you wish to receive. Specify the quantity desired, the sizes, the colors, and any other variable that may be applicable. This letter would be almost identical to an order letter (see Chapter 5) except that you would omit references to the method of payment, and you would *possibly* omit the reference to the method by which the items you are requesting are to be delivered.

If the person or organization that supplies a product you desire has indicated that you are to send an addressed envelope and pay the postage, you must enclose a stamped envelope. You should, of course, follow the good practice of referring in your letter to the enclosure. Often an organization that supplies free materials prefers to use its own envelopes for mailing these materials. When a firm uses its own envelopes, many people see the name and address of that organization; and this helps the organization to be better known. Banks, department stores, and other organiza-

519 North Oak Street
Pine Hill, NC   28060
June 18, 1973

Woodley Furniture Company
1222 State Street
Radford, NC   27965

Gentlemen:

Please send me a copy of the 28-page "Decorator's Guide" that you advertised yesterday in the Pine Hill Times. This book- let should be very helpful to my husband and me in selecting the furnishings for our house that is to be completed this fall.

Your mailing a copy of the "Decorator's Guide" so that it will reach me before we leave on a two-week vacation trip on July 1 will be very much appreciated.

Sincerely yours,

Mary Holbrook
Mrs. Paul O. Holbrook

tions frequently prefer to use their own envelopes when answering *routine* or *special* requests from customers or prospective customers.

The letter on page 118 is an example of a routine request for a product that is available without cost.

Routine requests for a service should be written in the same

HASTINGS COMMUNITY COLLEGE
Hastings, Colorado 81041

October 8, 1973

Colby Office Supply Company
402 East Broadway
Hampton, Colorado 80632

Gentlemen:

Please ask one of your servicemen to come to our campus sometime this week to repair the ribbon mechanism on one of our Hughes rotary calculators. This machine, which is covered by a service agreement with you, is in Room 327 in Greeley Hall.

Our buildings are open from 7:45 a.m. until 4:45 p.m. each day.

Cordially yours,

Clara Downing
Miss Clara Downing
Secretary to Mr. Robbins

manner as the request for a product. The specifics concerning the service desired should be included in the letter and so should such items as the exact location where the service is to be performed and the time and date that it is to be performed.

The service requested in the letter on page 119 has been paid

1151 Pebble Beach Road
Santa Fe, CA 93406
June 26, 1973

Dr. Raphael L. Wickleman
Director of Admissions
Central California College
San Juan, CA 95125

Dear Dr. Wickleman:

So that I can decide which college I shall attend next fall, will you please answer the following three questions for me?

1. Is a first-quarter freshman who lives in a men's dormitory permitted to operate an automobile on campus?

2. If I decide to move into a private home at mid-term, would the unused portion of the rent that I must pay when I register be refunded?

3. When must I register for the private golf lessons that are offered during September and October?

I shall appreciate your prompt answers to these questions. All of my other questions were answered adequately by the information in the brochure that you mailed to me on June 18. I thank you for sending it.

Sincerely yours,

Michael M. Sims

Michael M. Sims

through a maintenance contract between the school and the office supply company.

A letter that is written to request more than one item should be organized so well that the reader can readily see the number of items you are requesting. This good arrangement of the letter helps the reader, and it helps to insure that you receive each item requested. The letter on page 120 is presented in an easy–to–read manner.

SPECIAL REQUESTS

More persuasion is required in special requests than in routine requests. When you send a special request to one of your acquaintances or to an individual or an organization that has sent or is quite likely to send a special request to you sometime, less persuasion is needed than in other special situations. Although your referring to your compliance with your reader's earlier special request would ordinarily be an inappropriate thing to do, you may profitably refer to your willingness to comply with a future request for him. The letter on page 122 makes such a reference to a willingness to comply. Apparently the writer of this letter did not anticipate a particular request from the addressee of her letter, but she realized that a possibility exists for such a request. Notice the arrangement of that letter; the addressee could reply very easily.

Rather frequently a letter making a special request can be made effective by including references to one or more ways by which the addressee will profit by complying with the request. Some letters that are mailed to ask the recipients to complete questionnaires and return them contain promises to send summaries of the findings of the questionnaire survey. The writer can logically assume that the recipient would like to have a summary of the findings because the writer is sending the questionnaire to only those people who have a genuine interest in the survey that is being conducted.

In some instances a product may be offered as a reward for complying with a special request. The occasion prompting the request would dictate the appropriateness of such an offer. You must not write in such a manner that the reader could logically

CENTRAL HIGH SCHOOL
Spokane, OR 97067

April 4, 1973

Miss Ramona Ashbury
Chairman, Business Department
Ragland Senior High School
Ogden, OR 97644

Dear Miss Ashbury:

Mr. Robert W. Waverly, the McFarland Publishing Company representative who visited your school last Friday, made some very complimentary statements about your model office arrangement. We are drawing plans for a layout that is similar to the description that he gave of yours. To help us with these plans, will you please answer these three questions?

　　1. How many work stations are in your classroom?

　　2. How much aisle space is between each two rows
　　　　of stations?

　　3. What types of filing equipment do you use to
　　　　illustrate the three filing systems that are
　　　　covered in Study Guide 275?

As our classrooms are similar to yours in size and design, your answering these questions for us will be very helpful. I would welcome an opportunity to assist you in some way.

Cordially yours,

Jane Stephens

Mrs. John R. Stephens
Chairman, Business Department

jst

interpret your offer as a bribe, but your making that offer as a token of your appreciation can be appropriate and in good taste.

Almost always you should enclose a stamped, addressed envelope for the reply to your special request.

Seeking adjustments

Asking for an adjustment is actually making a special request; but because adjustment requests are so special, they are treated in this separate division of this chapter.

Even in the most efficient organizations, errors are made sometimes. "To err is human." Merely acknowledging the fact that an error was made through normal human behavior without making an honest, genuine attempt to correct the error is inexcusable. Repeated actions such as that would cause the businessman to lose the respect of his associates (and rightly so). The loss of respect through such actions would lead to business failure. Smart, successful businessmen recognize the importance of correcting errors; and although they dislike making errors, they appreciate the "injured" person's calling the error to their attention so that a satisfactory correction can be made.

Fair-mindedness is essential to success. Every citizen has an obligation to be fair to himself and to the other people with whom he communicates. When an error is made that causes you to suffer financially or to suffer some inconvenience, you owe it to yourself and to the person who made the error to call that error to his attention. As a general rule, perhaps, an honest, fair-minded person tends to believe that most other people are also honest and fair minded. Regardless of how honest and fair minded he may be, though, an intelligent person knows that a small percentage of people cannot be trusted. "Playing the law of averages," his first communication with another person is based on the assumption that he is associating with an honest, upright citizen.

When an error is made or some act that appears to be unjust is committed, call this error or injustice to the attention of the person responsible so that he will have an opportunity to make a satisfactory adjustment or proper restitution. Quite possibly that person is not aware that the error has been made. He may know that some particular thing has been done, but he may not realize that it is an unfair practice. When such an error or act is brought to his attention, he will (if he is a fair–minded individual) not only correct the situation, but he will also appreciate your calling his attention to the matter. Calling his attention to the error will enable him to avoid making that error again.

Sometimes a person may feel that an error has been made or that he has been treated unfairly only to learn later that he himself was at fault because of some misinterpretation. Misunderstandings should be "aired" so that good public relations can be restored to the benefit of all the people concerned.

Always give the person who made the error an opportunity to correct it. If a waitress gives you a check for $3.65 that should total only $3.45, ask *her* to correct it; do *not* wait until you present your check to the cashier to ask that the amount be corrected. A salesman in a department store should be given an opportunity to correct any type of error that he makes. Do not report the error to a department manager or to any other employee until the salesman has been given an opportunity to make the correction.

Publicizing errors to "outsiders"—people who are not employees of the organization in which the error was made—is one of the most inappropriate things that can be done. Not only is such an act a waste of time and energy, but it is also unethical. A person can suffer more from such unethical behavior than he would from the results of an honest error that seemed to be disadvantageous to him. Be ethical in all of your communications.

The tactful, diplomatic writer chooses his words carefully so that he maintains the goodwill of his readers. When requesting an adjustment, therefore, avoid using negative, unpleasant words such as *error, mistake, failed,* and *failure.* Put yourself in the reader's place. Compare the expressions in the two columns that follow and ask yourself how you would react to any one of them if it were used in a letter asking you to make an adjustment.

Positive	*Negative*
Please adjust the total on the enclosed statement.	Please correct the error on the enclosed statement.
Please correct the total on the enclosed statement.	Please correct the mistake on the enclosed statement.
Please credit my account with the $45 check I mailed to you on October 2.	Please credit my account with the $45 check you failed to record last month.

Positive statements are almost always more pleasant and more effective than negative statements.

You should request an adjustment only when you honestly believe that the adjustment is due you. And when you do believe that an adjustment is due you, you owe it to yourself and to the other person or group to ask for it. Request the adjustment confidently and courteously. The factors that led to your decision to write a letter should enable you to decide on the most appropriate way to organize the contents of your letter. You may present the request first or the explanation first, or you may present the message according to the time sequence that was involved.

REQUEST FIRST

When you feel reasonably sure that the reader will readily agree that your request should be granted, you may begin your letter by asking for the adjustment and then follow this request by giving whatever information you believe is necessary to explain your justification for writing. While your explanation must be clear and sufficient to justify your request, it should not include unnecessary details. As is true for all other letters, a tone of goodwill should permeate your message. The ending of the letter may very well refer confidently to your request and mention your appreciation for prompt action. The following letter is an example of a successful adjustment request.

Please adjust the balance of our account (No. 30762). As I mentioned in my letter of October 7 ordering 8 reams of stationery, my account had a $12 credit balance at that time. The current balance should, therefore, be only $2.50 instead of $14.50.

All of our office employees have been quite complimentary of the new letterhead that your artist designed for us. We are pleased that we let him plan this new stationery.

Your sending us a corrected statement of our account before the end of the month will be very much appreciated.

Notice that the tone of the preceding letter is positive and that goodwill is evident from the beginning to the end. Contrast with that letter the following message that contains negative wording and an accusing tone.

> Please correct a mistake you made in our account (No. 30762). The balance of $14.50 is the correct amount for the 8 reams of stationery that we ordered on October 7, but you failed to give us credit for the $12 credit balance that we had before we placed the October 7 order.
>
> We will pay our account in full when we receive a corrected statement.

Would such a letter as the preceding one do much to maintain or to promote goodwill? Although the facts are accurate and the letter is concise and is organized in an acceptable manner, the message contains nothing that contributes to good public relations.

Because the adjustment that was requested in each of the two preceding letters was unquestionably due, the writer of either letter would be successful in obtaining the adjustment. The courteous characteristics of the first letter would help set the stage for cheerful compliance with future requests. Such letters frequently help to establish or to secure a relationship that is beneficial to the writer in numerous unexpected situations at some time in the future.

While the writer of the second letter (the one with the negative wording and the accusing tone) would be successful in obtaining the requested adjustment, that letter may very likely have such an adverse effect on the reader that he would hesitate to adjust any future inaccuracy that is not *obviously* his fault. Such a letter can cause the reader to react negatively to business transactions that transpire in the future.

Explanation first

The nature of some situations is such that an explanation of the problem is needed to set the stage for the request for an adjustment. When the reader understands an existing difficulty, he is usually in a proper frame of mind to react favorably to the request. The letter on this page illustrates the explanation-first approach.

That letter brought a quick response stating that a new pair

---

509 North Cedar Avenue
Grand Forks, ND   58201
July 5, 1973

Mr. Wendell C. Riley
Floorshine Shoe Store
1104 Broad Street
Bismark, ND   58501

Dear Mr. Riley:

For no apparent reason the sole has separated from the upper portion of one of the Floorshine shoes I purchased at your store on May 6. I mailed the pair of shoes to you by parcel post this mornong.

I am confident that when you examine the shoes, you will realize that I have worn them only a few times during the two months that I have owned them. You will, of course, also notice the defect in the left shoe.

Having worn Floorshine shoes for the past twelve years (I have bought at least five pairs at your store), I am surprised that this difficulty has developed. I realize, however, that occasionally an item in any top-quality line of merchandise may be less satisfactory than its "peers."

I believe you will appreciate my calling your attention to these "10 1/2 C's," and I shall certainly **appreciate** your making the appropriate adjustment.

                Cordially yours,

                Martin F. Lyons
                Martin F. Lyons

of shoes (the same size, style, and color) had been mailed to replace the defective pair. The response also included a note of appreciation for being given an opportunity to make an adjustment.

TIME SEQUENCE

In seeking some adjustments, the writer may advantageously give the facts concerning the problem in the time sequence in which factors occurred. Such a plan is to be avoided usually, because it leads to wordiness by making necessary the inclusion of more details than are actually necessary, or desirable, to obtain the adjustment.

When you do not know the name of the person in charge of making adjustments, address your letter to the organization and add an attention line for the adjustment manager.

Soliciting

Letters are frequently used as the communication medium for soliciting funds or services. When you are soliciting funds or services for an organization that is well known to your reader, your letter–writing task is a great deal easier than when you have to describe your organization and its activities. A reader who has already been convinced that your organization is worthwhile needs little more than enough information to learn the kind of help you are soliciting. If it is feasible for him to help, he will usually do so.

The following letter was mailed to a civic–minded businessman who had contributed on several previous occasions to the group that mailed the letter.

> The local Homemakers Club is soliciting the help of the businessmen in our city again this year to send children of low–income families to summer camp.
>
> As you already know, this program, which lasts two weeks, includes educational and recreational activities that are especially

planned for the group. We have received applications from 36 deserving boys and girls from 9 to 11 years of age; and to permit all of them to participate, we must increase our existing fund by $700 before July 2.

Can you help us again this year? Any contribution you make to our fund will certainly be appreciated as much as ever.

Obviously, more information should go into a letter that is addressed to a person who is not already familiar with the organization or its activities. Special efforts should be made to keep the letter short yet complete, courteous, and interesting. Businessmen, as well as other private citizens, receive so many letters of this nature they may not read the entire letter if it is excessively long. On the other hand, they do not contribute the help that is solicited unless the letter contains adequate information in a well-written style.

Individually typewritten letters of solicitation are significantly more effective than are duplicated letters. Frequently, form letters must be used, however, when a large number of people are asked to contribute. (See Chapter 11 for more information on preparing form letters.)

An attention-getting device of some kind is needed for letters of solicitation. The attention-getting device is especially important when form letters are used. Pictures, cartoons, slogans, questions, colored stationery, and special placement on the page are some of the many devices that have been used to get the reader's attention. One large university alumni office has used special placement and a special color for the letter *u* as an attention getter; thus, "We must have U for a f nd."

Getting attention is obviously not enough. To be successful, the message must hold the reader's attention and convince him that the purpose for which the solicitation is being made is worthy of his help. Once you have convinced him that you are soliciting for a worthwhile cause, make it easy for him to contribute. Give him the exact name to whom his check should be written. Or if he is to contribute a service, give him complete instructions on *where, when,* and *how* the service is to be rendered. An addressed, stamped envelope may be enclosed to encourage him to respond quickly.

Collecting accounts

The credit system necessitates the creditor's establishing some type of collection procedure.

A major portion of today's business is transacted on a credit basis. Water, electric, and telephone services are provided on credit and are usually paid for once a month. Services of professional people—dentists, physicians, and attorneys—are usually paid for on a monthly basis or when a series of services has been completed. An item as small as a greeting card, or even smaller, can be purchased on credit in a store where the buyer has a charge account. Large items such as houses, farms, and ranches are seldom bought on a cash basis; instead, they are purchased on credit from an individual or from a bank or some other financial institution. Consumable goods—groceries, beverages, meals in restaurants—do not have to be bought on a cash basis. The buyer may have these items charged to his account with the seller, or he may use one of the many types of credit cards to defer payment. Rental plans on office machines such as typewriters or large electronic computers are forms of credit.

The size, the price, or the nature of an item or a service would not prohibit the user from obtaining that item or service on credit.

The credit arrangement is a great convenience for the user or purchaser of a service or a product, and it helps the supplier by simplifying his paper work. The necessity of carrying large sums of money or a checkbook is eliminated by using credit. Also, by paying for services, rentals, or products only one time each month, the user can easily maintain an accurate accounting of his payments. The supplier can keep a record of accounts due, mail periodic statements, and credit the accounts when payments are received more easily than he could handle all of the busywork that would be created by cash payments. Maintaining a system for cash payments rather than extending credit for such services as electricity and water would be almost impossible.

A major advantage to the creditor is that the credit system expands his business volume because more people can avail themselves of his services or products. Being able to enjoy the privileges of ownership of houses, clothing, and machines as well as many other items before the user can pay for them is, of course, a major advantage to the user. Retailers profit by being able to purchase merchandise and then sell part of it or perhaps all of it before having to pay for it.

The advantages of credit are so numerous and far reaching that an attempt to mention all of them is beyond the scope of this book.

Why can credit be used so extensively? Because an overwhelming majority of people are honest, one can assume that almost all accounts will be paid in full.

So that creditors can meet their own financial obligations and make a satisfactory profit, they must receive payments from their debtors when the payments become due. To encourage prompt payments, many suppliers issue invoices that bear a notation which offers a discount provided the merchandise is paid for within a specified time. A popular notation reads, "2/10, n/30," which means that the debtor is permitted to deduct a 2 percent discount from the invoice total if he pays for the merchandise within ten days after the invoice is issued or that he must pay the total amount within thirty days after the invoice date. To merit a discount of 2 percent, prompt payment is obviously considered important by businessmen.

Issuing the invoice is the first step that is taken by the creditor to collect the amount that is due him. Because most good businessmen take advantage of these prompt-pay discounts, issuing the invoice is frequently the only step that has to be taken to collect the amount that is due. For any one of various possible reasons—oversight, pressure created by peak workloads, and many others—"guilt-edge" debtors (those of unquestionable integrity and good business practices) occasionally do not make their payments on the due dates. When a payment is late, the creditor has to decide on the appropriate action that he should take.

When the payment is not made in time for the discount, the creditor mails a statement at the end of the billing period (usually at the end of a month). Mailing the statement may be considered to be the second step in collecting the account. If payment is not made at the end of thirty days, the creditor is alerted to possible reasons for the tardiness. He realizes that "to err is human"; and he, therefore, assumes that the tardiness in paying is caused by an honest error. He is constantly aware that his objective is *to collect the money and at the same time maintain the goodwill of the debtor.* He may, therefore, decide to delay taking action of any kind for several days with the hope that the debtor will pay his account without receiving any type of reminder.

The creditor may, though, have so many debtors that are tardy in making their payments that he simply cannot afford to wait many days to receive some of the payments. Under these circumstances a courteous and helpful step may be that of mailing some type of printed (nonpersonal) reminder that the payment should be made promptly. When you find yourself in this predicament, you may elect to mail to each of the debtors a duplicate copy of the statement of the amount due. This type of reminder is frequently all that is necessary to collect the money. If the account is not paid soon after the duplicate statement is mailed, another subtle reminder may be effective. Another duplicate statement bearing a brightly colored sticker containing such comments as "REMINDER," "JUST A REMINDER," "YOUR FRIENDLY REMINDER," or "FOR YOUR ATTENTION" may be mailed to the debtor.

When you are attempting to collect an account, remember to always begin the procedure with the "soft touch" and gradually go to the stern–action step only when sternness proves to be the only effective manner in which you can collect the money that rightly belongs to you.

Send any step in the collection process, regardless of whether it is a "soft touch" or a "stern–action touch," by *first-class* mail!

If, after mailing the invoice, a statement at the end of the billing period, a duplicate copy of the statement, and a duplicate of the statement with a sticker notation attached, the debtor still does not pay, at least one further step is obviously required. This next appropriate step may be a form letter that has been reproduced with blank spaces provided for filling in the address and a proper salutation for the debtor, the amount due, the date on which that amount should be paid, and possibly the dates on which previous reminders had been mailed. Seldom is the receipt of a form letter of this nature rightfully considered to be insulting to the addressee.

The tone of the form letter should be positive, friendly, and courteous. Including a sales pitch for some of your products or

---

WILLIAMSON WHOLESALE COMPANY
Muncie, Ohio 43262

Dear   :

Perhaps you have already mailed your check for $_____ to pay your account that became due on _____. If you have mailed your check, please disregard this reminder.

We're having a special sale this month on outdoor items for the home. The prices, which are shown on the enclosed leaflet, have been reduced as much as 20 percent on light-weight lawn furniture, charcoal grills, children's wading pools, and croquet and badminton sets. Perhaps you would like to send your order right away for a good supply of these items for your customers.

A stamped, addressed envelope is enclosed for your use in sending your next order and your check for $_____ if you have not yet mailed it.

Cordially yours,

J. Thomas Harley

J. Thomas Harley
Collection Manager

rne

Enclosures 2

services can be quite appropriate at this stage of a collection attempt. The sales pitch can often serve one or both of these two purposes: (1) to increase your sales volume and (2) to help you maintain the goodwill of the debtor at the same time that you increase the pressure on him to pay his account.

As the letter is duplicated rather than typewritten, the receiver realizes that the sender is treating him the same way that others who are delinquent with their payments are being treated. This evidence of identical treatment tends to help to maintain goodwill and to eliminate possibilities of embarrassment for the debtor.

The letter on page 133 may be an effective message to mail at this stage of a collection procedure. The second paragraph would have to be revised to suit the occasion.

A second and even a third duplicated letter could conceivably be mailed as further steps in the collection process. A more frequently taken step, however, is the mailing of a typewritten letter that has been composed especially for the specific debtor to whom the letter is addressed. In this letter you may wisely review the status of the past-due account and the steps that have already been taken to collect it. Resale or further sales promotional content should be omitted from this letter. You must concentrate more on collecting the amount that is already overdue than on attempting to increase your volume of business with that particular debtor. Appealing to the debtor's pride and to his good credit standing would ordinarily be more effective than other appeals. Tactful yet firm references to the necessity of his paying very promptly should characterize this letter.

Read the letter on page 135.

Enclosing a stamped, addressed envelope is appropriate for any mailing that you make in your attempt to collect an account.

Successful businessmen realize that in some instances they fare better by losing a small debt than by collecting the account and at the same time creating unfavorable publicity for themselves or the organization they represent. Being fair minded, they go to "great lengths" to avoid ill will for the debtor and the unpleasantness that would be generated for themselves if they were to turn an unpaid account over to a collection agency or take legal action against the debtor. A successful businessman is characterized not

WILLIAMSON WHOLESALE COMPANY
Muncie, Ohio 43262

Dear   :

You have reason to be proud of your fine reputation for paying your accounts promptly, and I am confident that you want to
maintain that reputation. Receiving a check for $_____ from
you before _____ would cause us to continue to sell to
you on the basis of your signature as well as for cash.

Until after we wrote to you on _____--the third reminder
that your account is overdue--we thought that perhaps your payment had been delayed because of a vacation, illness, or a business trip. We are convinced now that one of your capable assistants would have sent a check if you had been out of the office
for an extended time.

So that we can meet our own obligations and so that we can earn
the profit to which we are entitled by supplying high-quality
merchandise at fair prices, we must have your check for $_____.

Please use the enclosed envelope to let us hear from you before
_____.

                         Sincerely yours,

                         J. Thomas Harley

                         J. Thomas Harley
                         Collection Manager

rne

Enclosure

only by fair-mindedness but also by intelligence. He knows that
even though a large majority of people are honest, some are not
and that those who are dishonest have to be treated differently.
The successful businessman—considerate and intelligent—real-

izes that no one thinks more of him than he thinks of himself. He must take the steps that are necessary to protect himself and his associates. He must, therefore, resort to strong measures when necessary to collect accounts that are owed by inconsiderate or dishonest people.

Having gone through two of the collection phases—the friendly reminder phase, which ordinarily consists of the mailing of form messages, and the appeals to fair-play phase, which ordinarily consists of individually dictated letters—the creditor has *just* reason to take the stronger step of turning the account over to a collection agency or of turning it over to an attorney for collection.

As a businessman, you will constantly be aware of the fact that *your objective is to collect the outstanding account and to retain the customer,* provided the customer is trustworthy and therefore the type of person with whom you wish to transact business. Taking strong action to collect an account will in some instances cause the debtor to respect you. After such action, he becomes a better customer than before. You cannot expect such a reaction, however, from your debtor. Many of them will never return to you to transact further business. You should delay turning an account over to a collection agency or to an attorney until you are convinced that you would rather lose the customer than the money he owes you. If you are confronted with this situation, you have no other alternative than to become involved in some degree of unpleasantness.

An ultimatum must be stated firmly and clearly and without any threat or any type of comment that could rightfully be interpreted as slanderous. Word letters of this type carefully and keep copies for your possible use during the collection procedure.

A smart thing for a creditor to do is to prepare a series of messages to be mailed for the three phases of a collection procedure. You should not, however, use the same steps more than once for any particular customer; and you should not use exactly the same steps, beyond the initial phase, for any two customers. Because of extenuating circumstances, you may logically omit one or more of the steps that you have prepared; and you may also add one or more steps to your prepared series. When some customers believe from past experience or from the experience of one of your other debtors that you have a "set" procedure for collecting past-due accounts, they sometimes tend to wait until you reach a specific point in the series to send their remittances. Their waiting until this point is reached can cost you a considerable sum in mailing costs and in loss of interest that could have been earned on the money if you had received it when it became due.

Not only the steps but also the intervals between the steps should be varied. Debtors who are less considerate than they should be become aware of the time intervals as well as the various steps when a "set" pattern is followed in the collection process. Numerous factors help you to use good judgment in determining which steps to use and the time intervals that you should follow. You would obviously use more steps and longer intervals between the mailings for the first time that a debtor has been late in paying his account than you would for a large sum that is owed by a customer who has been late in paying earlier accounts.

For your own legal protection, be sure to mail by *first-class mail* any reminder that an account is due. Even the first friendly reminder must be sent by *first-class mail!*

Selling products and services

Selling is an organic business function. Regardless of the quantity and the quality of the products and the services that are available, they contribute nothing unless the people who could use them know about them. Sales messages, therefore, contribute to society in general; and they help the producers and the distributors of the products and services reap the financial rewards necessary to continue providing them.

Well-established retailers or wholesalers can operate at a given level by merely continuing to provide for their regular clientele adequate products at reasonable prices. For these establishments to increase their sales and for new businesses to acquire the needed customers to operate profitably, they must publicize their products and services. They can do this through such mediums as advertising in periodicals, on radio and television, and with billboards; distributing catalogs; and mailing announcements and letters.

Techniques of selling by mail are discussed in the paragraphs that follow. Conciseness, descriptive style, persuasiveness, and informality should characterize the letters that you mail to help sell a product or a service.

People are reluctant to read long, duplicated letters; and obviously, almost all sales letters must be duplicated. Keep your sales letters as short as you can and still include the information that is essential to accomplish your objective. You can usually enclose leaflets, pictures, and other material that will help you sell your product or service. Have your sales letters duplicated by some process that produces a high-quality copy.

Choose words carefully—especially adjectives, adverbs, and verbs—to describe vividly the item you are selling and to make it appeal to the people who receive your letters. Persuade them to *try* (or at least to *see*) your product or a demonstration of your service.

Informality is a desirable characteristic of a good sales letter. You can use contractions advantageously in this type of letter. Write in a clear, direct, cordial style. For the sales letters that must obviously be form letters, there is no need for you to try to personalize them by typing in the name and the address of the recipient. Merely use a salutation or other "attention-getting" remark that would be appropriate for each recipient and have your signature duplicated along with the letter.

Because people are reluctant to read duplicated letters, you must use some type of "attention-getting" device to encourage the recipient to read your short, informal, well-written letter. "Attention-getting" devices are limited only by the imagination of the letter writer. Choose the device that you believe will appeal to the particular group of people to whom you are writing. Some examples are described in the following paragraphs. You may wish to use one of them, a revision of one of them, or an entirely different type of "attention getter" for the sales letters that you will write. Among the almost unlimited number of devices are headlines, letter formats, alterations, attachments, and enclosures.

For some sales letters a "catchy" slogan, a question that creates interest, or some other type of headline may be used to get the attention of the recipient. These headlines may be near the top of the page, in the margin, in a diagonal position, or in some other position that will stand out. A special color may be used to make this headline more conspicuous.

For some letters this headline may be in the subject-line position for one of the many conventional letter styles. The letter

---

PAULETTA'S HANDICRAFT, INC.

Citrus Row, Florida

 Brightly colored yarn

September 4, 1973

Dear Homemaker:

Two 40-yard skeins of this 100 percent virgin wool yarn in neutral, white, or beige will be placed in your mailbox at <u>no cost</u> within <u>three</u> days after we receive your order for any needlepoint pattern that is described in the enclosed leaflet.

From this large assortment you can select the pattern that you believe will do most to enhance the charm of your living room, bedroom, dining room, or den. Your choice may be a picture to be framed, a bellpull, or a bench cover.

Use the color scheme of your own imagination, or choose from the recommendations that our talented artists have included in the descriptions in the leaflet. The special hard-to-believe <u>low prices</u> on these needlepoint patterns <u>are in effect through October 17</u>.

Your relatives and friends would treasure a needlepoint piece as a gift for Christmas or for any other occasion. They would treasure it not only because of its aesthetic value but also because of the sentimental value they would place on your handiwork.

Your creative friends who like to complete these popular needlepoint projects would be delighted to receive one of our patterns for them to complete; and at the TERRIFICALLY LOW PRICES that we offer <u>until October 17</u>, you can afford to give these rich-looking patterns this fall.

Just place a check mark by the catalog number for each one that you choose, specify the color of yarn you wish to use, and return the enclosed order form that already bears your name and address. You may enclose a check, or we will bill you next month.

And remember that <u>two skeins</u> of the yarn in the <u>color of your choice</u> will be mailed to you <u>without cost the day we receive your order</u>.

Cordially,

Elizabeth Alden

Mrs. Elizabeth Alden
Sales Representative

crs
Enclosures 2

styles described in Chapter 3 and in the reference section of this book can be used for sales letters. Other styles may also be used to get immediate attention. You should feel free to use your imagination in arranging the sales letter information in a form that will get immediate attention and create a favorable impression on those who read it.

You may even conceivably have your sales letter typed in an "up-side-down" manner (accomplished by inserting a sheet of carbon paper backward) so that it must be held before a mirror for easy reading. You would, of course, try to be reasonably certain that this letter would be sent to only those people who would have the time to spare for this reading arrangement and who would be fascinated by it. You would make special efforts to restrict the length of a letter with this unusual format.

One letter writer obtained the desired attention by having his secretary burn the upper righthand corner of his letter that began with the headline "This letter contains HOT NEWS!"

A piece of brightly colored yarn was attached to the letter on page 139. Copies of that letter were mailed to a large number of homemakers.

A well-chosen "attention getter" is of utmost importance in a sales letter; but that device alone cannot accomplish the purpose of the letter, which is to sell a product or a service. Follow the "attention getting" device with a carefully written message that intrigues the reader, causes him to become interested in the item you are attempting to sell, and stimulates him to respond in whatever manner you have established as your objective.

Some sales letters are merely announcements of sales, some are attempts to obtain orders, and others are introductions to products or services.

SALES ANNOUNCEMENTS

Suppose that you are planning to conduct a sale for a retail store whose operations you are managing. You may increase the volume of your sales significantly by mailing special announcements to your regular customers. These announcements may be short, simple fliers; or they may be letters that are duplicated in some manner.

FLIERS. The short, simple fliers would be most appropriate for sales of inexpensive merchandise or a large variety of merchandise —some inexpensive and some perhaps somewhat expensive. These announcements would go to a large number of people. You may send them to your customers (whose names and addresses you know) and perhaps to addresses in your region even though you do not know the names of the persons who reside there.

These announcements can be in a variety of forms, colors, and designs; and they can contain a variety of information. Some type of "attention-getting" headline is essential to call attention to the sales dates and the place. A list or a partial list of the items to be sold, pictures of some of the items, and perhaps some of the prices may be desirable information to include in these announcements to stimulate interest in the forthcoming sale.

An announcement for a department store mid-winter sale is on the preceding page.

LETTERS.   For sales of exclusive, high-priced merchandise, you may profit by mailing a letter to each of your charge-account customers. You may also mail letters to those customers letting them know about regular sales earlier than the general public is informed. Customers appreciate your giving them special attention, yet they want you to be fair with everybody.

The letters you mail should be short enough to encourage the recipients to read them, yet they must be long enough to include essential facts and "attention-getting" features. So that the length of the letter can be minimized, you may wish to enclose supplementary information on colorful leaflets.

Your letters may be duplicated by some process that produces a high-quality copy; or for announcements of sales of exclusive merchandise, you may send to a small number of customers letters that were typewritten by using an automatic typewriter. By using an automatic typewriter, you can mail letters that appear to be individually typewritten. Extenuating circumstances will help you to determine the content of the letter and the duplicating process that you should use for any particular occasion.

DIRECT SALES

Some letters are written to encourage the recipients to place an order by mail. Letters can be used quite successfully to sell some low-priced items. The lower the price, the greater is the effectiveness of this type of sales letter. Items priced at $5 or lower can be readily sold by mail provided the sales message is well written. Some items priced at $10 or somewhat higher can also be sold by mail. As the price rises, however, the effectiveness of direct-mail selling diminishes.

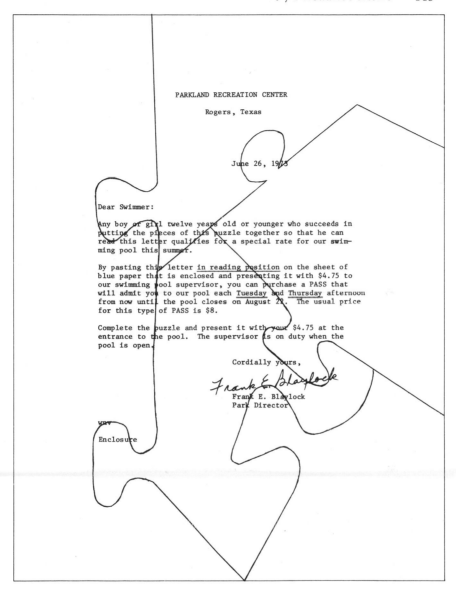

PARKLAND RECREATION CENTER

Rogers, Texas

June 26, 19__

Dear Swimmer:

Any boy or girl twelve years old or younger who succeeds in
putting the pieces of this puzzle together so that he can
read this letter qualifies for a special rate for our swimming pool this summer.

By pasting this letter <u>in reading position</u> on the sheet of
blue paper that is enclosed and presenting it with $4.75 to
our swimming pool supervisor, you can purchase a PASS that
will admit you to our pool each <u>Tuesday</u> and <u>Thursday</u> afternoon
from now until the pool closes on August 22. The usual price
for this type of PASS is $8.

Complete the puzzle and present it with your $4.75 at the
entrance to the pool. The supervisor is on duty when the
pool is open.

Cordially yours,

Frank E. Blaylock

Frank E. Blaylock
Park Director

WRV

Enclosure

The letter which is shown on the following page was written
to induce youngsters to respond by going to a neighborhood park
to purchase a ticket at a special price. A note typewritten on a
bright yellow note sheet served to call each recipient's attention to

the puzzle pieces that were enclosed to make up the sales letter.

Letters are also effective for selling subscriptions to periodicals and memberships in book clubs.

Some of the types of information that you should consider for inclusion in your sales letter are these:

APPEARANCE OF THE PRODUCT.   Using adjectives and adverbs painstakingly, describe the color choices, designs, shapes, and sizes in such a way that the reader will consider your product to be appealing. For some items that you wish to sell, you may compare the size of a particular item to some other item with which the readers are familiar. Such generalities are sometimes more effective in providing a vivid description than are specific dimensions.

NOVEL CHARACTERISTICS.   When the item you are selling has novel characteristics that would cause the buyer to enjoy it, stress those characteristics in your sales message.

USEFULNESS.   Tell your reader how he can use the item you are selling. Give examples of situations in which it can be used; and when appropriate, tell how other people (perhaps well-known personalities) are using the item.

PRICE.   Convince your readers that you are quoting a fair (and possibly even a bargain) price for your product or service. You may make fair comparisons with similar, comparable items.

EASE OF PURCHASING.   Make it easy for your reader to order the item you are selling. You can enclose an addressed, postage-paid card or envelope for him to use when mailing his order. You may even prepare the information on the order blank or card in such a way that all the reader will have to do is to place check marks by the color, design, and other such items to indicate his choices. When you simplify the ordering process to this degree, be sure that the purchaser's name and address are recorded on the order form; or *highlight* the need for his adding that information. If you enclose a card for him to use, you would obviously be willing to charge the item to his account or to mail the item C.O.D. If you do not sell the product on these terms, enclose an envelope rather than a card; and include clear, simple instructions on whether you will accept his personal check or whether he must enclose a money order.

Many sales letters are *too long!* Keep your sales letters short, and also minimize the number and the length of the enclosures that accompany your letters. Do, however, use whatever enclosures are needed to describe adequately the product or service you have for sale. Pictures, drawings, and descriptive writing on carefully chosen colored paper may be used advantageously to supplement the sales information in your short, carefully written letter.

Keep a record of the people who make purchases in response to your sales letter. Later you may wish to send a similar letter and the same enclosures to those people who do not respond to your first mailing.

You may wish to mail another letter that contains the same type of information but is stated differently for the third, fourth, and other mailings.

PRODUCT OR SERVICE INTRODUCTIONS

The purpose of some sales letters is to introduce a product or a service to the reader and to "build up" to a sale at some future time. Letters of this nature are usually used for high-priced items.

Like the letters that have been discussed in the preceding paragraphs, these sales letters must contain an appropriate "attention-getting" device. Such a device is perhaps more important in the first letter of a series for this method of selling than in the succeeding letters, but it is important in each letter. Perhaps the "attention getter" for the first in the series should be more dramatic than are those later in the sequence.

For some sales, only one introductory letter is sufficient; while for other sales, a series of two, three, or more letters should be written. The first letter obviously makes the initial introduction, and it contains descriptive information that causes the reader to want to know more about the item you are attempting to sell. Each succeeding letter may possibly repeat (but not verbatim) part of the information in the earlier letters of the series. This type of sales-letter series can be used effectively in a number of ways. One way is to continue to mail different persuasive letters until the recipient responds in some way. He may write or telephone for more information or for a demonstration of the product or service you offer. He may be persuaded to go to your store

---

NORTH PLAINS PRINTING COMPANY, INC.

North Plains, Texas

_____

_____
_____
_____

Dear _____:

With the new equipment that we installed last week, we can produce high-quality copy (the enclosed leaflet is an example) on any size paper up to 17 by 22 inches. We can print on any weight paper and can use as many colors as you wish.

Please study the prices that are shown in the second column of the leaflet. You will realize, I am confident, that these prices are lower than those that are quoted by any other printer for the same quality of work.

Ted Raulston, one of our representatives, will stop in to see you for a few minutes next week and will show you more samples of our work. He will also tell you more about the operation of our business and the <u>three-day service</u> we provide for almost all printing jobs that we perform for our customers.

Cordially yours,

Carlos E. Townsend
Manager

trm

Enclosure

or showroom to see the item you are selling, or he may be persuaded to invite you to bring the item to his home or office so that he can see it in the setting in which it would be used.

In some situations the series of letters is designed to cause the recipient to reply affirmatively when you ask him to let you come to his home or office to demonstrate the use of a product or a service.

For various reasons some recipients would obviously be ready for a demonstration or other additional information about your item at one stage of the letter series, whereas others would reach this point of interest at another stage. Once the demonstration or other goal that you have set has been accomplished, you would discontinue mailing the letter series for that prospective customer. Further correspondence with him would be contingent upon interest shown or action taken after the demonstration has been completed.

Some sales letters are written to introduce a product or a service and to introduce a representative who will call on the reader to give him additional information. The letter on the preceding page was written for that purpose.

Because sales letters go to so many people, you can justify spending a great deal of time in writing them. Write concisely, as well as vividly, and interestingly. Use enclosures appropriately to support the message that your short, well-written letter contains.

Questions for discussion

1. What are some of the *routine* requests that businessmen may make by writing letters?
2. What steps can you take to make it easy for the recipient of your letter to respond to your *special* request?
3. What information should be included in a letter from a charitable organization asking a businessman to lend equipment on a short-term basis?
4. How can you compose and organize a folder of the various messages that may be sent to collect an overdue account?
5. What are advantages of writing letters instead of making telephone calls or personal visits to collect accounts?

Exercises

Improve the following sentences that were taken from business letters.

1. I shall appreciate your returning the completed form as soon as possible.
2. I hope that you will be able to go to the meeting August 5.
3. You can get in touch with me by writing to the address given above.
4. I have received the check for which I thank you.
5. How many people were in attendance?
6. I extend this invitation to you to attend the meeting that will be held on the 28th.
7. The self-addressed envelope is enclosed for your use.
8. I believe that you will be able to complete the task in fifteen minutes' time.
9. Please send us the specifications at your earliest convenience.
10. I am writing this letter to ask you to be the speaker for our annual spring banquet April 16.

Problems

1. You are responsible for obtaining a speaker for the annual spring banquet for athletes at your college. Invite Coach Chuck Williams, who coaches track at the Lincoln College in Harrodsburg, Kentucky. Use your imagination and supply any information that you need to write a persuasive letter.

2. You are the manager of a bicycle factory that employs 275 people. If the existing parking space were used properly, it would accommodate all the cars that the employees drive to work. Several groups of employees have formed car pools.

   Because the space is not properly used (some cars are parked so that they use more space than is needed for one car), parking has become a problem for many workers. You have decided to appoint a committee of five people to study the problem.

   Write a letter to Dennis V. O'Neal, the supervisor of painting operations, and ask him to assume the responsibility of chairman of the committee. Make whatever suggestions that you wish to make to him and convince him that you believe that he is especially well qualified to be chairman of the committee. Tell him the names of the other four people who will be asked to work with him on this committee.

3. As program chairman of the Franklin, Maryland, chapter of the Administrative Management Society, invite Mr. Sam T. Collier to speak at your monthly chapter meeting in May. Because he has done a great deal of work in the word-processing area, you want him to talk on that subject. Many of the executives in your region have expressed an interest in learning more about this popular concept.

    Mr. Collier is vice president of Office Consultants, Inc. His address is 1126 Park Avenue, Bennington, New York 12783.

    Add any information that is necessary for you to write a good letter inviting Mr. Collier to speak to your group.

4. You are the salesman for Floor Care, Inc., of Selma, Colorado 80874. Prepare a letter to be sent with a full–color brochure to Mrs. James M. McCracken, 555 Northgate Drive, Crystal, New Mexico 87514, who had written asking for information on vinyl floors.

    We can now offer our softest, most durable cushioned vinyl for only \$5.25 a square yard. Thus a 9 by 12-foot floor could be put down for only \$63.45 (flooring only). Our corridor test with 125,000 people proved that Vinyl Floor is tough enough to withstand the rugged wear of your home and still look great.

    Install with seaming cement and spray adhesive. Patterns and colors of a wide variety are available.

5. As sales manager for the Christian Book Store, 1152 Seventh Avenue, S. E., Macon, Delaware 19968, write a letter to all regular customers announcing a special sale on a book published this month. This book, *Study of Christ's Life,* by M. B. Mays, contains more than 1300 pages and was published by Scotfield Publishers, Inc., and sells for \$15.95. We are offering it to regular customers for a limited time for only \$7.95.

    This volume was originally three separate editions dealing with the three themes: The Early Period, The Middle Ministry, and the Last Week. This edition contains all the information in the three previous volumes; but it has been printed on a thinner, better quality paper.

6. The double swag shower ensemble that you ordered from Seals, Holbrook and Company arrived today. However the white vinyl

liner which hangs behind the shower curtain was not included in the package. Write a letter asking that this liner be sent to you.

The double swag shower ensemble was No. 99W9875 in the catalog and your order number was 1052C. The merchandise had been sent C.O.D.; and of course, you paid before you opened the package.

7. For years you have wanted to have a social outing for the Stoneburg Community College faculty members who work with you (or your husband). Since you have recently built a vacation home out in the "wilds" (about a 45–minute drive from Stoneburg), you have decided to have a big picnic and invite all the teachers and their families. Write a letter that can be sent to everyone giving the particulars of the party and enclosing a map showing the way to your vacation home.

8. As Fred Stargel, chairman of the United Fund drive for Davis County, write a letter to Mr. Jerome P. Stinger, President of the United Laborers, asking for a donation from his group. Last year the United Laborers pledged $1,000 and gave over $1,400. This year your goal is a 10 percent increase over last year's gifts.

Mr. Stinger's address is P. O. Box 672, Frederick, Delaware 19937.

9. The Athens University drama department is in dire need of money to continue producing the three full–length plays they offer the public each year. You as chairman of the drama department decide that as a money–making project, you will write to all faculty members and interested townspeople and ask for donations. Each $10 donation would enable a person to be listed as a patron in the play program, and each $20 donation would enable a person not only to be listed as a patron but also to receive two tickets for each of the next three plays.

Write the sample letter to Dr. Ellis B. Brigham, Athens University, Athens, Oregon 97912.

10. You are the manager of the Abrams Wholesale Company in New Havelon, CT 06775. For the past seven months you have been selling merchandise on 2/10, n/30 terms to the Y and L Department Store, 247 Market Street, Stamps, CT 06809. The first five months that store paid its account within the 10–day period and took advantage of the 2 percent discount.

Last month you received payment at the end of 12 days. The 2 percent discount had been deducted, and the check had been dated two days before the end of the discount period. Even though mail has always arrived within two days from the Y and L store, you assumed that possibly the check had been delayed in the mail.

Yesterday, five days beyond the final date of the discount period, you received payment for merchandise. Again, the discount had been taken; and the check was dated within the discount period. The envelope had been postmarked two days ago.

You have justification to believe that the Y and L Department Store should not have taken the discount. Write them a letter and ask them to send you another check for the amount of the 2 percent discount on $742.81 worth of merchandise. You want to maintain their goodwill, but you must insist that they take the discount only when they pay within the 10 days. Write a firm, courteous letter to the store manager, Thomas E. Sells.

8

Securing employment

You MAY KNOW of some particular organization that you would like to work for. Your reason for seeking employment with that organization could be any one or a combination of two or more conditions such as these: opportunities for advancement, type of work for which you are especially well qualified, geographical location, opportunity to continue formal education, salary, and fringe benefits.

An important point to keep in mind is that if the job is good enough for you to seek, it is also good enough for many other well-qualified people to seek. And that is the way you want it to be. You certainly would not want a job that nobody else would like to have. Because others will apply for the job you are interested in, you must put forth your best efforts in applying. Also, you must submit your application as soon as you learn that the job opportunity exists.

No formula can be designed for writing a successful letter of application. This chapter does, however, contain some suggestions that you should consider when writing that particularly important letter.

The prospective employer knows that your application letter

represents your best efforts. In other words, he knows that no other letter that you would write would be better than the one you write to apply for a job. Your letter is your representative. A person who mails a neat-looking letter can be expected to look neat when he goes for an interview and when he goes to work each day.

Your choice of words should be appropriate for the occasion, and your letter must be written in the style that reveals *your* personality. Your grammar should be impeccable. You should strive for a good command of the English language when speaking; but even those minor errors that "creep in" occasionally in everyone's speech because of chance, changing thoughts before finishing a sentence, or for some other reason should be eliminated from the application letter. The writer has an opportunity to proofread carefully before mailing the letter, and he can ask some other well-qualified person to edit the letter for him.

The effectiveness of an application letter can be greatly enhanced by using a résumé, or personal data sheet. Preparing a résumé will be discussed before further suggestions are given for writing the application letter.

Résumé

The résumé, or personal data sheet, serves several purposes. First, it enables the applicant to give in an easy-to-read manner a great deal of information about himself. Second, it enables the applicant to minimize the length of his letter, yet still include all of the information that should be included in the written application. Third, and a very important purpose, the organization and the content of the résumé will enable the prospective employer to get a good idea of the applicant's ability to organize and his ability to determine what is important for including in the résumé. Ordinarily, the applicant who prepares a neat, well-organized data sheet is also a person who can organize his work well.

Information on the résumé is frequently shown under these four headings: personal, education, work experience, and references.

PERSONAL

The items of personal information that the data sheet should contain vary according to the types of jobs being sought and the applicant's background.

Almost always the applicant should include his date of birth. Marital status is another item that is usually given. Some other types of personal information that prospective employers may be interested in are height, weight, and general physical condition. The best step to take in deciding items of personal information to include is to study the requirements for the job and then "put yourself in your reader's place" and ask yourself, "What information would help me to decide whether or not I would like to interview this applicant for employment with our organization?"

The applicant should certainly include in some section of his résumé his name, address, and telephone number. Very often students and others who are residing away from home temporarily should list two addresses and telephone numbers—for their temporary residences and for their permanent residences.

EDUCATION

The record of your educational background should go back as far as high school graduation (give the graduation date and the name and the location of the school). A young person applying for a job within a few years after graduating from high school may profitably include data pertaining to his high school academic work and his extracurricular activities. His grade average, especially if it is good, may be included.

A complete record of college work—name and address of the college, academic major, and extracurricular activities—is important. The overall scholastic average or the average in the major field or for the final two years of study may be included. In some instances a list of courses of special interest may be an appropriate part of the record of college work.

WORK EXPERIENCE

Data pertaining to work experience should include dates, places, names of employers, and titles of the jobs or the nature of the work performed. Students or recent graduates who have had limited work experience should certainly include a record of part-time jobs and summer jobs. For those students who have had no work experience for which they were paid a wage or a salary may include work for which no monetary rewards were received. For example, such activities as typewriting copy for the school newspaper or yearbook would be good experience for the prospective secretary to include.

A young applicant who has had little opportunity to work should include such experience as delivering newspapers, even as a small boy. Such activity may help to give the prospective employer the impression that the applicant has been accepting responsibility for a long time. Jobs such as baby-sitting may be equally helpful for a young girl who is applying for employment of any type.

A record of any type of employment may be quite beneficial in securing an interview. The work experience does not necessarily have to be related to the job the applicant is seeking. If you have worked as a laborer part time after school, on Saturdays, or during summers, by all means include this work experience on your data sheet.

REFERENCES

Many prospective employers wish to write, telephone, or converse personally with the applicant's references—people who are well acquainted with the applicant's background. The applicant, therefore, should list the names, job titles, business addresses, and possibly the telephone numbers for three to five persons as references. These people should be those who know a good deal about the applicant's work experience, personal traits, or educational background.

Ordinarily, the job title of the reference should be included. When you feel that a reference's job title does not indicate to the prospective employer the reason you listed that person's name, you may appropriately add (perhaps in parentheses) a note explaining your relationship to the person. If no information is given to indicate the person's relationship to you, the prospective employer might conceivably think that the person is one of your relatives or one of your personal friends (roommate, boyfriend or girlfriend, sorority sister or fraternity brother, possibly) .

The name of a relative should be listed as a reference only when that person has been your teacher or an employer. Even in such cases as these, listing the names of nonrelatives would be a better practice in most instances.

Your listing of references will depend somewhat on your background. If you have had a considerable amount of work experience, you may wish to include the names of two or more employers—present or former. If you have had limited work experience, perhaps you should list the names of two or more teachers. With few exceptions, a recent college graduate should list the name of his major professor or faculty advisor. Personnel men usually expect this listing because the major professor or faculty advisor ordinarily knows a good deal about the applicant.

When applying for some jobs, the listing of character references is desirable. The name of your minister, your landlord, a neighbor, or some other person who knows about your personal habits could be listed for this purpose.

By all means, list the names of people who will give you a good recommendation. When choosing between two people who are somewhat equally well prepared to give you a good recommendation, choose the one who you believe can write the better letter and will write the letter promptly. Promptness in receiving recommendations can cause the personnel manager to give an applicant an "edge" over another applicant whose letters of recommendation are received later.

You should obtain a person's permission to use his name as a reference before you list his name on your résumé. Some reasons for getting this permission and some procedures that you should follow in requesting permission to use a name as a reference are discussed later in this chapter.

OTHER

The four divisions that have been discussed for the résumé are those that are somewhat basic to all résumés used in applying for a job. A person who has been out of school for some years would probably need to include additional divisions. Some other possible divisions that a businessman would wish to include are those that permit him to show appropriately his community activities (memberships; offices held; or special work in civic clubs, a church, or other organizations). He may also wish to include a section indicating his professional activities, speeches or consulting services, or honors received.

Stephen D. Lewis

Box 1118, Jackson College
Florence, Tennessee 38151
Telephone 615-526-7686

PERSONAL

		Permanent Address
Marital Status:	Married	
Birth Date:	May 1, 1951	126 Pine Street
Church:	Baptist	Macon, Alabama 36156
Height:	5 11	
Weight:	160	Telephone
Health:	Excellent	
Military Status:	2S	205 983-9655

EDUCATION

1966-1969　Macon High School, Macon, Alabama (diploma)

　　　　　Major: Mathematics　　　Average: B+

　　　　　Extracurricular Activities: Basketball, 2 years; Glee Club, 3 years

1969-1973　Jackson College, Florence, Tennessee
　　　　　(B. S. in Business Administration)

　　　　　Major: Accounting　　　Average: 3.45

　　　　　Extracurricular Activities: Accounting Club; Alpha Kappa Psi, President; Intramural Basketball, 3 years

WORK EXPERIENCE
(part-time)

1964-1968　Birmingham News, Macon, Alabama - Carrier

1968-1972　Hayes Construction Co., Inc., Marshall, Tennessee - Laborer

REFERENCES

Dr. Charles P. Hines
Associate Professor of Accounting
Jackson College
Florence, Tennessee 38151

Mr. James L. Zimmer
Instructor of Marketing
Jackson College
Florence, Tennessee 38151

Mr. Henry M. Johnson
Personnel Manager
Hayes Construction Co., Inc.
Marshall, Tennessee 38217

Mrs. Samuel L. Hubbard
803 North Peachtree Street
Florence, Tennessee 38151
(landlady)

An educator may very well include the sections that a business executive would have plus a special section for publications (books, articles in professional journals, and so on).

Make certain that through the information on your résumé you account for each year since you were graduated from high school.

Marcia McDonald

Apartment 31
2105 Windham Avenue
Sioux Falls, South Dakota

Telephone 808-673-2256

Education

Central High School, Sioux Falls, South Dakota – diploma	1967-1971
Sioux Falls Junior College, Sioux Falls, South Dakota – Associate of Arts Degree	1971-1973

Major: Secretarial Administration

Special Skills: Typewriting – 75 words a minute
                 Shorthand Dictation – 120 words a minute

Extracurricular Activities and Honors: President, Phi Beta Lambda; Treasurer, Future Secretaries Association; Outstanding Secretarial Student of the Year – 1973

Work Experience

Central High School, Sioux Falls, South Dakota (part-time receptionist in the principal's office)	1969-1971
Jameson, Heinke, and Wright Law Firm, Sioux Falls, South Dakota (part-time secretary)	1971-1973

References

Dr. Mary Lynn Fritz, Chairman, Department of Secretarial Administration, Sioux Falls Junior College, Sioux Falls, South Dakota

Mr. Clarke C. Jameson, Attorney-at-Law, 418 First National Bank Building, Sioux Falls, South Dakota

Mr. James M. Holtzmann, Principal, Central High School, Sioux Falls, South Dakota

Personal Details

Birth Date:	June 6, 1954	Church:	Church of Christ
Birthplace:	Jefferson City, Missouri	Weight:	110
Marital Status:	Single	Height:	5' 4"

The possible data sheet divisions discussed in the preceding paragraphs are not intended to be all inclusive. They are given as a guide in helping a job applicant plan a résumé that will be appropriate for the job for which he is applying.

One sample résumé is shown below. Others are to be found on pages 157, 158, and 160.

Walter Bayne Ramsey

856 Fifth Avenue
Richland, VA 23216

Telephone 703-653-1185

EXPERIENCE

1963-present	Hallmark Manufacturing Co., Inc., Richland, Virginia (Manager, Production Department)
1959-1963	Randall Products Company, Newman, New Jersey (Assistant Manager, Production Department)
1956-1958	Watkins Furniture Manufacturing Co., Newman, New Jersey (Supervisor, Sanding Operations)
1954-1956	Williams Manufacturing Company, Inc., Ramsey, Virginia (Management Trainee)
1949-1953	Wheatley State College, Wheatley, Missouri (Laboratory Assistant in the Management Department)

EDUCATION

1953-1954	Littleton State University, Littleton, West Virginia (M. S. Degree)
	Major: Management Thesis: "Production Control Methods in Morgantown Manufacturing Companies"
1949-1953	Wheatley State College, Wheatley, Missouri (B. S. Degree)
	Major: Management Minors: Accounting and English
	Extracurricular Activities: Delta Tau Delta, Social Fraternity; Beta Gamma Sigma, Honor Society; Alpha Kappa Psi, Professional Fraternity
1942-1946	Central High School, Columbus, Missouri (Diploma)

MILITARY

1946-1949	United States Army (Sergeant in Intelligence Corps - served in England and France) - Honorable Discharge

Walter Bayne Ramsey   Page 2

COMMUNITY ACTIVITIES

Elder, First Presbyterian Church, Richland, Virginia
Member of Ryan County School Board, Richland, Virginia, 1965-1971
Former President, Rotary Club, Richland, Virginia, Chapter
Member of local Parent Teacher Association

REFERENCES

Mr. Clarke L. Rodgers   Mr. William L. Maberry
General Manager   Manager, Production Department
Hallmark Manufacturing Co., Inc.   Randall Products Company
Richland, VA 23216   Newman, NJ 21802

Mr. Richard M. Greenbrier, Engineer Mr. J. Samuel Whitehead
Watkins Furniture Manufacturing Co. Personnel Manager
Newman, NJ 21802   Williams Manufacturing Co., Inc.
                                     Ramsey, VA 23211

                    Dr. Roger M. Thornton
                    Chairman, Management Department
                    Wheatley State College
                    Wheatley, MO 40133

PERSONAL

Birth Date: July 1, 1927   Marital Status: Married
Birthplace: Columbus, Missouri   Children: 3
Hobbies: Golfing, Camping, and   Height: 6 1
             Reading   Weight: 175

Requesting permission to use a name as a reference

Common courtesy dictates that you secure permission to use a person's name as a reference before you list his name on your résumé. Listing a name without getting permission to do so would be a breach of business etiquette. In fact, it would be un-ethical.

Even after a person has given you "blanket permission" to use his name as a reference at any time you wish, your letting him know the specific job that you are applying for will give him helpful information in writing the letter recommending you. By knowing a few days before he is to recommend you the type of job you are applying for, the person whose name you use as one of your references may have an opportunity to give adequate thought to the way he believes your qualifications relate to the job you are seeking. He may wish to refer to records in the personnel office if he is a former employer. Or if he is one of your former teachers, he may wish to refer to your record in the administrative offices of the school or to his own records of former students.

If a few years have passed since you have seen the person very often, you should tell him about your activities during that time. You should mention something that will help him to remember you. You can usually do this incidentally.

An incidental reference to some particular thing such as, "Your comments on my letter refusing an adjustment to the woman whose bedspread had faded have helped me on several occasions when customers have returned merchandise," may be sufficient to "jog" the person's memory. On the other hand, some such statements as, "I am the man who dropped the screwdriver in the air–conditioning unit that we sold to Mrs. Charles," may be just the remark that is needed to cause him to remember you.

Like all other letters, the content of this letter will depend on the *situation*. You must consider such things as these:

1. How well does the person know me?
2. How long has it been since we were closely associated with each other?
3. Is there some special item that I can refer to that will cause him to remember a good deal about me?
4. Is there another member of my family that he might confuse me with?
5. Is there some other person whose name is similar (or even identical) to mine that he may confuse me with?

When someone is recommending you for a job, he can write a better letter if he knows something about your activities during the years that have elapsed since he was closely associated with you. Tell him, therefore, the names and addresses of your present and former employers and the nature of the work that you have done.

517 South Cherry Street
Jacksboro, AL 35411
May 21, 1973

Mr. Clyde R. Armstrong
Armstrong Appliance Store
1146 Main Street
Macon, AL 35876

Dear Mr. Armstrong:

I shall use your name as a reference again next month when I apply for the job of salesman with J. Watson Company in Macon.

Hopefully, you will be asked to recommend me. As I mentioned to you just before my graduation from college in 1971, the recommendations you wrote for me then helped me to get favorable responses from prospective employers. Although my induction into the Army prevented my going to work as a salesman then, I am pleased to be completing a tour of military service. I shall be discharged from the Army on June 12.

I am eager to return to Macon. My four years there as a student at Denton College and as a part-time salesman for you during two of those years--1967-1968--were enjoyable. Fortunately, though, not all of the work experiences were quite so wild as my dropping the screwdriver into the airconditioning unit we sold to Mrs. Charles. Sometimes I doubted that you and Mr. Reed would let me live that episode down.

I hear that your business has grown very rapidly during the past two years. I congratulate you, and I wish you continued success.

If you are asked to recommend me for employment with J. Watson Company, I shall certainly appreciate your doing that. I shall come by your store to visit with you for a few minutes sometime next month.

Cordially,

Fred M. Hyder

Fred M. Hyder

Certainly, you will let the person know that you will appreciate his recommending you. Your letter should make it clear to him when he is to write the letter of recommendation. Even though you use his name as a reference, the prospective employer may not ask him to recommend you. If he is to wait until the prospective employer asks for a recommendation, you should state that condition clearly. If you want him to write before the prospective employer asks him to do so, make that point clear to him and give him the exact name, job title, and business address of the person who should receive the letter.

As has been said before, a *good* letter always lets the reader know what the next step is, or that no other step is to be taken.

The letter on page 162 was written by a young man who had been given permission to use a name as a reference. That letter was written to bring the recipient up-to-date on the activities of the writer.

The application letter

Remember that the prospective employer realizes that your application letter represents your best efforts in writing.

Always use plain white 20–pound bond paper of 25 percent rag content. The size should be 8½ by 11 inches. *Do not use letterhead.* Sign the letter with blue or black ink, and make doubly sure that the typewriter keys are clean and that the ribbon is dark. All errors must be erased and corrected so carefully that they can be detected only through extremely close scrutiny.

Write in a manner that will let the reader know that you are energetic and that you have the ability to think clearly and to organize your work well. The résumé (or data sheet) can be used to help display your ability to think clearly and logically and to organize, but you must continue to display these abilities by writing an appropriate letter.

You should make it clear at the beginning of your letter that you are applying for a *specific* job. Statements such as, "Please consider my qualifications for the job of accountant in your office," or "I should like to work as an accountant in your office," are much better than such statements as, "I should like to apply for a position in your office," or "Please consider my application for employment." You have an opportunity to use many *active* verbs when applying for a job. *Work* is an excellent verb to use.

When you know that a vacancy exists, tell the reader how you learned that the job is available. Many employers like to receive applications from friends, relatives, or acquaintances of present or former employees. When an employer advertises through such mediums as newspapers, magazines, or radio, he likes to know that the advertisement has received responses.

The first paragraph of your letter should be relatively short. By wording your beginning carefully, you can include a great deal of information in the first paragraph.

Try to learn the name and the job title of the person who is in charge of employing a person for the job that you are seeking. Address your letter to him. When you cannot learn the name of the person who will study your application, however, address your letter to the organization and use an attention line for the "Personnel Manager."

The last paragraph of your letter should ask confidently for a personal interview. If you can go for an interview at the convenience of the prospective employer, tell him that when you ask for an opportunity to discuss with him your qualifications for the job. When you know that peak-load periods in your present work schedule or examinations in school would preclude your going for an interview on certain dates, tell him that you can go any time at his convenience except on those dates. He will understand your need to make this statement, and he will appreciate your forethought and conscientiousness. Possibly, you will be in his vicinity during certain dates and would like to have an interview then. Feel free to mention this possible arrangement. Sometimes such an arrangement as this is advantageous to the prospective employer, especially if he is paying your travel expenses and your being close by for some other purpose would reduce the expenses he would have to pay.

By all means, type your return address above the date. The reader will know that a letter sent to that address will reach you. Suggesting that he "write to the address given above" would, therefore, insult his intelligence. If you believe that you will be at some other address when he replies, tell him the address that he should use.

Those paragraphs between the first and the last will vary greatly among applicants and among various jobs that any one applicant may seek. In these paragraphs you should try to convince the reader that you are well qualified for the job and that you can contribute to the success of his organization (firm, business, or other). Do all that you can to show him that you have the proper blend of self–confidence and modesty to succeed. No employer wants an employee to be overly timid. Neither does he want an employee to be overly aggressive. What is *your* "happy medium" that suits *your* personality and the job you are seeking?

Convince the prospective employer that you are especially interested in working for him and give some good reasons (other than selfish ones) for your interest. Remember that you are attempting to sell your services. Spell out these *services* as *specifically* as you can, and relate them to the requirements of the job. You must let him know that you understand what the job requires but be careful to state your understanding of what he requires without *telling* him what they are. As has been stated earlier, when you must tell the reader something he already knows, subordinate the "telling." Following this principle is especially important in the letter you use to initiate your application for a job.

The résumé contains in outline form important facts concerning your work and educational background. You can profitably emphasize in your letter some particular fact on the data sheet that you feel is a strong point in your qualifications. Although you should not make a big issue of the fact that you are enclosing a résumé, you should mention in some incidental way that the data sheet is enclosed. A photograph can be considered a part of the data sheet and therefore should not be mentioned in the letter.

Keep the letter reasonably short—never more than one page. An attractive, well-written "medium-length" letter (less than one full page) commands favorable attention.

If you wish to attach your résumé to your letter, do so by using a paper clip so that the letter and the résumé can be easily separated if the reader wishes to separate them. If your résumé is longer than one page, staple the pages together. Place the staple diagonally in the upper left–hand corner.

The application letter and résumé are usually mailed in a plain white No. 10 envelope. Some applicants prefer to mail their applications in large manila envelopes so that folding the letter and the résumé will not be necessary. When this procedure is used, the application presents a better physical appearance than

```
                                    P. O. Box 451
                                    Cutbank State College
                                    Cutbank, Wyoming
                                    April 17, 1973


          Boise Central Bank
          1128 Market Street
          Boise, Montana

          Attention:  Personnel Manager

          Gentlemen:

          Please accept this letter as the initial step in my application
          for one of the management trainee jobs that are open in your
          bank.  Mr. Wayne R. Goodwin, Placement Director at our college,
          told me about the job openings you have announced.

          On June 4 I shall be graduated with a B.S. Degree from Cutbank
          State College.  My major is business management, and my overall
          scholastic average is 2.81 on a 4.00 scale.  As is indicated on
          the data sheet that I am enclosing, I have been quite active in
          a number of extracurricular activities in college.

          As night manager of a busy local service station for the past
          two years, I have continued to accept responsibility, which I
          began accepting as a newspaper carrier when I was fifteen years
          old.

          May I have an opportunity to talk with you personally to tell you
          more about my qualifications for a trainee assignment with you?
          I can come to your office at any time that is convenient for you,
          except during final examinations week, which is May 26 through
          June 3.

                                    Sincerely yours,

                                    Ralph W. Tillman
                                    Ralph W. Tillman

          Enclosure
```

when folding is necessary. Neat appearance cannot be over-emphasized. Appearance alone is not enough, however. Appearance must be accompanied by good, well-organized, easy-to-read content.

Some application letters are illustrated on pages 166–168.

```
                                    P. O. Box 1715
                                    Northern Indiana State College
                                    Denton, IN  41706
                                    May 1, 1973



        Randle Manufacturing Company
        2445 Walnut Ridge Road
        Akron, OH  44309

        Attention Personnel Manager

        Gentlemen:

        Can you use another stenographer whose basic skills have been highly
        polished by hard work in the capstone course that is offered for sec-
        retarial students in our college?  I am taking that course this term,
        which ends on June 4.  Please consider my application for a steno-
        graphic job.

        I can transcribe rapidly and accurately the shorthand notes that I
        take from dictation at 130 words a minute.  Our teacher dictates sci-
        entifically constructed letters, memorandums, speeches, and reports
        that require us students to make many decisions to determine the proper
        punctuation marks to use, to verify mathematical computations, and to
        spell correctly.

        She includes each day a few hard-to-spell words that are not familiar
        to us so that we will be well prepared to take dictation from almost
        any executive.  Because only the perfect copy is accepted for credit, I
        have learned to be a better-than-average proofreader.  Additional infor-
        mation about my background and preparation for stenographic work is on
        the enclosed resume.

        My fiance, who last week accepted a job as chemical engineer for Sci-
        entific Industries, Inc., in Akron, will begin working on July 1, two
        weeks after our wedding date.  I am very eager to work in Akron, too.

        May I have an interview with you any time that is convenient for you,
        except between June 1 and June 25?

                                    Cordially yours,

                                    Mary Ellen Hart
                                    Miss Mary Ellen Hart


        Enclosure
```

P. O. Box 1146
Morrison University
Morrison, KY 40506
May 2, 1973

Mr. Edward M. Hunt
Hunt and Oliver Accounting Firm
1126 Meadow Lake Road
Haleyville, KY 40201

Dear Mr. Hunt:

I should like to work in your Haleyville office. Mr. Joseph H. Hale,
my faculty advisor, told me this morning that you plan to employ a
junior accountant to begin working on June 15. Please consider my
application for that job.

For the past three years I have worked part time for Aaron and Long
Accountants in Morrison. This work fascinates me; and I am challenged by the demands that are made, especially during the rush season for income tax returns.

Although this part-time job has forced me to sacrafice some of the leisure time I enjoyed as a freshman, I have continued to participate in
a social fraternity, as well as in a service fraternity, and have maintained a 3.32 scholastic average on a 4.00 scale. As you can well imag-
ine, I have learned to budget my time. I would like to continue with a
full-time schedule by redirecting my efforts to performing the tasks
that are required in your accounting office.

Mr. Hale and the other three men whose names are listed as references
on the enclosed resume said they will be glad to give you an evaluation
of my qualifications for the vacancy that you will fill next month.

May I have an opportunity to talk with you about the possibilities of
my working for you? I could come to your office at almost any time that
would be convenient for you.

                            Cordially yours,

                            David J. Rhea

                            David J. Rhea

Enclosure

After you have proofread your letter and data sheet as carefully
as you can by reading aloud, ask some other well-qualified person
to read it and to search for any error that you may have overlooked. Accuracy is important in any letter; and this is especially

true for the application letter. Once your letter has been typed, signed, proofread, sealed in the envelope and the envelope stamped and mailed, you can then give some additional thought to the interview that you requested in the last paragraph of the letter.

If you are invited to go for an interview, you have been successful in your first step—writing the initial letter—in the job application. The next steps—confirming the plans for the interview and the follow–up—are discussed next.

Confirming the interview

When the prospective employer grants you an interview, he will either designate a specific date or give you some alternative dates. Acknowledge his letter *immediately*—within twenty-four hours if possible. Again, use plain paper of the same type you used for the application letter and the résumé.

Be *specific* in your reply. Tell him the specific date and the time of day that you will meet him for the interview. Confirming these points in writing impresses the prospective employer and avoids some possible misunderstandings. Also, confirm the place. The office of the personnel manager is frequently the location for the beginning of the interview, but sometimes arrangements are made for the interviewer and the interviewee (the applicant) to meet at some other place. Interviews are frequently conducted at conventions and sometimes even at airports. In your letter you should also repeat the title of the job for which you are to be interviewed. This is especially helpful for personnel men who conduct numerous daily interviews for a variety of jobs.

These comments are made on the assumption that a letter was used to grant your interview. When the prospective employer gets in touch with you by telephone to invite you to meet him for an interview, the telephone conversation may be sufficient confirmation for all of these points. Even then, writing a confirming letter that afternoon or the next day would be a good thing to do if at least a week's time is to elapse before the interview date.

The letter on page 170 was written to confirm an interview.

```
                              P. O. Box 451
                              Cutbank State College
                              Cutbank, Wyoming
                              May 5, 1973




        Mr. James T. Thomas
        Personnel Manager
        Boise Central Bank
        1128 Market Street
        Boise, Montana

        Dear Mr. Thomas:

        I look forward to talking with you on Friday, May 18, about my
        qualifications for the management trainee job in your bank.  I
        shall arrive at your office at 9:30 a.m. as you suggested.

                              Cordially yours,

                              Ralph W. Tillman
                              Ralph W. Tillman
```

The interview

The prospective employer would not ordinarily offer employment without interviewing the applicant. Seldom would an applicant accept employment without having a personal interview.
When a prospective employer invites you to come for an inter-

view, you know that he has been impressed by your letter and your résumé and by the recommendations submitted by the people whose names you listed as references. Now, you must continue to sell yourself.

Some suggestions that may help you prepare for a job interview are presented on pages 459–461 of the reference section of this book.

Regardless of the outcome of the interview, you should follow up by writing a letter to the interviewer thanking him for discussing with you your qualifications for the job. This letter should be written promptly—usually within twenty-four hours after you return to your home. The exact time that you write, as well as the contents of the letter, will be governed by the results of the interview.

If you were offered the job and you accepted that offer, you should write immediately and after thanking the interviewer for the enjoyable visit with him, state the exact title of the job that you have accepted, the starting salary, and the date that you will report for duty. As in all other letter-writing situations, subordinate the "telling" when you tell him what he already knows. Of course you will tell him that you look forward to working for him. Even though you would not have accepted the job offer if you had not believed that you would like it, telling him in writing provides a courteous, goodwill ending for your letter.

In perhaps rare instances you will be asked to sign a contract that specifies your job title, terms of payment, and beginning date of employment. In these instances you will not need to restate all of these points in your letter. You will usually need to restate the job title to remind him immediately of the particular job you have accepted if you think that he has employed persons for several job classifications within the past few days. Too, you could hardly express genuine enthusiasm for working without stating the title of the job you are to perform.

To accept the job later

If you were offered the job and you promised to let the interviewer know by a certain date whether or not you will accept the offer, write to him within twenty-four hours after you return home and after thanking him for discussing the job with you, confirm your promise to let him know your decision by that date (and specify the date). In this letter you should state the title of the job.

Read the letter on this page.

If you were given forms of any type (job application, insurance,

---

Apartment 317
Woodland Towers
1216--21 Street
Salem, TN 38915
May 17, 1973

Mr. Duane E. Fisher
Personnel Manager
Sterrett Aircraft Corporation
1144 Ridgewood Parkway
Salem, TN 38915

Dear Mr. Fisher:

Thank you for interviewing me yesterday for the secretarial job that is open in your purchasing office. I am convinced that I would be challenged by the work that you and Mr. Atkins, the chief purchasing officer, described; and I am very favorably impressed by all of the employees that I met.

As I mentioned to you, though, I am committed to go out of town next Monday for another interview. I appreciate your offering me the job, and I will certainly let you know my decision by Thursday, May 24.

Sincerely yours,

Hazel Springer
Miss Hazel Springer

personal data, and so on) to complete, you would return them with your letter and mention them in whatever way is appropriate for the occasion. Remember that ordinarily when something is important enough to be enclosed, it is important enough to be mentioned in the letter. In some cases you may have to wait three or four days to obtain all of the information necessary for completing the forms. When that is the case, you may delay writing the letter to thank the interviewer until the forms can be enclosed. If you must wait several days to obtain some of the information, write the "thank you" letter immediately and mention the date on which you expect to return the completed forms.

If the interviewer tells you that he will let you know by some specific date whether or not he will offer you the job, you should write him immediately after you return home and, after thanking him for the opportunity to discuss your qualifications with him, tell him that you are looking forward to hearing from him by the date he mentioned. Specify the date in your letter. Try to add something about your qualifications that will help to convince the prospective employer that you are the person for the job. You must, of course, use discretion to keep him from thinking that you are overzealous or that you are trying to exert pressure on him.

The letter on page 174 was written by an applicant who was very much interested in the job for which she had been interviewed.

Suppose that even though you were very much interested in the job, it was not offered to you. Write the interviewer immediately and thank him for discussing your qualifications with you. The courtesy you display in this letter may impress him so much that he will wish to consider you for a future vacancy that he believes you are qualified to fill. Also, he may be inclined to recommend you to someone else who has a vacancy for which you seem to be well suited.

Personnel men try to employ persons they think will be happy in certain jobs. Sometimes an applicant is rejected because the interviewer realizes that the applicant would not be challenged by the job that he has applied for. Not being accepted for some jobs would be a favor to you, but always be courteous and make that good businesslike impression that is necessary for climbing the ladder to the top of the organization chart.

The job may have been offered to you during the interview and you declined at that time, or you may have promised to give the prospective employer your decision at a later time. In either case be sure to write the "thank you" letter immediately. The tone of this letter should be just as cordial as that of any other letter that you write. If you wait to decline the offer until writing the letter, perhaps you should give a reason for declining.

P. O. Box 1715
Northern Indiana State College
Denton, IN 41706
May 29, 1973

Mrs. Opal M. Rhyne
Personnel Manager
Randle Manufacturing Company
2445 Walnut Ridge Road
Akron, OH 44309

Dear Mrs. Rhyne:

Thank you for giving me an opportunity yesterday to discuss with you my qualifications for a job in your stenographic pool. I enjoyed the entire visit, including the nice lunch in the company cafeteria with the two private secretaries.

The tour through your office building was most impressive; and I am very excited about the possibilities of my working in such a pleasant, stimulating environment. I am confident that my preparation and the four months' experience you require in the stenographic pool will qualify me to do top-level work as a private secretary for your company.

I look forward to hearing from you by June 26.

Cordially yours,

Mary Ellen Hart
Miss Mary Ellen Hart

Accepting an offer

Promptness is important in accepting an offer of employment. When you write a letter accepting a job offer, direct that letter to the person who made the offer unless you are instructed to direct

```
                                        P. O. Box 1146
                                        Morrison University
                                        Morrison, KY  40506
                                        May 16, 1973




        Mr. Edward M. Hunt
        Hunt and Oliver Accounting Firm
        1126 Meadow Lake Road
        Haleyville, KY  40201

        Dear Mr. Hunt:

        I accept your offer of employment as a junior accountant in your
        Haleyville office at a salary of $9,000 a year.

        Thank you for sending the information on apartments.  This morn-
        ing I wrote to the manager of the Terrace Apartment Building and
        sent the required deposit.  I shall move to Haleyville on June 12
        and will be ready to go to work in your office at eight o'clock
        on Monday morning, June 15.

        I look forward to working for you.

                                Cordially yours,

                                David J. Rhea
                                David J. Rhea
```

it to someone else. Be sure that in your letter you state definitely and cheerfully that you accept the offer. State the title of the job, the salary, and the date on which you are to begin working. Existing circumstances may, of course, necessitate your including additional information in your letter.

The essential characteristics of a job acceptance letter are included in the illustration on page 175.

Declining an offer

In many instances a job is offered to the applicant a few days after the interview. If you receive a letter offering you a job that you wish to decline, write a letter immediately (within twenty-four hours) telling the person that you have decided to decline the offer. Here again, make sure that before you begin writing the letter you have thought about the situation as much as you need to to make your decision to decline. You may wish to give the reason for your decision, though you do not have to. If the reason is a pleasant one such as a better job has been offered to you, you may very well include the reason. As there is no need to mention unpleasantness when you decline an offer, *do not* do that.

Promptness in declining an offer is extremely important. By declining promptly, you make a favorable impression on the "would-be" employer. He will appreciate your thoughtfulness and fair-minded attitude in declining quickly so that he can employ someone else soon. Quite possibly, he has considered some other person who also has good qualifications for the job; and your promptness in declining his offer may enable him to employ the other well-qualified person before that person accepts employment with another organization.

Notice the promptness with which the letter on page 177 was written.

Businessmen do discuss among themselves good applicants they have interviewed, and favorable comments about you may lead to your being given special consideration by some other organization that could offer you special opportunities. But if for no other reason, decline offers promptly and courteously simply for the sake of fair play.

```
                                      123 White Avenue
                                      Jasper, VA  22031
                                      May 18, 1973



     Mr. Ernest J. Miles
     Personnel Manager
     Riggs Manufacturing Company
     1426 Longview Road
     Anchorage, MS  39614

     Dear Mr. Miles:

     Yesterday afternoon, before I received your letter offering me
     employment in your management training program, I accepted a
     similar job with a company in Louisiana.  That company pays a
     higher salary than you offered me, and the working conditions
     and the opportunities for advancement are somewhat the same.

     I appreciate very much your offer.  I feel confident that the
     person you employ will enjoy working for you.

                              Sincerely yours,

                              Craig L. Hastings
                              Craig L. Hastings
```

Resigning

Almost all people change jobs at least one time during their lives. You hope, of course, that you will change jobs only because you have an opportunity to go into a better situation. The situation may be better because you are going to a job that pays a higher immediate salary, offers a better chance for advancement in salary or prestige, provides an opportunity to use your skills and knowledge to greater advantage, or provides an opportunity to do the kind of work that is most interesting to you; or you may be going to a geographical area that is especially desirable to you.

Some young women resign from their jobs because they get married and will no longer work for pay. Others may leave their jobs to rear children, and still others may move from one job to another because their husbands move to a new organization or transfer within the organization to a different locality. These reasons for resigning are only a few of the many possible reasons that a person may resign a position under pleasant circumstances. You will have very little difficulty in writing a letter of resignation when you leave under pleasant conditions.

As is the case with all other letters, make up your mind definitely to resign before you begin writing the letter. State specifically the last day that you are to work on the job you are leaving. You may or may not need to state the title of your job; this will depend on such factors as the type of job, the size of the organization, the length of time you have worked there, and the person to whom you address your letter. You should, ordinarily, address your letter to your immediate supervisor. In many possible situations, though, you may need to address your letter of resignation to some person other than your immediate superior. In some organizations all such letters are addressed to the personnel manager. The way the group for which you work is organized will help you to determine the officer to whom your resignation letter should be addressed.

Perhaps it would be appropriate for you to include in your letter your willingness to help train the person who will replace you. You may, conceivably, feel that it is appropriate for you to suggest the name of a person to replace you. On the other hand, suggesting a person as a replacement may be inappropriate. The conditions that exist at the time you resign will help you determine just what to include in your letter. By all means, write a letter that will leave a good last impression on the people who will read your letter. Your letter will be filed in your personnel file and may be read by several people at various times in the future.

The letter on this page which was written under very pleasant circumstances, left a good impression of the writer.

Occasionally, the most efficient, most ethical, most capable, hardworking persons encounter unpleasant conditions that cannot be remedied. They must, therefore, resign under unpleasant

---

BRADLEY MANUFACTURING COMPANY
Waterford, NJ 08099

September 18, 1973

Mr. Ellis G. Graham
Personnel Manager
Bradley Manufacturing Company
2455 Handley Road
Waterford, NJ 08099

Dear Mr. Graham:

Because the Westfield Manufacturing Company has offered me a job that affords especially good opportunities for advancement as well as a starting salary that is considerably higher than I am earning here, I am submitting this resignation from my present job. Friday, November 27, will be my last working day here.

I have certainly enjoyed my work here as assistant manager of the production department; and I appreciate the courtesies that have been shown me since I joined this company on July 1, 1968. The experiences I have had here are invaluable, and I shall always value highly the friendships that I have developed with the other employees.

I shall be glad to assist in any way you suggest in orienting my successor to the job.

Cordially yours,

T. Martin Lambert

T. Martin Lambert

circumstances. The resignation letter is perhaps as important as the application letter because in many instances this letter is the last document that is placed in the person's personnel file of the organization he is leaving. Regardless of the kinds of conditions that exist at the time you resign, make the tone of your resignation letter pleasant, specific, and firm yet diplomatic.

If you should resign because of some unpleasant circumstances, the tone of your letter of resignation must be just as pleasant as the tone of a letter that you would write when leaving under pleasant conditions. Stated negatively *for emphasis,* under *no* conditions can you afford to refer to—or even hint at—unpleasantness in a letter of resignation! This is true regardless of the degree of seriousness of the circumstances that have been unpleasant for you.

When you have a grievance (and some grievances do occur in the best run organizations), you owe it to yourself and to the other person involved to discuss that grievance with him. Often the person who you feel is responsible for the conditions does not realize that the conditions he has created are unpleasant for you. When that is the case, he will gladly make whatever adjustments are needed to correct the situation; and he will appreciate your calling the matter to his attention.

Sometimes a situation seems unpleasant to you because you do not fully understand the conditions that exist. Here again, the fair thing to do is to discuss the grievance with the other person involved so that the matter can be explained. Because you are a fair-minded person and have an open mind, you will dismiss the grievance once you understand that it is something that you should not be offended by. You may wish to state a simple oral apology for your misunderstanding. If you feel that you should apologize, you should do so simply and then forget about the matter. The other person involved will certainly appreciate your giving him an opportunity to explain the situation so that pleasantness will be restored. You should remember that a simple apology (when an apology is appropriate) exemplifies character. Repeating the apologetic remarks, however, can cause the person to think that you are "weak kneed" or that you were unfair in even asking for an explanation.

While almost all people who attain supervisory or executive status are ethical, some, unfortunately, are not. If you should encounter some difficulty with a superior who is unethical or who will not attempt to correct a situation that imposes undue hardship on you, you certainly have a right to disagree with his refusal. You owe it to yourself and to your subordinates (if you have subordinates on the job) to "stand up for your rights." An intelligent person of strong character controls his temper so that he does not throw tantrums as an immature person would do, but he should "fight the case" and even take the grievance to personnel further up the organization chart when he knows that he is right and wants to continue working in his present position.

Any disagreeable situations should be discussed only with those persons who can do something to remedy the inequity. Do *not* discuss such matters with friends or fellow workers who cannot help effect a settlement of the dispute. Gossip would hurt rather than help you, and you should not lower your standards of conduct to such behavior.

The point to be stressed is that regardless of the degree of unpleasantness that exists and regardless of what you say or do about an unpleasant situation, you must not include any reference to unpleasantness in your letter of resignation!

The tone and the content of a letter of resignation that is written because of unpleasant conditions leading to your decision to resign must be the same as the tone and the content would be if the letter were written under the most pleasant circumstances.

Questions for discussion

1. Why should a letter of application be written on plain paper rather than on letterhead?
2. What are appropriate ways of producing copies of a résumé?
3. Why is it important that you list your experience as a laborer (if you have had such experience) when you are preparing a résumé as a part of an application for a job in management?
4. What action should you take if you do not receive a reply within thirty days to your application letter?

5. When applying for some types of jobs, you may need to include such details as your height, weight, and coloring. For what types of jobs should you include these details on your résumé?

Exercises

Improve the following sentences that were taken from business letters.

1. When you decide whether or not you will accept the job offer with us, please advise me.
2. I should like to thank you for recommending me for the job of assistant buyer for the Hamilton Department Store in Knoxville.
3. Please inform us of your plans within ten days' time.
4. I hope that this arrangement will not be inconvenient for you.
5. A copy of our agreement is attached hereto.
6. A survey of my college work can be found on the enclosed résumé.
7. Why not contact us before December 1.
8. Due to the fact that Jack and Fred could not serve on the committee, the chairman asked Jeanie and myself to accept that responsibility.
9. I shall be more than happy to be of assistance to you.
10. The completion of this test will only require a short period of time.

Problems

1. The following advertisement was in the *Jackson Times* yesterday.

WANTED

Secretary, salesman, management trainee by June 1, Jackson Office Equipment Company, 1104 Natchez Road, Jackson, Mississippi.

Write a letter of application for one of these three jobs. Enclose a data sheet (résumé).

2. Assume that the letter you wrote for Problem 1 was successful. You received a letter today inviting you to come for a personal

interview. The date and the time of day for the interview were specified in that letter.

Reply to the letter.

3.   You had a personal interview this morning. As another applicant is to be interviewed next week, you are to be notified within two weeks as to whether or not you will be offered the job.

Write a letter thanking the person for the interview and letting him know that you are still very much interested in obtaining the job. Having had an interview, you know the name of the person to whom you are writing.

4.   At the conclusion of the interview you had last Friday, the personnel director (and of course you remember his name) told you he would let you know within two weeks whether he would offer you the job.

You received his letter today offering you the job. *Accept* the offer.

5.   Assume that your application letter (see Problem 1) was successful. You had a personal interview last Friday, and you wrote a letter the next day thanking the person for the interview and telling him that you will let him know within two weeks whether or not you will accept the job.

Yesterday another company offered you a job that (for any reason or reasons you wish to assume) you prefer. Write a letter declining the offer for the job you were offered as a result of the application letter you wrote and the subsequent interview.

6.   Assume that for the past two years you have been working for the Thomas Manufacturing Company. You will need to make some reference to the kind of work you have been doing.

You have an opportunity to take a better job with another company. *Use your imagination!* Why is the job better? When will you resign? What is the name of the other company? Have you profited by working two years for the Thomas Manufacturing Company? Add anything that is appropriate.

Write a letter of resignation.

Remember that this letter will be placed in your personnel file. Perhaps this letter will be the *final* good impression that you will make on the people who work for Thomas Manufacturing Company.

7.   You have been working as assistant manager of the production department of the Whaley Manufacturing Company since Sep-

tember 15, 1967. Things went along nicely until last August. Since that time many annoyances have hindered your work. You have discussed these legitimate grievances with your immediate superior and with the personnel director. Each person agreed with you that your requests for adjustments are in order.

You're *fed up!* and you have a right to be! Resign. Write the letter of resignation.

9

Disappointing news

BUSINESS ACTIVITIES involve frequent requests for both products and services. Some of these requests are for free assistance of some type, and some of them are for products or services for which the person making the request expects to pay. As has been pointed out earlier in this book, no one can survive as an isolated individual; everyone must call on others from time to time for assistance. Successful business executives realize the importance of helping others, and they are eager to help at appropriate times. When a person can help by complying with a request that is made, he has no problem in writing his response. Letters of this type—complying with requests—were discussed in Chapter 5. Review that chapter for writing affirmative responses.

Regardless of how efficiently your organization is run or how much you are interested in helping other people, you will occasionally receive requests with which you cannot comply; or it may be possible to comply though you feel you should not. Your response to such requests are somewhat more difficult than the responses would be if you were complying, but you can reply to these requests in such a manner that you will still maintain the goodwill of the people who made the requests. Letters of this type are discussed in this chapter.

Good public relations is essential for success in any business endeavor or in any activity involving associations with other people. Your personal reputation and the reputation of the organization you represent are established and maintained by handling all transactions efficiently and tactfully. Your attitude is always reflected in your well-written letters. When you believe in yourself, others tend to believe in you also, provided of course you have reason to believe in yourself because you are honest, competent, tactful, and genuinely interested in the welfare of others. When you possess these qualities, you can decline a request and at the same time maintain the goodwill and friendship of the person making the request.

A very high percentage of the requests that are made of business executives are made by people who are fair minded and who request only those products or services they honestly believe you can provide. Human nature being what it is, however, some people make unreasonable requests that you cannot afford to respond to affirmatively. The requests that are made by fair-minded individuals, however, are the ones you must treat with great care; and they are the ones that you want to decline in such a manner that will cause the person making the request to feel just as good toward you and your organization as he would feel if you granted his request.

Declining a request is disappointing news for the receiver of your letter. As you prepare to write a letter containing disappointing news, bear in mind the basic principle that when you cannot do what the reader would like for you to do, tell him *first* what you *can* do.

Some of the letters that have some element of disappointing news are those offering substitutes or other alternatives or promises to comply later. Some refer to the need for additional information in order to comply, and some recommend another source of supply. Still other letters express outright refusals to comply with requests.

Substitutes or alternatives

Suppose that you are working for a department store, a wholesale house, or some other supplier of merchandise who receives orders by mail. You know that the person who orders some item from you hopes to receive that item promptly; and you know that when he receives a letter from your organization, he hopes that the letter contains information telling him that the item he ordered has been sent or that it will be sent very soon. Any information other than this will be disappointing news for him.

As a competent communicator, you will understand the purpose of the letter that you will write as a reply to his request; and you will write promptly. You will decide specifically what you must say to him; and by keeping your reader in mind and by anticipating his mood, you will *begin with good news* by telling him what you *can* do *before* telling him what you cannot do. Applying these principles as well as all of the other basic principles presented in Chapter 2, write a letter that has a positive, pleasant beginning and a positive, pleasant ending with any necessary disappointing news subordinated within the body of the letter. (Remember that the beginning is the most important part of a letter and that the ending is the second most important part.)

When you receive an order for merchandise that you cannot ship by the date specified by the person ordering, study the *situation* thoroughly to determine the most appropriate action to take. You may send a substitute item, you may tell when you can supply the particular item he requested, you may ask another supplier to ship the item, or you may suggest that the person ordering the merchandise submit his order to another source. The more you know about the situation and the person ordering the merchandise, the better you can choose the step that would be most appropriate for you to take.

SUBSTITUTES

By studying the situation carefully, you may learn that the particular item that was ordered must be used by a specific, early date. That being the case, you can appropriately suggest a substitute item, provided you honestly believe the substitute you suggest is satisfactory for the use that is to be made of the item that was ordered. You may need to give a sales pitch for this product. You should give some *specific* reasons why you believe the substitute will be satisfactory. Merely telling your reader that the substitute should be satisfactory is not sufficient unless he is already familiar with the substitute or unless he already has a great deal of confidence in your judgment concerning the matter under consideration.

Even when suggesting a substitute, you have many avenues among which you must choose. If the product is needed very

---

THE FARM AND GARDEN SHOP
Livingston, AL 35470

July 2, 1973

Mr. Randall N. Gray
1151 Rosemount Drive
Macon, AL 36267

Dear Mr. Gray:

We have a Model 8 riding lawn mower that is more popular this year than the Model 6 because it has a two-inch wider cutting area and has a quieter motor. The new model has all of the other features that the Model 6 has and sells for only $15 more, which is a small sum when applied to a purchase of this amount.

We can send the Model 8 to you immediately. August 17 is the earliest date on which we can send a Model 6. A strike in the manufacturer's plant last month has prevented our obtaining a supply of that model.

Considering the size of your lawn and the rate at which the grass grows in your area, you are wise indeed to replace your old mower with a riding model. After mowing the whole lawn in one afternoon, you will still feel up to eighteen holes of golf; and by the way, one recent purchaser of a Model 8 is using it as a golf cart. That can be done easily, as only one nut has to be removed to detach the cutting blade.

A Model 8 riding mower will be on its way to you the day we receive your approval to send it.

Cordially yours,

Eugene T. Hollingsworth

Eugene T. Hollingsworth
Sales Manager

grm

quickly, you may send the substitute at the same time you write the letter explaining your reason for sending something other than the exact item that was ordered. In a case such as this, perhaps you should give the recipient an opportunity to return the product at your expense if he wishes to do so. You would, however, encourage him to keep the substitute as you would send it only because you believe he will be pleased to receive it. Because negative wording may cause him to choose to return the merchandise, write in such a manner that your letter expresses a positive, confident, courteous tone. The letter on page 188 was written to offer what the writer believed was a good substitute for the item that was ordered.

Continue to be mindful of the fact that sales are successful so long as the purchaser is satisfied with the product he purchased.

Provided a considerable length of time is to elapse before the item that was ordered will be used, you may appropriately write to the person who submitted the order and give the sales pitch on the substitute you suggest and allow *him* to decide that you send the merchandise. When a person has an opportunity to contribute to a decision, he tends to be happy with that decision. Writing a letter *before* shipping the product may be extremely important when the product involved is heavy or is otherwise difficult to transport.

A number of reasons exist for the necessity to suggest substitutes. Among such reasons are these:

1. Inadequate inventory.
2. Discontinued item.
3. Lost franchise.
4. Better item available.

INADEQUATE INVENTORY. Your inventory may be low because of an oversight or because of a strike in the plant of the manufacturer or a strike among the railroad, truckline, airline, or other carrier group responsible for delivering your supply of merchandise. Your inventory may be low because of an oversight in your own organization (occasionally an error is made in the most efficiently run organizations), or the inventory may be low because of inaccurate estimates of requirements. Estimates cannot be 100 percent accurate all of the time. Your inventory may be low because the manufacturer's production may be behind schedule for one of numerous possible reasons. One or more of various other reasons could cause your inventory to be inadequate.

DISCONTINUED ITEM.   The manufacturer of a particular item that was ordered may have discontinued the production of that product. He may have discontinued production entirely, or he may have started producing a different model. If a new model is being produced, chances are good that it is superior to the earlier model; but you oftentimes have to *convince* the reader of your letter that the later model is an improvement.

If a product has been discontinued without being replaced by another model, you must *sell* an entirely new product as a substitute when you believe such a substitution is advisable.

LOST FRANCHISE.   If you no longer have the franchise for the product that was ordered, you obviously cannot supply it. Because you want to continue supplying other merchandise to the customer, you may suggest a substitute item and give him the facts that would convince him that your product is as good as and possibly even better than the one he requested. You should, after giving him your sales pitch, tell him why you are not sending the specific item he ordered. You cannot afford to seemingly ignore his original request. Your explanation would, of course, be followed by a pleasant, specific ending.

BETTER ITEM AVAILABLE.   You may have, in addition to the specific item that was ordered, a similar product that you believe would better suit the needs of the person who placed the order. The similar item may be more durable; it may sell for a lower price; it may have a longer guarantee; it may have a better appearance; or it may be superior because of some other characteristic. Suggesting that the purchaser accept this substitute would be doing him a favor, and he may appreciate your thoughtfulness in calling his attention to the proposed substitute.

Any time you suggest a substitute for an item that was ordered, you should *begin* your letter with the good news of *what you can do for the reader*. Add enough sales talk to convince him that he will be pleased with the substitute. Even though you write well enough to convince him that the substitute is as good as *or* is better than the item he ordered, you must refer in some appropriate way to the reason for suggesting an alternative. To seemingly ignore his request for a specific item would be a poor business practice. *Present your explanation positively!*

Almost always this explanation can be presented quite well without using a single negative word or negative connotation. Omit such negative terms as *unfortunately, regret, sorry, cannot, not, will not be able,* and *unable.* Contrast the positive expressions with the negative expressions in the two columns that follow:

Positive	*Negative*
We can send the merchandise on November 5	We cannot send the merchandise until November 5.
By considering this item, you	Why not consider this substitute
. . . will be ready to mail on	. . . will not be available until . . . .

Sales talk for other merchandise or services and some other types of pleasant information may be included in your letter; but whether or not such additional information is included, end your letter with something that is pleasant, positive, and specific. Many otherwise well–written letters suggesting a substitute are spoiled by using such words as *hope, trust,* or *if* in the last paragraph in such a manner that causes the reader to doubt that the substitute will be satisfactory. Contrast the positive and the negative ending paragraphs in the two columns that follow:

Positive	*Negative*
Our representative for your area will bring you a supply of our revised order forms when he comes to your office next Thursday morning.	I hope that you will be pleased with the Model 22, which we believe is superior to the model you ordered.
A fall edition of our catalog will be mailed to you on June 4.	We trust that you will be pleased with this substitute.

Positive	*Negative*
We look forward to receiving another order from you.	If you like this new model as much as the one you requested, we will be happy to fill other orders for it.

Note that in each of these positive endings the next step to be taken is implied or is spelled out in detail.

ALTERNATIVES

Some requests for services or contributions of money or other materials, as well as some of the requests for products, must be declined. The technique for declining these requests is the same as for declining the requests for products: when you cannot do what the reader wants you to do, tell him *first* what you *can* do.

SPEECHES.   When you are asked to speak to a group, to participate in some other way in a program, or to perform any other type of service, remember that the person making the request wants your reply to begin by accepting that responsibility. Obviously, you will sometimes be faced with invitations or requests that you cannot comply with even though you would very much like to do so. When you can offer some alternative (and usually you can), you should present the alternative first and then subordinate the refusal of the original request. One or more alternatives may be suggested. Any alternative that is suggested must be one that you sincerely believe may be a possible satisfactory substitute. Obviously, you have to have adequate information pertaining to the situation out of which the request originated in order to suggest appropriate alternatives.

Suppose that you have been asked to speak on a selected topic to a group that is scheduled to meet on a specified date. If you have another commitment for that date, you may logically agree to speak at some other time, provided of course you are familiar enough with the group to know that the meeting could be conveniently rescheduled or that the group has regularly scheduled periodic meetings. In this case your offering to speak at a later time may be an appropriate alternative to suggest before you tactfully decline the invitation as presented to you. An example of this can be seen in the letter to Mr. Edwin A. Rogers shown below.

If you know enough about the group of people to know that they are especially interested in having a particular topic discussed on the date you have been invited to speak, you may sug-

---

HASTINGS COMMUNITY COLLEGE
Hastings, Colorado 81041

January 7, 1974

Mr. Edwin A. Rogers, Chairman
Business Education Department
Norfolk Senior High School
Norfolk, Colorado 81422

Dear Mr. Rogers:

Could the Southern Colorado Business Teachers Association meet at some time other than Thursday evening, May 12? I would be very glad to speak to that group on the topic you suggested, "Enthusiastic Teaching," at any time that I am free.

I have accepted an invitation to represent the Association of Colorado Community Colleges at a national meeting in Houston, Texas, on May 11, 12, and 13.

I realize that for any one of various possible reasons you may have to stick to the May 12 date for your meeting. If so, you will no doubt have ample time to obtain another speaker for that occasion.

Cordially yours,

Wendell W. Robbins

Wendell W. Robbins, Chairman
Business Education Department

pjf

gest an alternate speaker if you know a person who you believe could present a good speech on that particular topic. Under some circumstances you may appropriately consult the person you wish to recommend before you recommend him. You would, however, exercise special care to handle the situation in such a manner that the alternate you suggest will not be embarrassed or offended if the person in charge of obtaining a speaker does not invite him. You would also make your suggestion in such a way that the reader of your letter would not feel obligated to invite the person you recommend. Oftentimes program chairmen have more than one speaker in mind so that they can choose an alternate if the person they invite declines the invitation.

When you suggest an alternate speaker, you should make it easy for the person in charge of the meeting to invite the alternate if he chooses to do so. Sending the alternate's full name and mailing address is usually sufficient information. His telephone number could be included in the data you supply, and you may conceivably offer to get in touch with the alternate if you are asked to do that.

Certainly, you should give some reasons for recommending him. Tell some of his characteristics—his knowledge of the subject and his ability to speak or his reputation as a speaker, and so forth—when you say you believe he would present a good speech.

When you offer to speak on another date, give as much consideration to your reader as you do when you recommend another speaker. He may have already made plans for the future meetings and would not wish to have you speak on any date other than the one he specified. To avoid placing the reader in an embarrassing situation, make it easy for him to proceed with any plans he may choose without feeling obligated to accept your offer to speak at a subsequent meeting. Always avoid forcing someone into an embarrassing situation. You can make suggestions diplomatically without putting pressure on your reader to accept any alternative you suggest.

Study the situation thoroughly to determine whether you can suggest one or more *appropriate* alternatives *before* you decline a request of any kind.

CONTRIBUTIONS. Organizations are frequently asked to contribute money, services, or materials to various groups—schools, civic clubs, and charitable organizations. They are also asked to help some professional groups by advertising in convention programs and other publications or by renting space to exhibit their products at professional conventions. You may welcome an opportunity to participate in these ways. If, however, you do not wish to participate in the manner requested, you are under no obligation to do so; and of course you can decline without hesitation. Being an effective communicator, you will apply the basic principles of telling what you *can* do *before* you tell what you cannot do.

You can choose from several alternatives. One alternative would be to offer (provided you are sincere in making this offer) to comply the next time the group meets or the next time a drive is sponsored. You may conceivably recommend that others participate. For example, you may place a note on the company bulletin board inviting your employees to contribute individually to a fund drive if your funds allocated for such purposes have been depleted. A thorough understanding of the existing conditions will enable you to suggest an appropriate alternative before you *state in a positive, cordial manner* the reason you must decline the original request. Follow this reason with a pleasant, positive ending for your letter. Contrast the positive and the negative endings in the two columns that follow:

Positive	Negative
We wish you the best of luck in your fund–raising campaign.	We sincerely regret that we must decline your invitation.
Please give us an opportunity to exhibit our machines at your next annual convention.	We are sorry that we cannot exhibit our machines at your convention this year.
We heartily endorse the work that your organization does.	We apologize for any inconvenience this may have caused you.

Negative statements such as these at the end of an otherwise good letter cause the reader to concentrate more on your declining his request than on your willingness (and possibly even eagerness) to help him in whatever way you mentioned in the beginning of your letter.

CREDIT.   A person who seeks credit obviously believes that he or the organization he represents would benefit by being granted the credit privilege. When you must decline this request, you must present the disappointing news as tactfully and cordially as you can. You would want his business because when all business operations are efficient, increased sales volume can be expected to increase profits. You therefore have a selfish interest as well as an interest in the prospective customer in adding his name to your list of current customers.

A good beginning for such a letter may be the explanation of special consideration you can give to cash customers. When you can offer a cash discount, for example, make this arrangement sound as attractive as you can by including some specifics. Perhaps your doing some arithmetic that involves figures that seem appropriate for the amount of the order he has placed or you expect him to place would help convince him that your cash discount arrangement is worthy of his consideration. The writer of the letter on page 197 stressed the advantages of cash purchases until a satisfactory ratio of assets to liabilities could be attained.

Present your figures in such a manner that will cause him to concentrate on the saving you are pointing out rather than cause him to think that you are simply doing arithmetic for him. *Specific* figures such as $6.39 as a saving on an order for $219.43 worth of merchandise are much more meaningful than general figures such as $6 as a saving on an order for $200 worth of merchandise. Specific figures can be used, of course, only when an order has been received. General figures may seem appropriate for estimates of orders that you anticipate his sending.

In either instance the amount of the actual *saving*—$6.39 or $6.00—means more than would merely stating that he qualifies for a 2 percent discount. Use specific, positive, cordial statements that are well written to "sell" the alternative that you suggest for granting credit.

In declining an application for credit, you have to give some reason. Make whatever complimentary statements you can about the applicant before you state the reason for declining. His personal habits or reputation, his bill–paying habits, or his selling ability may be qualities that you can compliment sincerely. Your mentioning these items can possibly cause the reason for declining to be obvious. He will, therefore, be in a good mood before he actually reads the reason you have given.

WILLIAMSON WHOLESALE COMPANY
Muncie, Ohio 43262

July 7, 1973

Mr. Reginald R. Chambliss
Manager, Scott Clothiers, Inc.
Lakeview, GA 30635

Dear Mr. Chambliss:

Our 3 percent discount on purchases of $300 or more is somewhat larger than that offered by any other clothing supplier in this region. We encourage you to take advantage of this liberal discount.

We can--except for very rare occasions--ship merchandise within twenty-four hours after we receive an order. This prompt shipping would enable you to borrow money from a bank at the beginning of a month and then sell the merchandise before that money has to be repaid.

By borrowing $350, the amount you mentioned in your letter of July 5, you would have to pay only the minimum that is charged for one month; and by paying cash for the clothing you order from us, you would save $10.50. The markup on the merchandise would afford you a sizable profit without having to use any of your own money. I urge you to take advantage of our cash discount plan until the ratio of your assets to liabilities is 2 to 1.

The people whose names you gave us as references for our routine investigation of your credit application were very complimentary of your selling ability, as well as your personal character. I am confident, therefore, that your assets to liabilities ratio will be in fine condition very soon.

Until then, Mr. Chambliss, let us supply your clothing requirements through our 3 percent cash discount plan. Please remember that we can almost always ship any of the merchandise described in the enclosed catalog within twenty-four hours after we receive an order.

Cordially yours,

Merrill E. Watson
Merrill E. Watson
Credit Manager

dlb

Enclosure

Certainly most applicants for credit realize that their backgrounds will be investigated before their applications are approved or disapproved. Even though this procedure is generally understood, referring to your investigation as a *routine* matter may be good psychology to use. Remember, too, that the information that was given to you in your investigation *must be treated confidentially.* You must, therefore, generalize to some extent on the complimentary statements you include in your letter; and you must omit identification of any person who supplied the information even though your reader knows the people whose names he gave to you as references.

Whether or not you can encourage the reader to reapply for credit later, end with a positive, pleasant statement or question. Contrast the positive and the negative endings in the following columns:

Positive	*Negative*
We can ship any item listed in our catalog the day we receive your order.	We regret that we cannot approve your application for credit at this time.
We shall be glad to receive another credit application from you when. . . .	Why not send us another credit application when. . . ?

Delayed compliance

When you cannot provide the requested product or service and have no suitable substitute to recommend, you may wish to encourage the person making the request to permit you to comply with his request later. You should study the conditions thoroughly enough to know that he could conveniently wait until the time you can comply.

Begin your letter by telling *when* you can fill the order or comply in some other manner with whatever the request may be and then explain in a positive, tactful manner the reason necessitating the delay. An explanation presented in a positive manner will omit such negative words as *delay, inconvenience,* and *failure.*

A sales pitch on some additional item may very well be included in some of the letters explaining delays. Resale information on the product that was ordered is also desirable in some letters of this type. The entire situation would, of course, enable you to decide whether to include a sales pitch or resale information.

RANCHLAND DEPARTMENT STORE
Spring City, Kansas 67083

February 16, 1974

Mrs. Kenneth E. Odlund
247 East Walnut Street
Lawrence, Utah 84730

Dear Mrs. Odlund:

As a supply of the best seller <u>Cascade Adventures</u> by Walter E. McMillan is scheduled to arrive at our store on February 28, we can send a copy to you that day so that it will reach you before your nephew's birthday on March 5.

I am confident that he will be pleased with your gift selection. This book has received some of the best reviews of any publication within the past eight years. Because it has been enjoyed by so many adults as well as by teenaged boys, I suspect that you, too, would enjoy reading it.

The demand for this book has been so great that our first supply, which we received last Monday, was exhausted before the end of the week.

We will gift wrap your copy of <u>Cascade Adventures</u> with a paper that appeals to many young men so that it will be ready for you to present to your nephew before March 5.

Sincerely yours,

Louis G. Waddell

Louis G. Waddell
Manager, Book Department

btb

As the ending of a letter is second in importance only to the beginning, write an appropriate ending to any letter you send to explain a delay in compliance. Notice that the positive tone is evident in the final paragraph of the letter on page 199.

Need for more information

If you need more information in order to comply with a request, begin by telling the reader that you can comply when you receive the additional details. Be specific in asking for the additional data. Always write tactfully and positively and minimize the use of negative words, phrases, or ideas.

Contrast the positive and the negative statements in the two columns that follow:

Positive	*Negative*
Which do you prefer—Model No. 3 or Model No. 4?	You neglected to specify the model you prefer.
Please specify your color preference	You did not specify your color preference.
Please complete the column for model numbers.	You failed to complete the column for model numbers.

One or more sentences assuring your reader that you will grant his request promptly when you receive the additional information you have asked for will lessen the impact of the disappointing news that any letter bears that does not fully comply with the request.

Resale information is on some occasions quite appropriate for this type of letter. A few sound courteous statements reassuring the reader that he will be well pleased with the product he has ordered may be very helpful in motivating him to send the needed information quickly so that you can fill his order. If his interest in the product may have waned somewhat since he placed the order, resale information may provide the stimulus he needs to send the data you must have to comply with his original request.

Another source

Perhaps you will at some time be asked to supply a product that you do not carry in stock and you do not have a suitable item to offer as a substitute. In a case such as this, you are wise to suggest another source rather than mention a possible substitute. You will make a much more favorable impression on the person who requested the item by telling him where he can obtain it than by even suggesting another item that would not please him as much as the one he ordered. Two alternatives from which you may choose are: (1) to tell him the name and address of a supplier who can furnish the item desired or (2) to get in touch with another supplier and request that the item be sent to the person who requested you to send it.

The alternative you choose will depend somewhat on such factors as the urgency of obtaining the item, your relationship with the person requesting the item, your relationship with the other supplier, and the location of the other supplier. If the person ordering is one of your regular customers and he needs the product in a hurry, you would probably do him a favor by getting in touch with the other supplier and asking him to send the product by the date that was specified in the original request. This procedure would certainly seem to be the proper action to take if the other supplier is in your city or is in a nearby city.

Under certain conditions you may appropriately ask the other supplier to send the requested item and charge it to your account. You would then charge that amount to the account of the customer who requested the product. You should begin your letter to the person who ordered the product by telling him that you have asked another supplier (identify him by name and address) to send the product by the time it will be needed. An explanation, stated in positive terms, of why you asked someone else to supply the product should follow your explanation of the action you have taken. Because you have done as much as you feel you should do, you do not need to offer any kind of apology. This letter, like all other letters of this nature, should end with something pleasant and specific. Study the letter on page 202.

WILLIAMSON WHOLESALE COMPANY
Muncie, Ohio 43262

May 20, 1973

Mr. Guenther H. von Braun
Manager, Byland Department Store
122 South Main Street
Oxford, GA 30267

Dear Mr. von Braun:

This morning I called Mr. William R. Chadwell, manager of the
Stevens Wholesale Company in Muncie, and asked him to send you
three dozen 52-inch plastic wading pools in assorted colors.
He said that he will ship them to you by truck tomorrow afternoon. The price is the same as ours.

We sold the last one in our warehouse on Monday. As our next
supply is scheduled to arrive on June 3, two days after your
sale will begin, we called the Stevens Wholesalers immediately
after receiving your order so that you would have the wading
pools for the sale.

We will have an ample supply of wading pools after June 3, and
of course we still have our usual large variety of merchandise
ready to ship when we receive your next order. I will send you
one of our fall catalogs when they come from the printer next
week.

We wish you the very best of luck with your special sale, and
we look forward to hearing from you again soon.

Cordially yours,

Clyde R. Bingham

Clyde R. Bingham
Sales Manager

wjl

Promptness in writing this letter is extremely important. To
have the merchandise arrive from the other source before your
letter of explanation arrives would be embarrassing to you and
the organization you represent.

When you choose to send the name and address of another supplier to the person requesting an item so that he can place the order, you should begin by giving this information. You will, of course, follow this information with a cordial, positive explanation of your action. Except for the first paragraph, this letter and the one telling the purchaser that you have asked another supplier to send the desired product would be somewhat the same. Both letters would begin by telling the action you have taken, followed by an explanation of the reason you took that action, and ended with a pleasant, specific statement.

The importance of maintaining good public relations cannot be overemphasized. Your taking the action necessary to enable a person to obtain a product or service he needs is as important as your supplying that product or service. For success in business, always observe the principle of keeping your reader in mind.

When writing a letter that contains an element of disappointing news, resist the temptation to begin with a trite "Thank you for . . . ." and, of course, omit any variation of the trite ending "If I can be of further assistance to you, please do not hesitate to contact me."

By telling *first* what you *can* do, you can minimize the effect that the disappointing news has on your reader.

Outright refusals

A major portion of requests are legitimate, though some are not. Some of the legitimate requests are those with which you cannot comply or that you choose to decline without offering a substitute or some other alternative. For example, you may be asked to contribute to a fund that you do not wish to support because you do not agree with the objectives of the group conducting the fund–raising campaign. You may be requested to grant credit to a person whose reputation is such that you do not wish to transact business with him even on a cash basis. You will receive still other requests with which you will not wish to comply or to offer an alternative of any type.

The letter on page 204 was written to decline a request to contribute to a charitable organization.

WILLIAMS MANUFACTURING COMPANY
Pinehurst, TN 37094

October 8, 1973

Miss Anita Fine, Chairman
Lancaster Charity Society
P. O. Box 265
Lancaster, TN 38569

Dear Miss Fine:

I have heard some complimentary statements about the work that
your organization has been doing, especially in the Upper Cum-
berland area.

For the past five years, we have contributed to "Joint Efforts"
the entire amount of our money that was budgeted for charitable
organizations. Because our employees support this plan so en-
thusiastically, we expect to continue with it indefinitely.

We appreciate your inviting us to participate in your campaign
this year, and we wish you much success.

Cordially yours,

Samuel F. Manley
Samuel F. Manley
Public Relations Director

dlm

Remember always that as a person of strong character you will
uphold your convictions. People will respect you for such strength
of character. When you receive a request with which you do not
wish to comply, you can decline that request in a firm, clear,

tactful, straightforward manner. Tact is an essential characteristic of successful business people.

Whether you are complying with a request, offering a substitute or other alternative, or making an outright refusal, apply the basic principles of letter writing to each letter that you mail.

Questions for discussion

1. Suppose that you do not have the materials that someone ordered from you and you do not have anything that seems to be an acceptable substitute. You do not know where such materials can be obtained. What should you tell the person when you acknowledge his order?

2. What are some of the requests that businessmen may likely receive that they would have to refuse to comply with?

3. What are some advantages of granting some adjustment requests that you feel should not have been made by the customer?

4. What are some disadvantages of referring a customer to another source when you cannot supply the merchandise he has ordered from you?

5. What are some reasons other than the ones listed in this chapter that may cause you to have to delay shipping merchandise that has been ordered from you?

Exercises

Improve the following sentences that were taken from business letters.

1. You asked me to return the enclosed form by June 26.

2. Would April 29 be more inconvenient for you than April 30?

3. I should like to be of assistance to him in some way.

4. At the present time I do not know how much time will be required for the installation of the computer.

5. I have received your invitation, and I regret to inform you that I shall be unable to accept.

6. We cannot send the books you ordered until May 30.

7. I hope that you will be pleased with the substitute, which is superior to the product that you ordered yesterday.

8. Please do not hesitate to get in touch with me at any time that I may be able to help you.

9. We are conducting the campaign for the purpose of financing a summer camping program for children of low-income families.

10. Mr. Riley W. Holtsman is the party who called you this morning.

Problems

1. You are one of six students who spent the Christmas holidays at a ski resort in Switzerland. Each of the six people performs well on the ski slopes, and each one made many excellent slides during the holidays in Switzerland.

    Charles Y. Olson, who is president of the Cumberland Ski Club, wrote a letter to you yesterday asking you to speak at a luncheon meeting at the Skyland Resort Hotel on Wednesday, December 13. (The Cumberland Ski Club has a luncheon meeting once a month —on the second Wednesday of each month.) You would like very much to speak to the group on December 13, but you have two final examinations scheduled for that day. One examination is scheduled for 10:30 A.M.; the other, 1:00 P.M.

    Write to Charles in Cumberland, Tennessee, and *decline* the invitation to speak in December. Offer to help him in some way.

2. Today you received a letter from Charles E. Ramsey. The letter was an order for thirty copies of a book entitled *Writing Business Letters* by Harold O. Richards. You cannot fill the order immediately. You have sold all of your copies of the book, and you will not receive another supply until the end of two more weeks.

    You regret this unfortunate circumstance because Mr. Ramsey is one of your best customers. You want to continue to serve him well because you want to keep him as a good customer. His book sales are usually very good during this season.

    He works for the Longfellow Department Store in Dayton, Ohio. He is the manager of the book department. The store is located at 122 South Jefferson Avenue, and the ZIP number is 43221.

    Write to him.

3. The principal of a high school 60 miles away has asked you to speak to the forty–two seniors in that school who are interested in majoring in business in college. The occasion for your speech is

the annual high school career–day program, which is scheduled for 9 A.M. on the first Tuesday of next month.

You would like to speak to that group; but you will be at home, which is 250 miles away, for a one-week vacation at that time. Write to the principal.

4. On December 1 James E. Riley sent you an order for three dozen Model 27 Recordex tape recorders. These small tape recorders were good sellers in his store last year during the Christmas shopping season. Your wholesale price was $33.75 each.

    No Model 27 tape recorders are available anywhere as that particular model is no longer manufactured. You now supply a Model 33 Recordex that is superior to the Model 27 (use your imagination to determine the specific characteristics that make it superior to the old model) and wholesales for $34.50.

    Write to Mr. Riley. You want him to handle the new Model 33, and you want him to receive the three dozen tape recorders in plenty of time for sale during the Christmas season.

    The address of his store, The Gift Shoppe, is 2206 Broadway, Richmond, Kentucky 40475.

5. You are the credit manager of a wholesale house in St. Louis, Missouri. Three weeks ago Keith L. Sharp opened an appliance store in Xenia, Ohio. This is his first business venture. You received a letter from him today asking you to sell small appliances to him on credit.

    You would like to have him as a customer, but you grant credit to only those businesses that are already well established.

    You have added several new appliances to your line of merchandise this fall. Among them are a new electric drill, an especially attractive hair dryer, and a polishing machine.

    Reply to his letter.

6. You are the manager of Stockdale Wholesalers, Inc., in Midland, Illinois. Today you received from the Ratcliff Sewing Center in Phoenix, New Mexico, an order for twelve Model 9 Whistler Sewing Machines. You do not have any sewing machines in stock and do not expect to receive another shipment until the end of six more weeks.

    Mr. Bradley F. Bush, manager of the Ratcliff Sewing Center, wants the machines for a special sale that will begin in four weeks. You know that the Swathmore Wholesale Company in Lake Charles, Minnesota, handles the Whistler machines and probably has them in stock at a price that is comparable to yours.

Write to Mr. Bush and suggest that he order the machines from Swathmore.

7. You cannot fill order No. 57W2110 from Mrs. Omar W. Childers, until you receive some essential information. The infant's snow-suit that she ordered comes in two styles. One style has elastic stir-rups on the pants and has a separate hat. The hat has a leather–look vinyl trim on the earflaps and peak and matches the coat. The second style has knit anklets and an attached drawstring hood edged in the pile which trims the coat.

Make it easy for Mrs. Childers to send you the information you need and assure her that the snowsuit will be sent promptly as soon as you receive her reply. Remind her that these plush pile snowsuits are easy to care for, warm, and long wearing. Mrs. Childers' address is 55 North Shore Drive, Alma, New Hampshire 03411.

8. You are the assistant manager of Lee Walls, Inc., a mail–order nee-dle art and creative crafts center. Mrs. Althea Bond sent in her first order for No. NN33–40, a decoupage purse kit that was fea-tured in your spring, 1974, catalog. In July, 1974, this purse kit was discontinued; and a similar one, No. NN33–44 was added. A double catch lock was added to the new purse. The same charming prints depicting the world of children are used; and, of course, the kit includes the prints, decoupage finish, and all hardware and materials needed to complete the purse. The new purse kit is, how-ever, 50 cents higher. You would expect to pay at least $13.99 for this unique accessory kit, which is now only $8.33.

Write Mrs. Bond at 2399 South Maple, Cranston, Rhode Island 02856, and suggest the substitute purse. Make it easy for her to order by enclosing a card and any other literature you think would be appropriate.

9. Today you received an order letter from Mrs. Donald Lee Smythe, 401 Cedar Drive, Katlas, Indiana. She ordered several decorator rods for windows, drapery holdbacks, and two vinyl–coated de-signer stripe shades. You can send the rods and the holdbacks im-mediately, but Mrs. Smythe failed to indicate the color of shades she desires. The shades come in four smart colors: red/white, gold/white, black/white, and green/white. All are white on street side, of course.

Write to Mrs. Smythe to find out what color shades she would like to have.

10

Personnel administration

OF THE four major functions of a business organization (production, distribution, finance, and personnel), *personnel* is the most important. People handle the *finances* of the organization, and they *produce* and *distribute* the goods and the services that the organization must provide for society.

Effective personnel administration is essential for any successful enterprise. So that employees can perform at a level near their maximum potential, goodwill must be established and maintained within the organization as well as between that organization and its outside forces. Because goodwill within a group contributes a great deal to the public relations element that exists between the group and its outside contacts, personnel administration merits the special consideration that top executives give to it. Successful executives realize that efficient personnel administration is based on good communication—written and oral. They recognize the necessity of exerting special efforts to communicate effectively with prospective, present, and former employees.

Effective personnel administration involves some very pleasant, cheerful situations; and it also involves, from time to time, situations of a less desirable nature that must be handled firmly, yet diplomatically. Among the many messages that must be written in administering personnel are those that:

1. Invite prospective employers to come for interviews.
2. Make offers of employment.
3. Welcome new employees.
4. Reject applicants.
5. Accept resignations.
6. Dismiss employees.
7. Recommend employees.

Inviting to an interview

As has been said earlier in this book, a personal interview is a significant factor in the employment process. In a high percentage of cases, the applicant would not accept a so-called permanent job without first visiting the location in which he would work if the interview should lead to employment. He would, of course, want to see the specific place (office, store, factory, and so forth) in which he would spend the workday; and when the geographic area is not familiar to him, he may very likely wish to see enough of the city to become acquainted with some of its characteristics such as residential areas, schools, shopping areas, and recreational facilities.

The prospective employer, too, usually wants the applicant to be aware of the environment in which he will work if the interview should lead to employment. Both the applicant and the prospective employer realize that regardless of how much a worker likes a job for which he is well qualified, he will continue to be happy and to do his best work only when he is satisfied with his surroundings. The prospective employer realizes that the applicant, the employer and his staff, the job that is to be filled, and the local environment are all under close scrutiny during a job interview. He wants to put his best foot forward, therefore, when he begins negotiating with a prospective employee; and of course he expects the prospective employee to do the same thing.

Because inviting an applicant for an interview is a compliance with his request and is therefore a good-news letter, it is an easy letter to write. When you write this type of letter, *begin with the good news.* This letter should include—in addition to an invitation—the date, the time of day, and the exact location for the interview. In most instances, perhaps, the job title under consideration should also be mentioned. Other information that should be

---

JACKSON MANUFACTURING COMPANY, INC.
P. O. Box 4783
Colliersville, TN 38211

October 15, 1973

Miss Margaret Anne Kyle
P. O. Box 1714
Fairview Junior College
Colliersville, TN 38211

Dear Miss Kyle:

You are one of four applicants that we are inviting to come to our plant for an interview for the job of secretary to the production manager. We should like for you to come to my office at 10:30 a.m. on Thursday, October 26.

After you complete the Wonderlic Personnel Test and our usual dictation and transcription exercise, you will have an opportunity to discuss the job requirements with Mr. H. B. Chandler, the production manager. Please come prepared to stay until about 2 p.m.

We look forward to having you visit our plant on October 26.

Sincerely yours,

Claude L. Francis

Claude L. Francis
Personnel Manager

dbf

included in this letter will depend on the particular situation. The examples shown on this page and on the preceding one contain some of the other items of information that seem appropriate for the occasions they represent. Still other items would be applicable for other situations.

```
                    JACKSON MANUFACTURING COMPANY, INC.
                              P. O. Box 4783
                          Colliersville, TN  38211




                              May 25, 1973




        Mr. Stephen J. O'Mary
        P. O. Box 1428
        Randolph Community College
        Randolph, AR  72359

        Dear Mr. O'Mary:

        We would like for you to come to my office at 9 a.m. on June 7
        to discuss your qualifications for one of the four management
        trainee jobs that are open.  The three men whose names you gave
        as references have recommended you very highly.

        We have reserved a room for you for Wednesday night, June 6,
        at the Holladay Hills Motel, which is only seven blocks from my
        office.  The interviews with the training supervisor and me and
        tours of our factory and of the city can be completed by 4 p.m.

        May we expect you that day?  We will reimburse you for your
        room, meals, and traveling expenses.

                              Sincerely yours,


                              Claude L. Francis

                              Claude L. Francis
                              Personnel Manager


        dbf
```

When your schedule is especially tight, you may feel that it is necessary to have the applicant confirm his plans to come for the interview. You would, therefore, ask for his confirmation. Under some circumstances, however, you may wish to omit a request for a confirmation so that on the basis of whether or not he sends a confirmation at an appropriate time, you may learn more about the applicant's thoughtfulness, promptness, and acceptance of responsibility.

Offering employment

Because a letter offering employment bears good news, that letter is an easy one to write. Simply follow the principle of beginning with good news. This type of letter should ordinarily specify the title of the job that is being offered, the salary, and the date on which the new employee is to begin working. When a formal contract is enclosed for the new employee's signature, some of these details can, of course, be omitted.

The information that has already been exchanged during the interview and through previous correspondence will naturally help the writer to choose other appropriate statements to be included in the letter offering employment. The plans (locating adequate housing, arranging for a physical examination, and so on) that you know the new employee will have to make may also be mentioned appropriately in this type of letter.

As you will offer employment only to those persons who you believe will be assets to your organization, you will look forward to having them join your group. Telling them so in this letter may be good psychology. Most people do their best work when they are motivated through *positive* action. Letting a new employee know that you are favorably impressed by his abilities and his personal attributes can pay rich dividends. Compliments in the letter offering employment can be beneficial to your organization and to the new employee. He, like all other intelligent human beings, can sense the difference between sincere compliments and flattery. Confine your comments, therefore, to those that are sincere and will likely be accepted as sincere compliments rather than attempts to flatter.

Use this easy-to-write letter to establish early a good rapport between the new employee and the personnel with whom he will work.

The letter below was written to a young man who was completing the requirements for a college degree.

ARNOLD AND WILLIAMS ACCOUNTING FIRM
Madison, Michigan

May 22, 1973

Mr. Donald H. Robinson
Apartment 257
Terrace View Apartments
2114 Lake View Drive
Canton, Michigan

Dear Mr. Robinson:

We would like to have you join our staff as a junior accountant on June 15 at a salary of $10,500 a year. Insurance provisions, vacations, and other fringe benefits are described in the booklet that we gave you when you were here for an interview on May 10.

All of us who had an opportunity to talk with you on May 10 are very favorably impressed by you as a candidate for this job, and we look forward to receiving your acceptance of this offer.

Good luck with your final examinations next week.

Sincerely yours,

Merrill L. Patterson

Merrill L. Patterson
Senior Accountant

lar

Welcoming a new employee

In a small organization the officer who writes the letter offering employment to a prospect who has been interviewed is perhaps the person who will work rather closely with the new employee.

RUTGERS MANUFACTURING COMPANY, INC.
P. O. Box 1714
Creekmore, OK 73639

July 2, 1973

Miss Claire Richards
255 Whitehall Avenue
Amherst, OK 73014

Dear Miss Richards:

You will certainly be a welcome member of our staff when you join our stenographic pool on September 1. I congratulate you on your excellent performance on our dictation and transcription test.

I am confident that you will enjoy working with the eight other stenographers. They, too, are highly skilled; and we appreciate their efficiency.

Sincerely yours,

Herman M. Alexander
Herman M. Alexander
Administrative Assistant

srf

In such a case a sentence or two in the letter offering employment is enough to welcome the new person to the organization. In large organizations, however, the letter offering employment is often written by a personnel officer who may seldom see the new employee after he begins working. Or at least he may not be

RUTGERS MANUFACTURING COMPANY, INC.
P. O. Box 1714
Creekmore, OK 73639

August 3, 1973

Miss Jane N. Harrison
Box 1112
Watterson Community College
Watterson, CO 80082

Dear Miss Harrison:

We look forward to your joining our staff on September 1. As secretary to the purchasing officer, Mr. Joseph H. Wellington, you will have an opportunity to meet many people and also to use the skills that you have developed during the past two years of college.

Because Mr. Wellington will be on vacation from August 25 to September 8, you will begin working at an ideal time. As you already know, Miss Rainey, who is working for him now, will continue to work until September 12. She will have ample time to help you become acquainted with the specific tasks that are performed in that office.

I hope that the vacation you have planned for the last two weeks in August will be especially pleasant.

Sincerely yours,

Herman M. Alexander
Herman M. Alexander
Administrative Assistant

srf

closely associated with him on the job. In a situation such as this, the immediate supervisor or someone else who expects to be closely associated with the new employee when he begins working may wish to write a short letter welcoming the newcomer to the group. Such a letter can contribute greatly to helping the newcomer get off to a good start on the job.

This letter would probably contain some of the same types of good-will information that would be in the letter written by a personnel officer offering employment. While the size and the nature of the organization and the existing conditions will help you to decide what to write in your letter welcoming a new employee, remember to limit your comments to those that are sincere.

The two letters on pages 215 and 216 were used by one first-line supervisor. Notice that the second letter contains some items that would not have been appropriate for the person to whom the first letter was addressed.

Rejecting an application

Except for the few jobs for which only a very limited number of people can qualify or in times when existing jobs exceed the number of available personnel, at least two (and oftentimes more than two) applicants will be interviewed for each vacancy. And as was said in the chapter on letters concerning employment, an applicant seldom wants a job that no one else is interested in. Applicants realize, therefore, that in most instances more than one person will be interviewed for a job; and they know that only one can be employed. Each one who is genuinely interested in obtaining the job hopes, of course, that he will be the one who is selected.

A letter telling an applicant that another person has been selected is obviously a bad-news letter. You should begin this type of letter by telling the applicant what you can do for him. You may appropriately mention that you will keep his application in your active file so that you can consider him for a similar job in the future, or you may tell him that you would like to consider him for another job that will be open in your organization and ask him to allow you to consider his application for that job. Whatever offer you make must be sincere and something you believe is appropriate. Whether or not you can do anything for him that would interest him, you do want to maintain good public relations with him and with the people with whom he will be as-

---

HATHAWAY WHOLESALE COMPANY
Minot, MN 55571

April 28, 1973

Mrs. Ruth Taylor Moore
305 West Seventh Street
Blue Lake, MN 56341

Dear Mrs. Moore:

We are keeping your application in our active files so that we can get in touch with you when we need another typist, which will probably be about September 1. Your 70-words-a-minute typewriting speed is impressive indeed, and so are your general clerical scores and your courteous manner.

Yesterday we employed a young woman for the receptionist job for which you were interviewed. She can take dictation rapidly; and as we told you during your interview, the receptionist in our office will be given some dictation almost every day.

I am glad you plan to study shorthand this summer. The ability to take dictation combined with your typewriting skill will help you to land a more challenging, higher-paying job.

Cordially yours,

Robert E. Ford

Robert E. Ford
General Manager

awb

sociated. You will, therefore, be courteous to him; and never will you allow your letter to sound curt or rude.

For the applicant's sake you would not want to discourage him unduly. He may very likely possess good qualities for other jobs that are open elsewhere. A courteous letter from you may help him to develop or to maintain his self-confidence when applying for employment with other organizations.

Establishing, maintaining, promoting, or reestablishing good public relations should be a characteristic of each letter that you write.

Although you should try to soften the blow as much as you can when you write a letter rejecting an applicant, you must in all fairness make it clear to him that you have decided to employ someone else rather than him and therefore not cause him to have some false hope of obtaining the job that you cannot offer him. When you must write a letter of this type, follow the basic principles presented in Chapter 2 and the suggestions in Chapter 9. As a skillful writer, you can reject an applicant for a job and still maintain his goodwill. Write so clearly that your message cannot be misunderstood, but say "no" in such a manner that your reader will like it. You can achieve this objective by putting your reader's interest foremost in your letter.

The letter on page 218 was written to a young woman who was well qualified for a typist's job, but she lacked the ability to take dictation.

Accepting a resignation

Maintaining an accurate record of employment for all personnel is quite important. These records are maintained in a variety of ways. Some organizations file printed forms bearing the dates of initial employment and termination, others file copies of letters written by the employee and by a personnel officer, and others maintain less formal records. The size and the nature of an organization help determine the type of personnel records that are maintained. In some small organizations people are employed on the basis of an oral agreement, and their employment is later terminated by means of a letter of resignation submitted by the employee, or a letter of dismissal has to be written by an employer.

When a letter of resignation is received, some officer of the organization should in most instances write a letter to the employee accepting his resignation. A cordial tone should characterize this letter. Pleasantness can permeate the message regardless of the circumstances under which the resignation was submitted. If the person is a satisfactory employee, you will perhaps be sorry to lose him from your group; but you will be pleased to have him get an opportunity to better himself elsewhere. Rather than exemplify a selfish attitude by *emphasizing* your regrets that he has decided to resign, let him know that you are pleased that he has an opportunity to move to a more favorable job. You should, of course, let him know that you are sorry that he is leaving; omitting any reference to your regrets could cause him to believe that you are pleased that he is resigning. Creating such a feeling would deflate his ego and would not be beneficial to you or to him.

You should acknowledge his resignation from the specific job that he holds, and you should make it clear to him that you understand the date of his last workday for your organization. Perhaps there will be statements that you should make about the way in which he is to receive his final paycheck. Other financial matters such as insurance and retirement benefits should be mentioned when applicable. Numerous other matters such as keys, tools, uniforms, and so on, that are to be turned in may also be mentioned in the letter accepting the resignation. Such matters as these will be determined by the policies and the practices of your organization.

The letter on page 221 was written to a valued employee who had decided to accept an employment offer that he had received.

If the person submitting a resignation is not a satisfactory employee, you may be pleased that he has decided to resign. Even then, your letter should carry a tone of cordiality. You will be happy if he has obtained a job that he prefers over the one he now holds, and you can congratulate him on that achievement if you feel that a note of congratulations is in order. Although congratulatory comments may not seem to be appropriate for your particular letter, you can at least wish him good luck in his future endeavors.

Honesty is always the best policy. You should not express re-grets that an employee has submitted a resignation if you are not

---

BRADLEY MANUFACTURING COMPANY
Waterford, NJ 08099

September 19, 1973

Mr. T. Martin Lambert
Assistant Manager
Production Department
Bradley Manufacturing Company
Waterford, NJ 08099

Dear Martin:

I congratulate you on being chosen for the job with the Westfield Manufacturing Company. Through talking with one of my friends there, I learned that they interviewed some high-calibre candi-dates; and I agree with them that you were the best choice.

Their gain is our loss. Although we do regret losing you, we are pleased that you have been offered a better situation than we can afford now. We appreciate the fine work you have done for us.

You can leave your office keys at the payroll window when you go by to pick up your November paycheck. The payroll clerk is glad to write the check three days early for you as you will be leaving us on November 27.

We wish you the best of luck in your new job. Remember that you can always count on us for a top-notch recommendation at any time.

Sincerely,

Ellis B. Graham

Ellis G. Graham
Personnel Manager

msb

pleased with his behavior or his performance on the job, yet there is no need for you to express your feeling of elation that he has decided to resign. The employer who wrote the letter on this page was completely honest, yet cordial, in accepting a resignation from an employee whom the employer would have

BRADLEY MANUFACTURING COMPANY
Waterford, NJ 08099

July 16, 1973

Mr. George S. Folger
Department of Accounting
Bradley Manufacturing Company
Waterford, NJ 08099

Dear Mr. Folger:

We accept your resignation from the job of junior accountant.
As your last work day with us will be July 31, you will have
earned another week's vacation. An extra week's pay, therefore, will be added to your final salary check.

We wish you the best of luck in your new job and in all your
other future endeavors.

Cordially yours,

Ellis G. Graham

Ellis G. Graham
Personnel Manager

msb

dismissed if the employee had not resigned within thirty days. Possibly the employee realized that he would probably be dismissed in the near future, but no one had told him that such action had been planned.

When you write a letter of any type, remember that good public relations is a genuine asset to any organization.

In some situations you may wish to try to persuade the person who has submitted a letter of resignation to reconsider his decision and to continue working for you. If this is to be done, it should be done *before* the letter accepting a resignation is written. Hopefully, your personnel administration will be so efficient that you will have an opportunity—and will take advantage of that opportunity—to make whatever negotiations that you may wish to make for keeping the person in your employment *before* he submits his letter of resignation.

Dismissing an employee

Dismissing an employee is an unpleasant task for both the employer and the employee. The employer who has to dismiss someone he was responsible for hiring must frequently admit that he made a poor selection when he offered employment to the person who must be dismissed. Sometimes, though, when there is a shortage of personnel available for screening, an employer has to employ workers whose ability to perform the duties assigned to them or their ability to work well with their associates is questionable. Even under circumstances such as these, the employer faces the problem and the sometimes great financial burden of finding, employing, and training a replacement for the worker whose services must be terminated. The employer has other concerns that also contribute to the unpleasantness of firing an employee. He is perhaps genuinely concerned about the personal welfare (financial, social, and psychological) of the employee; and he is concerned about the effect that his action will have on the employee's family and friends and the other members of the employer's organization.

The employee who is dismissed stands to suffer financially and psychologically now and possibly for a considerable length of time in the future. He realizes that this action becomes a part of his permanent record of employment, and he knows that his dismissal will have to be explained to his future prospective employers. His morale will, therefore, be greatly affected by being dismissed from a job.

Because the task of dismissing an employee is difficult, regardless of the manner in which it is handled, the letter announcing a dismissal or confirming such news that has already been released is one that is very difficult to write. Writing such a letter requires a great deal of thought and finesse.

When personnel matters have been handled appropriately, an employee will be partially prepared to receive a dismissal letter. Before the letter is written, his superiors will have discussed with him the fact that his work is substandard and the ways in which he should improve his job performance in order to be a satisfactory employee. If he has a good attitude, the employer will help him to improve his skills and knowledge; and if he cannot become proficient in his present job, he will be transferred to another job within the organization, provided his skills are needed in some job. In many instances employers are eager to retrain workers. When no other suitable job is available within the organization, the employer is usually eager to help a hardworking, dependable worker obtained employment with some other organization.

When you must write a letter terminating an employee's services, follow the principle of telling *first* what you *can* do for him. Obviously, circumstances will be such that you can offer to assist a deserving person in some specific way.

The letter on page 225 was written to an employee who, although she seemed incapable of performing satisfactorily in her present position, possessed the qualifications for another job within the organization for which she was working.

The letter on page 226 was written to an employee who had a good attitude toward his work and his associates and had tried to improve his abilities to the level required. He could not, however, acquire the skills necessary for acceptable performance on his present job; and no job for which he was qualified existed within his organization.

Whether a person is dismissed from his present job because

BRADLEY MANUFACTURING COMPANY
Waterford, NJ 08099

June 15, 1973

Miss Yvonne E. Bowman
Planning Department
Bradley Manufacturing Company
Waterford, NJ 08099

Dear Miss Bowman:

Perhaps you know that Miss Sherry Moss is leaving our company
on August 1. We should like for you to replace her as receptionist in our administration building.

With your pleasant disposition and ability to converse with the
company visitors, you would represent us well in that job. Your
salary would be the same as for the job you have now as secretary
to Mr. Wheatley.

As Mr. Wheatley's added responsibilities require him to have a
secretary who can write shorthand, we must remove you from your
present job so that he can employ someone who has that skill.

You may begin working as receptionist on July 23, a week before
Miss Moss leaves. Please let me know by July 1 whether or not
you wish to accept the receptionist job. I believe you would
enjoy working in that office.

Cordially yours,

Ellis G. Graham

Ellis G. Graham
Personnel Manager

msb

of inability to perform satisfactorily, unwillingness to cooperate
with others in the group, reduction in the work force, or some
other reason, the letter bearing the news of dismissal must contain certain items of information. The letter should state clearly,

BRADLEY MANUFACTURING COMPANY
Waterford, NJ 08099

January 15, 1973

Mr. Thomas C. Adfield
Auditing Clerk
Bradley Manufacturing Company
Waterford, NJ 08099

Dear Mr. Adfield:

You are well liked by your associates, and your efforts to perform the tasks that are assigned to you are appreciated. I hope
that you will return to college to acquire the knowledge necessary for you to realize your potentials in accounting or in
whatever field you may choose to work.

As you know, the volume of our business has increased so much
that we must employ someone who can handle more work without supervision than you are prepared to handle. We have employed a young
man who has a college degree and a CPA certificate to do the jobs
you are doing plus others that require the high degree of training that he possesses. He will join us on March 1, which means
that we must terminate your employment with us on February 28.

The paycheck you will receive that day will include an extra week's
pay for the vacation time you have earned since July 31.

I am glad to know that you are interested in returning to college.
When you get ready to go to work again, both Mr. Bradford, the
senior auditor, and I will be happy to recommend you for any job
for which you are qualified to perform. Please feel free to use
our names as references.

Sincerely yours,

Ellis G. Graham
Ellis G. Graham
Personnel Manager

msb

yet as tactfully as possible, that the addressee's employment will
be terminated. The last day that he is to work for the organization
must be specified. The reason for his dismissal should also be
included, even though the reason may be obvious to him.

You must certainly refrain from making any statement that could validly be interpreted as being accusing or slanderous. Write so carefully that if the employee contests his dismissal, no arbitrator, attorney, or union official can use the letter to your disadvantage.

Other information that may be appropriate for your letter would perhaps depend on the existing conditions. You may need to mention the last paycheck he is to receive as well as other financial matters. Much of the content of the dismissal letter may be similar, or even identical, to the content of the letter that is written to accept a resignation.

Exert sincere effort to maintain the goodwill of all former employees. Much of the credit for success in any business endeavor can be attributed to good public relations. Exhibiting your willingness to be fair and considerate of others will help you to maintain a good image with the general public.

Recommending an employee

Some people work for one person or one organization throughout their entire lifetime; that is, they remain in their initial employment until they reach retirement age. These people constitute only a small minority of the work force, however. Most workers change jobs two or more times; some change jobs many times during their working years.

Managers of personnel are called upon frequently to recommend their employees or their former employees for promotions within their organizations or for employment with other groups. In some instances these letters of recommendation carry a great deal of weight in determining whether or not the promotion or the job offer will be granted to the person under consideration. Promptness in writing these letters is very important. When two people who seem to be equally well qualified for a job are being considered, the applicant whose letters of recommendation are received somewhat earlier than those for the other applicant has a decided advantage over the one whose letters are received later. This advantage is, of course, more pronounced when the vacancy is to be filled within a short time. Bear this fact in mind when you are asked to write a letter of recommendation. Write as quickly· as you can.

Some requests for a recommendation state specific qualities that are to be evaluated. You may be asked to evaluate the person's ability to perform the duties that will be assigned to him, or you may be asked to comment on his personal characteristics. In many cases you will be asked to comment on both ability and personal factors. When the factors you are to cover in your letter are specified, your recommendation letter will be considerably easier to write than when you must make the decisions as to what kinds of information will be given the greatest attention by the reader.

If specific types of information are requested, you will have an opportunity to add comments that you believe should be added. These additional comments can include further details, or they can serve as explanations for your remarks.

When you must make the decisions as to the types of information to include in your letter, study first the job for which the applicant is being considered. Consider the qualifications that a person should possess to do the job well and then think about his preparation, experience, and personal characteristics in relation to the job.

If you are fair minded and sincerely interested in the welfare of the person you are recommending, you will try to help him obtain a job for which he is well suited. Only when a worker is satisfied with an assignment that he can fill satisfactorily can he do " a fair day's work for a fair day's pay." Proper adjustment on the job is extremely important for both the employee and the employer.

Honesty is always the best policy. Although you will want to compliment the person you are recommending and emphasize his best qualities, you cannot afford to exaggerate. The tone of your letter and your writing style have a great bearing on the effectiveness of your letter of recommendation. A flowery style or insincere tone will tend to cause the reader to believe that you have overrated the person. Specific, positive statements are as important in this letter as in any other letter that you can write. Choose your words carefully. Well–chosen adjectives that describe the person under consideration can be quite helpful to him. Among the almost limitless number of adjectives that you may wish to use to describe a person are these:

energetic	enthusiastic
amiable	versatile
industrious	hard-working
congenial	neat
polite	polished
courteous	well-mannered
frank	candid
tactful	diplomatic
dependable	trustworthy
resourceful	strong
punctual	receptive
self-confident	modest
creative	imaginative
intelligent	fair-minded
skilled	skillful
competent	capable
educated	vivacious
even-tempered	witty

Certainly, you would use only a few of these adjectives to describe any one person. And as has been said already, this list is only a small sampling of the words that you can use to describe various individuals.

While your appropriate usage of adjectives would help the reader to know something about the nature of the person you are recommending, references to specific incidents can carry a great deal of weight in convincing the reader that your evaluation of the person is accurate.

When recommending his secretary for another job for which she had applied, a college professor gave the following comments as support for his statement that she was competent and that she had initiative:

> When a long-distance telephone call delayed my going to class yesterday, she went to my classroom and told the students why I had been detained and that they could expect me within the

next few minutes. Thoughtful acts such as this combined with her skill, courteous manner, and genuine pride in her work make her a valued assistant.

The writer of the letter on page 231 pointed out the good traits of punctuality and dependability by stating that the employee he was recommending was always at work on time and that he had not missed a single day. He supported his statement that the employee was energetic by saying that he completes his assignments cheerfully and promptly. These specific references and others combined with the description of Mike Hanson helped the reader of the letter to be most favorably impressed by the young man.

When you are asked to comment on specific characteristics of a person, your mentioning each of the specified characteristics will, in most cases, be more effective than if you omit a reference to some of them. Omitting references to an attribute that you were asked to evaluate may likely cause the reader to believe that you rate the person low on that particular factor.

To be completely honest to the reader and to the person you are asked to recommend, you must in some situations mention some negative traits the person possesses if you sincerely believe the prospective employer should know about them. Those traits can be mentioned discreetly and can be subordinated so that the reader will become aware of them but will not be overly concerned by them on the basis of your letter.

Under some special circumstances you may write a recommendation letter and give it to the person whom you have recommended so that he can present it at an interview. This practice is followed *very rarely,* however. Letters presented in such a manner would obviously omit any references to a negative characteristic the person recommended may possess, and it may not cover the specific characteristics that the prospective employer would like to have evaluated. While the time factor is often very important, the interviewer seldom needs a written evaluation of the applicant's personal characteristics or job competency at the time of the interview unless he has already had sufficient opportunity to obtain such evaluation by contacting directly the person writing the recommendation.

MONTGOMERY CREDIT ASSOCIATION
Montgomery, GA 31365

July 8, 1973

Mr. Lee J. Carter
Regional Manager
McConnell Publishing Co., Inc.
1242 Palmetto Road
Athens, SC 29821

Dear Mr. Carter:

Mr. Michael E. Hanson, about whom you inquired, seems to possess
the qualities needed by a representative for a publishing company. He is a clean-cut, well-dressed, well-mannered young man
who gets along well with his associates.

Perhaps he told you that next month he will complete a one-year
appointment with us as a replacement for a clerk who asked for a
year's leave. We are pleased with Mike's work. He is always at
work on time; he has not missed a day. He completes his assignments cheerfully and promptly. Not only is he energetic, but he
also has the proper blend of self-confidence and modesty to sell
himself and, I believe, McConnell publications.

I have no reservation in recommending Mike Hanson for the job of
sales representative.

Sincerely yours,

Ronald L. Christian
Ronald L. Christian
Manager

bks

If a person requests that you let him deliver personally the
letter you have written to recommend him, explain to him that
the letter will be much more beneficial to him if you mail it
directly to the prospective employer.

Other personnel messages

In addition to the letters that have been discussed in this chapter, letters and memorandums must be written that pertain to numerous other personnel administration matters. Among the personnel affairs for which messages are frequently written are those that pertain to vacations, appointments, grievances, anniversaries, promotions, and announcements.

Some of these matters can be handled appropriately by writing letters, yet for other matters intraoffice memorandums would be more appropriate. The content and writing style for memorandums and for letters addressed to persons within an organization are almost identical. These two types of messages—letters and memorandums—differ primarily in format. Format and the uses of intraoffice memorandums are discussed in Chapter 14, "Informal reports."

Questions for discussion

1. What are some of the personnel administration letters that must be written from time to time that are not mentioned in this chapter?
2. What types of employment tests are given to applicants for various types of jobs?
3. Why do personnel directors request some applicants to bring their wives with them for part of the job interview?
4. What specific types of information would you like to receive from an applicant's references before you interview the person for a job?
5. What are some of the first questions you would ask an applicant to answer during a job interview?

Exercises

Improve the following sentences that were taken from business letters.

1. Why not come in to talk with us about those plans before October 1.
2. Group A will hold its meeting in Webb Hall.

3. In order to be eligible, you must declare your intentions not later than August 2.

4. I should like to welcome you to our staff.

5. Please inform Mr. Hanson that I appreciate his writing the recommendation letter for me.

6. I should like to express my appreciation for your help.

7. You may reply by writing to the above address.

8. I wish to send you this confirmation of your reservation for a single room for July 8.

9. I will get in touch with you at a later date.

10. In the event that a longer period of time will be required, the meeting will be rescheduled.

Problems

1. Randle W. Swain has been working as a salesclerk in your department store for the past twenty-two months. He was an excellent salesman and had a good rapport with his customers until about three months ago. Several customers have indicated to the department manager that Mr. Swain had been rude to them on more than one occasion. He was late arriving for work several mornings, and he took longer lunch breaks than were allotted.

   After the department manager talked with him, he performed better until two weeks ago. Because he did not improve his performance after the department manager talked with him again, you talked with him. Because he still is doing a very poor job, you must terminate his employment at the end of this month—two weeks from now.

   Write a firm yet courteous letter to him and tell him that his employment with your store is being terminated. You are the personnel manager for the store.

2. You are the administrative services manager of the Wakefield Wholesale Company in Tacoma, South Dakota. During the past several weeks, four of your customers who frequently get in touch with your office by telephone have complimented your receptionist, who answers the telephone. They say that she is courteous and very efficient.

   Write a short letter to her and tell her you appreciate her helping to project a good image for your company.

3. As personnel director of the Thomas Manufacturing Company in Greenfield, West Virginia, reply to James L. Hay's letter applying for the job of junior accountant that was filled last week. Mr. Hay, who will be graduated from the Greenbrier Community College, in Greenbrier, Virginia, next June, sent a well–written letter and an impressive resume.

4. Harold L. Gray, an accounting clerk in your office, has asked for permission to take a two–week vacation the last two weeks of March. He has an opportunity to travel to the West Coast then with members of his family. Because that period is an unusually busy time for your firm, decline his request. In January you and he had scheduled his vacation for the first two weeks of July.

   As chief accountant for Hobart and Sams Accountants, write to Harold and decline his request.

5. Virginia Sue Rose, who worked as your secretary from June 1, 1968, until May 31, 1973, has applied for a job as secretary to the personnel manager of the Dayton Manufacturing Company, Dayton, Michigan—an organization similar to yours. She was an outstanding secretary. As personnel manager of your organization, write a letter recommending her.

6. Fred E. Daley, who is to be graduated from the Greenbrier Community College, Greenbrier, Virginia, next June, has applied for the job of assistant cashier in your bank. He has listed four names as references on his résumé. Write to one of those four persons, Mr. Charles B. Cobb, instructor of business, Greenbrier Community College, and ask him to recommend Mr. Daley. So far you are very favorably impressed by the applicant.

7. After Mr. Jon E. Ramsey, manager of your production department, announced his resignation effective August 31, the assistant manager, Ralph M. Lyles, was promoted to the job of manager. Bart W. Reynolds has been selected as the person to be promoted to the job of assistant manager of the production department.

   As personnel manager of your organization, write to Bart and tell him he is to be promoted. Supply any information that should be included in this letter.

11

Form messages

Letters are essential to conducting personal affairs, privately owned businesses, partnerships, corporations, and nonprofit organizations. Letters—whether they are written to transmit information or emotions or merely to provide records of messages previously transmitted—are quite expensive.

Many writers of books and articles in periodicals pertaining to written communications have mentioned approximate average costs for business letters. Some of these estimates of average costs have ranged from less than $5 to more than $12. While many people have used similar approaches to determine the average cost of a business letter, apparently no two have used exactly the same criteria. Salaries of the letter writers make up the most significant contributor to the letter–writing cost. The salary of the executive who dictates a letter is obviously the greatest cost factor, which is followed next by the salary of the person who transcribes the letter. A few of the other numerous expenses that have to be considered in arriving at the total cost are these:

1. Stationery (letterheads, envelopes, carbon paper, and copy paper).
2. Postage.
3. Machines (typewriter, postage meter, and so on).

Some approximate costs have included a portion of such office expenses as lighting, heating, cooling, and insurance; a portion of the office space that has to be rented; and the cost of the desks and the chairs used when dictating and transcribing letters. When one makes a thorough study of expenses incurred in writing business letters, he can easily see that the figures derived by various individuals should vary somewhat.

Regardless of the degree of accuracy of the cost that may be determined, the important fact that should be borne in mind is that *business letters are expensive!* This cost factor and the increased importance of transmitting high-quality messages rapidly have led to the word-processing concept that is increasing in popularity among business executives. To keep up with the rapid pace at which data are being processed, businesses must speed up their communication processes (both internally and externally) by using methods that are practical and economical. Frequently, large sums of money can be saved by using form letters. When form letters are used appropriately, they can contribute to—rather than detract from—the goodwill that the sender wishes to establish, maintain, promote, or reestablish.

In the remaining portion of this chapter, various types of form messages and some examples of the conditions under which they may be used advantageously are presented. Types of form letters included are those that are duplicated with spaces provided for fill-ins, those that are duplicated in their entirety, those that are made up of form paragraphs that can be presented in various sequences, and form paragraphs that are interspersed with individually dictated paragraphs. Some examples of forms that are used for intraoffice communications are also presented and discussed in this chapter.

Duplicated letters with fill-ins

Everyone likes to know that he receives special consideration at times and that he is considered as an individual rather than as merely a name or an account number in some set of records. At the same time, however, he likes to know that for some situations he receives treatment identical to that which is given to the other people in his particular category (whatever that category may be).

Suppose that, because of an oversight, a regular customer who always pays his account when it becomes due fails to send his payment on time. You may logically suspect that the payment was misplaced in the mail; and because you know that no one is perfect, you may also logically suspect that the customer needs to be reminded that his payment is due. Under some conditions a printed or duplicated reminder may be attached to a duplicate statement and mailed to the customer. This action is described in the section on collecting accounts in Chapter 7. Under other conditions, though, you may believe it desirable to write a cordial letter to the customer and to include the amount due and possibly other specific details such as the date on which the amount became due or the date on which the purchase was made. When a letter of this nature is mailed, one that is obviously a form letter will probably have a much better effect on the reader than would one that is individually dictated or one that is a form letter but appears to be individually dictated.

By duplicating a letter and leaving spaces so that the amount due and other special entries may be filled in with ink, the addressee realizes that the type of error he has made is also made by many other customers. He will probably feel that you are treating the incident as a routine matter and that you are not greatly disturbed by his honest mistake. Everyone errs occasionally; and knowing that others make similar errors provides some consolation for the conscientious person who may be embarrassed by an oversight.

The letter on page 238 is an example of a form letter with spaces provided for fill-ins. The spaces may be filled in by longhand, or they may be filled in with a typewriter. Regardless of the method you use to fill in the spaces, you should make it obvious to the addressee that the letter is a duplicated form letter that is used for many customers.

A duplicated form letter such as this has these advantages over an individually dictated letter or one that appears to be individually dictated:

RANCHLAND DEPARTMENT STORE
Spring City, Kansas 67083

Dear Customer:

Because you always pay your account so promptly, we suspect that your check for _____ for last month's purchases has been misplaced in the mail or that through some oversight you are waiting later than usual to mail your payment.

If the check has been lost in the mail, perhaps you will want to stop payment at the bank and mail us a duplicate. I suspect you will appreciate this "memory jogger" if the check is yet to be sent.

We are always glad to have you visit our store or to mail your order to us.

Cordially yours,

Tim C. Allen
Accounting Department

hsk

1. The addressee is less likely to be embarrassed or offended by receiving the message.
2. A considerable amount of time and money can be saved in mailing the letters.

For many occasions form letters must be used, even though the writer would prefer to send individually written letters if he had sufficient time and money to send different letters to the people who are to receive the message that is being mailed. Quite often the recipients of form letters realize that the writer's sending individually prepared letters would be impractical for the occasion, and they feel that a carefully prepared form letter is appropriate. Under such circumstances you can let your reader know that you have given him the personal consideration that your resources will allow by using a high-quality duplicating method (offset duplicating can produce excellent copy) and by adding his name, inside address, and salutation with a typewriter.

When you follow this procedure, your typewriter should be equipped with a ribbon that will produce copy that closely parallels the quality of the copy produced by the duplicator. The two types of copy (typewritten and duplicated) can be so nearly alike that the reader will not be readily aware that the letter was duplicated unless he gives it close scrutiny. Your aim should be to let the reader know that you have given him the individual attention you could afford under the existing circumstances rather than to try to deceive him and to try to make him think that you have typewritten the letter. When the number of letters is small enough to make it feasible for you to sign them with ink, your personal signature can help to let the receiver know that you have given him personal attention. When the number of letters to be mailed at one time is so large that you cannot spare the time to sign them individually, you may sign the master copy so that your signature will be duplicated. The writer's signature—whether it is written with pen or is duplicated—should appear on each letter.

The letter on page 240, which was mailed to ninety-four people whose names and addresses had been supplied by an employment office, was duplicated on letterhead stationery by using an offset duplicator. An electric typewriter, equipped with a carbon ribbon and the same type style used for typewriting the letter, was used for filling in the name, the inside address, and the salutation. The typewriting and the duplicating matched almost perfectly. The writer, Mr. Ellis G. Graham, signed each letter with a pen.

Regardless of whether or not you want your letter to be obvi-

BRADLEY MANUFACTURING COMPANY

Waterford, NJ   08099

March 2, 1973

———————————
———————————
———————————
———————————

———————————:

To complete the information that we must have to decide whether
to open a branch office in Sidney, will you please fill out the
enclosed questionnaire?

We were pleased to learn from your local employment office that
you are available for office work. If we decide to open an
office in Sidney, we will send you an application form by May 1.

The addressed, postage-paid envelope that is enclosed is for
your use in returning the questionnaire, which will require only
a few minutes of your time to complete. Your returning the completed questionnaire by March 10 will be very much appreciated.

Cordially yours,

Ellis G. Graham

Ellis G. Graham
Personnel Manager

msb

Enclosures 2

ously a form letter, use great care in duplicating it. Always
remember that your letter represents you. You must, therefore,
give due consideration to the content and the quality of presentation.

The occasions for which form letters with fill-in spaces can be used appropriately are almost limitless. They vary among the groups that use them.

Entire messages

Many messages can be duplicated in their entirety; that is, no information is to be filled in in the body; and no special parts

---

RANCHLAND DEPARTMENT STORE
Spring City, Kansas   67083

July 5, 1973

Dear Charge Customer:

Our annual Mid-Summer Sale will begin on July 15 and will continue through July 20.

Prices on all of our summer clothing will be reduced as much as
20 percent. Greater price reductions will be made on picnic
and camping items and on yard and garden tools.

We will announce this sale in the local newspapers on July 12,
but we want you to know about it earlier. We look forward to
seeing you in our store sometime during the week of July 15-20.

Cordially yours,

Robert F. Weston
Robert F. Weston
Assistant Manager

wnv

such as name, inside address, and salutation are to be added. Occasions for which this type of form message is appropriate are almost countless. To mention only a few, there are those that:

1. Serve as announcements for meetings, sales, and so on.
2. Solicit funds and other types of donations.
3. Serve as reminders.
4. Attempt to sell a product or a service.

The recipients of such messages as these do not expect to receive individualized letters. These messages contain no variables in amounts, dates, names, or addresses; and the events which prompt the mailing of these messages make it obvious to the reader that mailing anything other than a form would be impractical.

A postal card bearing a duplicated message can be used more advantageously than a form letter for some purposes. Postal cards are used frequently for sending announcements and reminders and for acknowledging routine orders, as well as for many other reasons. The use of cards effects savings in postage, supplies (paper and envelopes), and time required for folding and inserting letters into envelopes.

The letter and the postal card on page 241 and below typify these types of mailings.

October 15, 1973

Dear Member:

The Hartsell Investment Group will meet again at 7 p.m. on Thursday, October 22, at our regular place. Mr. Lee S. Vanderford will discuss some stocks that he believes will be of special interest to us.

Cordially yours,

Fred R. Ramer

Fred R. Ramer
Secretary

For some postal cards that are duplicated in their entirety, the sender's signature may be omitted. If a salutation is used, the signature is used. If the salutation is omitted, perhaps the signature should be omitted also.

Typewritten form letters

Some form letters should be individually typewritten. Your decision as to whether the letter should be typewritten or duplicated will, of course, be contingent upon the various factors involved in the situation at hand. A typist can typewrite from a typewritten copy much more rapidly than from notes taken from dictation or from dictation that has been recorded on a machine. When the same information is to be sent to different people, therefore, a master typewritten copy should be prepared from which the typist can copy. Such a practice saves time not only for the typist but also for the dictator. There is no need for him to dictate the same information repeatedly.

The letter on page 244 is an example of a form letter that is individually typewritten for each person who receives a copy.

That particular letter is used as a follow-up for a routine inquiry that is made as a result of a college recruiting representative's visit with high school groups. When the recruiter talks with a group of high school students, he gives each one a form postal card that is addressed to the admissions director of the college. The card contains a list of the major fields of study available at that particular college. Each student who is interested in attending the college is asked to place a check mark beside the field of study he wishes to pursue and to mail the card to the admissions director. The information that is underlined in that letter is revised to suit the occasion for which each letter is written. No underlining appears on the copy that is mailed.

The admissions director, upon receipt of one of these cards, sends a college catalog and an admissions form to the high school student; and then he forwards the postal card to the chairman of the department the student has chosen for a major field of study. When the chairman of the office administration department receives one of these postal cards from the admissions director, his

HASTINGS COMMUNITY COLLEGE
Hastings, Colorado 81041

_____

_____
_____
_____
_____

_____:

You can expect to receive sometime this week a letter from
Dr. Alfred E. Thompson, who is chairman of our department of
office administration. He can give you specific information
about the program that is offered in that department.

This morning I mailed you a copy of our college catalog, which
contains a form on page 8 that we would like for you to fill
out and return to us as soon as you can. The enclosed stamped
envelope is for your use in returning the form.

Miss Carolyn Winningham enjoyed talking with your high school
graduating class last Friday morning. She was especially impressed by those of you who attended her group meeting that
afternoon.

We would be very happy to have you as a student next fall. We
would also be pleased to have you visit our campus at any time
before then.

Sincerely yours,

Ray E. Brock
Ray E. Brock
Admissions Officer

hsr

Enclosure

secretary sends a neatly typed copy of the letter on page 245 to
the student.

Using this form letter speeds up the communicating process
and accomplishes the same purpose that individually dictated

letters would accomplish. The volume of this type of correspondence involving the office administration department is small enough to make the practice of typewriting these form letters a practical procedure.

When the volume of such correspondence is too great to per-

HASTINGS COMMUNITY COLLEGE
Hastings, Colorado 81041

_____

_____
_____
_____

_____:

We would be very glad to have you enroll in our department next September.

Our secretarial curriculum, which leads to an Associate of Arts degree, is designed specifically for the student who wants to be well qualified for secretarial work at the end of two years of college. The graduates of this curriculum are in great demand throughout this section of the country. During the past five years, they have taken jobs that pay from $450 to $500 a month in law offices, retail stores, colleges, industry, and government offices.

The credits that you earn in this program can be transferred to a four-year college or university. Some of our graduates have continued in school to receive a bachelor's degree before accepting employment.

A list of the courses that are required for completing the secretarial program and a list of recommended electives are on pages 3 and 4 of the brochure that I am enclosing. I believe that you will be interested in reading the entire brochure.

Please come by my office on registration day, September 10. I should be glad to have you come to visit in our department at any time before school opens on September 10.

                    Cordially yours,

                    Alfred E. Thompson
                    Alfred E. Thompson
                    Department Chairman

jam
Enclosure

mit typewriting each letter, one of the many brands of automatic typewriters may be used. A typist inserts a letterhead sheet into the typewriter and typewrites the date, the name and address, and the salutation and then engages the mechanism which causes the automatic typewriter to typewrite the rest of the letter— body, complimentary close, signature line, reference initials, and any other applicable notations. A properly prepared master insures accurate copy, thus enabling the sender to sign the letter without the necessity of proofreading.

Some types of form letters contain variable data (dates, amounts, names, and so on), such as the one on page 244. For a letter of this type, the automatic typewriter can be programed to stop at the point where the variable begins so that the typist can supply the information applicable to that particular addressee and then engage the mechanism which causes the typewriter to continue until the next variable is reached or until the letter is completed. The speed of the automatic typewriter is at least 135 words a minute (and is usually faster).

The extent to which typewritten form letters can be used advantageously is governed by the nature of the activities of the organization, the imagination of the personnel involved, and the availability of word-processing facilities.

Form paragraphs

For some correspondence, especially replies to recurring types of inquiries, a set of form paragraphs can be used advantageously. One example of an office that receives many similar inquiries is a college admissions office. Hundreds of prospective students write to that office each year, and many of them ask the same questions. They inquire about programs of study, expenses, living accommodations, part-time employment, scholarships, and so on. These four benefits are realized from the use of a set of well-written form paragraphs—a paragraph for each question that is asked by a large number of prospective students.

1. The prospective student receives a prompt response to his inquiry. Because this routine information does not have to be dictated for each reply, a typist can copy a form paragraph that has been prepared for each question that was asked. No time has

to be spent in dictating that reply, and the typist can typewrite much more rapidly from typewritten copy than she can transcribe from any type of recorded dictation.

2. The prospective student receives a well–written response. Because each paragraph is used for many different letters, the writer can afford to spend the time required to cover every detail adequately and clearly. When a person is unduly pressed for time, he sometimes omits some details or does not write quite as clearly as he does when he has adequate time to devote to each letter.

3. The office sending the replies makes a real saving in time, and therefore in cost, in replying to these letters, which are quite important to the school as well as to the prospective students.

4. The writer creates a better impression for his school by sending a carefully written reply *promptly*. Promptness in mailing this letter and the care with which the letter is prepared can have a significant bearing on the prospective student's choice of the college he will attend. Oftentimes, prospective students send inquiries to more than one college. The college that sends a good response early very likely has an edge over another college that would like to recruit the prospect.

For letters of this nature, form paragraphs are more effective than complete form letters because the information in some of the paragraphs will not apply to some of the inquiries. The admissions officer knows, for example, that some prospective students will reside off campus. He would, therefore, omit from his reply the paragraph pertaining to on-campus housing. He knows that some inquirers will not be interested in part-time employment. He would obviously not include the paragraph pertaining to part-time employment in his replies to those persons. Including information that the addressee would definitely not be interested in may cause him to realize that the letter he receives is a form letter and would therefore probably give him the impression that he has been given little or no personal consideration.

Well-constructed form paragraphs should not be used in an attempt to deceive the recipient of a letter. Actually, though, they can be used in such a way that the addressee benefits more from them than he would from a less carefully prepared paragraph that is dictated especially to reply to his inquiry.

Some letters may be made up entirely from form paragraphs.

When an office has a form paragraph for each question that is raised in an inquiry, the reply may be made very well from these paragraphs. The paragraphs may be presented in different sequences for various letters. A good practice to follow when sending information that has been requested is to reply to the questions in the order in which they were asked. This plan makes it easy for the writer to make certain that he replies to each question, and it helps the addressee to see quickly that each of his questions has been answered. Sometimes, too, the person requesting the information may expect to use it in the order in which he asked the questions.

For the answers to inquiries from prospective students, the college admissions officer may have prepared the following form paragraphs:

1. *Programs of study*

   Each of the five colleges of our university offers from three to seven programs of study that lead to a bachelor's degree. These programs, which are listed on page 7 of the enclosed catalog, are described in detail on the pages that follow that list.

2. *Expenses*

   The total expenses for a year in college vary, of course, from student to student. The average last year was $1300 for dormitory students, $900 for off–campus students, and $1100 for the married students who lived in apartments. These figures include clothing, recreation, transportation, fees, etc.

3. The expenses for tuition, fees, meals, and lodging are explained on page 67 of the catalog that is enclosed. Textbooks, which are available in the university bookstore, cost about $45 a quarter. You can obtain used copies for some of your courses.

4. *Living accommodations*

   You can rent a single room in a dormitory for $115 a quarter or a double room for $85. We provide linens and maid service for all rooms.

5. The dormitories, which are air-conditioned, are in excellent condition. To reserve a room, complete the form on page 6

of the enclosed brochure and mail it with a $25 deposit to the address that is on that form.

6. *Part-time employment*

   Part-time jobs are available in the library, in the cafeteria, in the dormitories, in the gymnasium, and in various offices on the campus and downtown. As Mrs. Vera Stamps is in charge of part-time employment, I suggest that you write to her and tell her about your qualifications. Address your letter to Mrs. Vera Stamps, Placement Director, Central State University, Midtown, TX 75639.

7. *Scholarships*

   The scholarships that we offer range from $350 to $1,000 a year. I have asked Miss Julia Ann Pryor, who processes the scholarship applications, to write to you. I am confident she will write to you within the next two days.

8. *Courteous ending*

   We would be very glad to have you enroll in our university.

If a prospective student inquires about programs of study, expenses, and part-time employment only and states that he has made arrangements to reside with a relative while he attends college, the reply to his inquiry may appropriately be only those three paragraphs that answer his three questions. Possibly, the form paragraph on scholarships would be written in such a manner that including it in the letter to a particular student would be appropriate.

The message on page 250 is the reply to a letter from a prospective student who said he has a scholarship that will cover all of his expenses. His major will be accounting. He inquired about on-campus living accommodations and asked for an estimate of the expenses for one year of college. He will not decide until a short time before school opens as to whether he will reside on campus or with an aunt whose home is only a few blocks from the university campus. For this reply the typist merely had to copy form paragraphs 4, 5, 2, 3, and 8.

The paragraphs on programs of study and scholarships should definitely be omitted. Including that information would make

CENTRAL STATE UNIVERSITY

Midtown, Texas 75639

July 2, 1973

Mr. James T. Rawlings
Route 2
Landmark, TX 75431

Dear Mr. Rawlings:

You can rent a single room in a dormitory for $115 a quarter or
a double room for $85. We provide linens and maid service for
all rooms.

The dormitories, which are airconditioned, are in excellent condition. To reserve a room, complete the form on page 6 of the
enclosed brochure and mail it with a $25 deposit to the address
that is on that form.

The total expenses for a year in college vary, of course, from
student to student. The average last year was $1300 for dormi-
tory students, $900 for off-campus students, and $1100 for the
married students who lived in apartments. These figures include
clothing, recreation, transportation, fees, etc.

The expenses for tuition, fees, meals, and lodging are explained
on page 67 of the catalog that is enclosed. Textbooks, which
are available in the university book store, cost about $45 a
quarter. You can obtain used copies for some of your courses.

We would be very glad to have you enroll in our university.

Cordially yours,

Larry E. Clark

Larry E. Clark
Admissions Officer

wen

Enclosures 2

it obvious to the addressee that very little special attention had
been given to his letter.

Quite often form paragraphs are excellent for part of a reply;
but more information is essential, or is at least desirable, for the

reply. That additional information can be given in individually dictated paragraphs. Some letters may very well begin with an individually dictated paragraph that is followed by form paragraphs. For some other letters an individually dictated paragraph could be placed between two form paragraphs or at the end of

---

CENTRAL STATE UNIVERSITY

Midtown, Texas   75639

July 17, 1973

Miss Marie Welch
P. O. Box 348
Longhorn, TX   75138

Dear Miss Welch:

You may enroll for only twelve hours if you wish. Many other
students who work part time take this minimum load for full-
time students.

The total expenses for a year in college vary, of course, from
student to student. The average last year was $1300 for dormi-
tory students, $900 for off-campus students, and $1100 for the
married students who lived in apartments. These figures include
clothing, recreation, transportation, fees, etc.

The expenses for tuition, fees, meals, and lodging are explained
on page 67 of the catalog that is enclosed. Textbooks, which
are available in the university book store, cost about $45 a
quarter. You can obtain used copies for some of your courses.

You can rent a single room in a dormitory for $115 a quarter or
a double room for $85. We provide linens and maid service for
all rooms.

The dormitories, which are airconditioned, are in excellent condition. To reserve a room, complete the form on page 6 of the
enclosed brochure and mail it with a $25 deposit to the address
that is on that form.

We would be very glad to have you enroll in our university.

                              Cordially yours,

                              Larry E. Clark
                              Larry E. Clark
wen   Admissions Officer
Enclosures 2

the letter. The content of the inquiry and the extent to which form paragraphs have been prepared will help the letter writer to determine how the individually dictated paragraphs and the form paragraphs should be interspersed to arrive at a message that would be appropriate for the occasion.

The letter on page 251 is a reply to a prospective student who will work in a downtown office while she studies office administration. She asked whether she could enroll for only twelve quarter hours' credit each term. She will live on campus until the middle of the second quarter when she is to be married to a local resident. (Tuition is based on a load of twelve to twenty quarter hours a term; this plan is described on page 67, which is referred to in the paragraph on expenses.) Note that this reply consists of an individually dictated first paragraph that is followed by form paragraphs 3, 2, 4, 5, and 8.

Another example of the many occasions for which form paragraphs can be used advantageously for replies to recurring types of inquiries is a hotel that hosts many convention groups. The hotel has prepared the following paragraphs that describe such facilities as meeting rooms, exhibit areas, bedrooms, catering services, and tour services:

1. *Meeting rooms*

   We have meeting rooms for just about any size group. Four of the rooms seat from 15 to 25 each when a conference arrangement is used or 25 to 40 with the chairs arranged in theatre style. Each of the largest five rooms seats up to 375 with the chairs arranged in theatre style.

2. Six other rooms are arranged so that any two of them can be combined by simply opening folding doors. Each of these six rooms seats 125 for meals or 225 with theatre style seating.

3. *Exhibit areas*

   A large exhibit area 150 by 175 feet is well lighted and is wired so that any type of appliance can be shown at any position in the room. For a small number of exhibits, any portion of this large area can be separated from the rest of the room by merely closing attractive folding doors.

4. A highly talented decorator who works closely with our supervisor of convention arrangements can help you develop a plan that will be especially attractive as well as convenient for your exhibitors.

5. *Bedrooms*
    Our bedrooms are spacious and are luxuriously furnished. Just specify the type of bed you prefer—double, twin, queen size, or king size. Shag carpeting in all of the bedrooms contributes to the appearance of the color scheme that helps to make our hotel a showplace in this region.

6. *Catering service*
    All of the banquets, luncheons, and the like at our hotel are catered by the nationally acclaimed Peggy Coker Catering Service. A menu for any occasion can be arranged at reasonable prices. Our food service director works very closely with the representatives of the groups for which the meals are planned.

7. *Tour service*
    Our hotel is a regular stop for Buffline Tours, Inc.; and tickets as well as descriptive brochures are available at our tour service desk. You can arrange special tours by working with the clerk at that desk.

8. *Courteous ending*
    We look forward to hearing from you again soon. We would enjoy having your group meet at our hotel.

By using these specially prepared paragraphs and by adding some personally dictated paragraphs, the sales manager who is in charge of convention arrangements can handle most of his routine correspondence very quickly at a minimum cost.

Paragraphs 1, 6, 3, 4, and 8—in that order—were used in the letter on page 254 as a reply to a letter from a small group of local people who are planning a one-day meeting. They inquired about meeting rooms, meal service, and exhibit space. Because the participants are local, they would not be interested in receiving information concerning bedrooms or tours.

Like the complete form letters discussed earlier in this chapter, the form paragraphs can also be typewritten by using one of the many brands of automatic typewriters. Fill-in spaces can be included in these paragraphs, and individually dictated paragraphs can be interspersed with the forms when using an automatic type-

---

INLAND CITY HOTEL

Inland City, Florida 32852

February 6, 1974

Mrs. Geraldine R. Caldwell
President, Professional Women's Club
129 West Lakemont Drive
Inland City, FL 32851

Dear Mrs. Caldwell:

We have meeting rooms for just about any size group. Four of
the rooms seat from 15 to 25 each when a conference arrangement is used or 25 to 40 with the chairs arranged in theatre
style. Each of the largest five rooms seats up to 375 with
the chairs arranged in theatre style.

All of the banquets, luncheons, etc., at our hotel are catered
by the nationally acclaimed Peggy Coker Catering Service. A
menu for any occasion can be arranged at reasonable prices. Our
food service director works very closely with the representatives of the groups for which the meals are planned.

A large exhibit area 150 by 175 feet is well lighted and is
wired so that any type of appliance can be shown at any position in the room. For a small number of exhibits, any portion
of this large area can be separated from the rest of the room
by merely closing attractive folding doors.

A highly talented decorator who works closely with our supervisor of convention arrangements can help you develop a plan
that will be especially attractive as well as convenient for
your exhibitors.

We look forward to hearing from you again soon. We would enjoy
having your group meet at our hotel.

Cordially yours,

Dwight R. O'Neal

Dwight R. O'Neal
Sales Manager

rmo

writer. The volume of correspondence of this nature and the availability of machines would help to determine the desirability of using automatic typewriters.

The use of form paragraphs is not limited to replies to inquiries. The extent to which they are used would—like the use of complete form letters—be governed by the nature of the activities and the imagination of the personnel involved.

Although minimizing correspondence costs has been stressed throughout this chapter, cost reduction is not the only reason for using form messages. Getting the carefully written message into the hands of the person who will benefit by reading it is of primary importance. You can use these pre-prepared messages to help your reader achieve his goal and at the same time give him the prompt attention a reader of your correspondence deserves.

Study the correspondence of your own organization to determine whether or not you can increase the effectiveness and also reduce the cost by maintaining a file of well-constructed form paragraphs and letters. Such forms should be prepared after studying your correspondence over a considerable length of time. When you realize that you can use form messages advantageously, spend the time necessary to write them well. Repeated use of them will justify your spending a good deal of time and effort preparing them.

Routing slips

Routing slips can be used quite effectively in many offices to speed up the circulation of letters, reports, memorandums, and other messages within the organization. Such a slip usually contains the names of people who are to receive these types of messages frequently, and it may contain short messages such as those in the illustrations on pages 256 and 257.

To route a message to any group of people, you merely place a check mark beside the name of each person who is to receive it. The first person who receives it reads it, initials the routing slip, and sends the message to the next person whose name is checked on the list. The person who attaches the routing slip to the message that is to be circulated may transmit whatever message

Office of the Sales Manager

Michael H. Ross

June 19, 1973

_____ Mr. Allen

_____ Mr. Baker

_____ Miss Brownlow

_____ Mr. Harris

__✓__ Mr. Hayes

_____ Mrs. Jacobs

__✓__ Mr. James

_____ Miss Townley

_____ Mrs. Walker

__✓__ Mr. White

_____ Mr. Yearwood

_____ please see me

_____ for your files

_____ for your signature

_____ please prepare reply for my signature

__✓__ for your information

_____ please handle

_____ for your suggestions

Comments:

he wishes to transmit by simply placing a check mark beside the message that is duplicated or by writing a note in the space provided at the bottom of the slip.

In the example above, the message "for your information" was

```
                    Ronald E. Beach

                    General Manager


    To                          Initials      Date


    _____  Miss Adams          _____      ____

    _____  Mr. Clinton         _____      ____

    _____  Mr. Colburn         _____      ____

    _____  Mrs. Hathaway       _____      ____

    _____  Miss Madison        _____      ____

      ✓     Mr. Mason           _____      ____

    _____  Mr. Whitehall       _____      ____

    _____  Mr. Woolworth       _____      ____

    _____  Mr. Zane            _____      ____


    _____  please see me

    _____  for your files

    _____  for your signature

    _____  please handle

    _____  for your information

    _____  for your suggestions

    Comments:
```

Please go to our Gadsden plant to negotiate with the contractor.

sent to three men—Mr. Hayes, Mr. James, and Mr. White. In the second example (see illustration), the executive who routed the report asked Mr. Mason to go to one of the branch offices to transact some business.

Records of calls

The use of printed forms for recording messages from visitors or telephone calls can effect savings of time and effort by the person taking the message. Pads of such forms as the one that is

```
                                NOTE

         To_____

         From_____


         While you were

         _____  out of the office

         _____  talking on the telephone

         _____  in conference


         M_____

         _____  called on the telephone.

         _____  came by the office.


         _____  He will telephone.

         _____  He will return.

         _____  Please call him.

         _____  Please write to him.

         _____  He left the attached message.

         Comments:
```

illustrated on the preceding page are frequently placed beside office telephones and on the desks of secretaries, receptionists, and others who may accept messages for some other office employee if that employee is absent when the message is received.

Numerous other forms can be used very effectively for internal communication. Study the activities of the organization for which you work so that you can introduce the forms that will enhance the communication effectiveness.

Questions for discussion

1. What are some specific situations for which form letters and form paragraphs can be used advantageously?
2. What are some of the recent mechanical and technological developments that contribute to the effective use of form letters and paragraphs?
3. What are some of the form messages that the teacher of this course could use effectively to transmit information to the students?
4. What steps should you follow in developing form paragraphs or letters for the department in which you are employed?
5. Why can a typist copy more rapidly from typewritten form messages than she can transcribe from shorthand notes or from dictation that has been recorded on a tape, belt, or some other medium?

Exercises

Improve the following sentences that were taken from business letters.

1. You will find a picture of the Model 8 on page 63.
2. We cannot ship the books you ordered until December 8.
3. Enclosed is my check for $9 in payment of invoice number 7673.
4. You will be enrolled in a training program for a period of one year.
5. Thank you for your check in the amount of $11.00.
6. The second pamphlet you requested will be mailed to you at a later date.
7. Do you think that I should enclose a self-addressed envelope?
8. I am happy to send you this information in reply to your inquiry.

9. I will send the catalog under separate cover tomorrow morning.
10. I am sure that he will be glad to be of assistance to you.

Problems

1. As personnel director of a large manufacturing company in a town that has a large business college and a state university, you receive many applications for secretarial jobs. As you can employ only a small percentage of the well-qualified applicants, prepare a form letter that you can have produced in your word-processing center for prompt mailing to each applicant that you cannot grant a personal interview.

2. As placement director for student employees on your college campus, you receive inquiries about part-time work for many prospective students. You have a printed form that you ask each person to complete for your files before you offer him employment or place his name on a waiting list for a job.

    Prepare a form letter that can be typewritten for mailing to each prospective student who inquires about a part-time job.

3. As editor of your college weekly newspaper, write a letter to the president of each club on your campus and request his reactions to a new format that you are proposing for the college newspaper.

4. As credit manager of a large department store, prepare a series of three form letters that you would write to collect an overdue account. Assume that these letters would be mailed after you have mailed the monthly statement, a second copy of the monthly statement with a reminder notation attached, and an obvious form letter.

    This series that you will prepare will be used before you mention turning the account over to a collection agency or to an attorney for collection.

5. You are the circulation manager for *Family's Best* magazine that has a very large circulation. Many subscribers neglect to renew their subscriptions at the proper time. You send them a card reminding them to renew and then mail another copy of that card if they do not renew their subscriptions before the expiration date.

    Prepare a form letter that you can use to encourage them to renew their subscriptions. Resell the magazine and perhaps tell them something about what to expect in forthcoming issues.

12

Dictating

WHEN YOU dictate a letter, you should use the same basic principles and writing style qualities that you would use if you were writing it. Dictating differs from writing in only one respect: the person composing the message *speaks* the words instead of *writing* them. To dictate well, you must learn to write well. Anyone who has had very little experience in *writing* business letters should prepare a rough draft of his message and then revise it so that it will be properly organized and properly worded. This process of writing and then rewriting helps the writer to become adept in preparing effective letters.

Having studied the preceding chapters of this book, you are ready to begin *dictating* letters.

The ability to dictate well is essential for any successful business executive. As was pointed out in the preceding chapter, business letters are expensive; and the factor that contributes most to the cost of a letter is the salary of the executive who composes it. The executive's taking the time to write the letter in longhand, in shorthand, or on the typewriter can be justified in only very rare instances.

For an unusually difficult letter, the composer may sometimes profitably spend the time required to prepare a rough draft and even some revisions of that draft before dictating the letter. The beginner who may feel somewhat ill at ease, only because dictating is new to him, may be justified in writing his letters before dictating them for the short time that is required to overcome his so-called stage fright and to develop the self-confidence he needs to dictate from brief notes only.

The following twelve suggestions are given to help you become a skillful dictator of effective business messages:

1. Collect the needed information before you begin to dictate.
2. Jot down notes in margins or on slips of paper so that you will include all of the information you intend to include.
3. Dictate most of your messages during a specified period each day.
4. Number the letters to which you reply and give them to the transcriber so that she can copy the names and addresses.
5. Spell proper names that cannot be copied from the letters you give to the transcriber.
6. Verify the accuracy of dates and other figures.
7. Dictate numbers in groups rather than individually.
8. Pronounce all words clearly and slowly enough so that the transcriber can hear them well.
9. Supply the punctuation marks for special or unusually difficult situations.
10. Give special instructions *before* you dictate a message.
11. When you dictate to a recording machine, follow the special instructions that the manufacturer has prepared for operating the machine.
12. Dictate in a conversational tone.

Collecting information

Once you have decided to send a letter and have determined the objective you wish to achieve by sending it, you are ready to collect the information that is needed. Collect whatever information you need for your letter *before* you attempt to begin dictating. Possibly, you will need to take one or more of the following five steps to gather that information:

1. Refer to other correspondence in your files.
2. Confer with other personnel.
3. Make one or more telephone calls.
4. Request information from a computing center or make some calculations at your desk.
5. Consult a calendar to verify dates *(very important)*.

You may have to take still further steps to gather some of the required information.

Outlining

You can enhance the effectiveness of your dictation by jotting down notes (dates, names, addresses, arithmetic computations, and other details) for almost all of the letters that you write so that you will not have to interrupt your dictating to locate this information. You can easily record notes of this nature in the margin of the letter to which you are replying, or you can record them on a scratch pad. You may also profit by recording brief notes (one word may be sufficient as a reminder of a good deal of data) concerning extraneous information such as a sales pitch, a special goodwill paragraph, and so on, so that you will remember to include it in the letter that you will dictate.

For the simplest, routine types of letters, though, notes would obviously be of very little help. Any notes that you use should be listed in the same order as the information to which they refer will be presented in the letter. This informal outline will not only serve as a reminder to you to include all the information that you wish to include, but it will also help you to present that information in a well-organized manner.

For some of the most difficult types of letters you have to write, you may profit from preparing a somewhat detailed outline. A topical outline is usually sufficient, but scribbling a few complete sentences is sometimes worthwhile. As is true with other activities, a person's depending on some type of support is largely a matter of habit; and everyone must strike a happy medium on the degree to which he depends on a support. Use as your support for dictating whatever outline best suits the occasion for which you

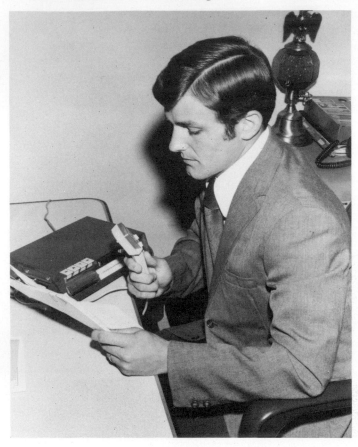

Brief notes in the margins serve adequately for outlines for replies to most correspondence.

are composing the message, but cultivate the habit of dictating mostly from notes that serve only as a cue.

Dictating efficiency

Dictating efficiency should contribute to transcribing efficiency. No matter how carefully a message has been organized and worded, it is of value only when it reaches the intended recipient. As you dictate, therefore, do so in a manner that will facilitate transcription. The salary of the transcriber is the second greatest contributor to the cost of a business letter. By dictating in such a manner that the message can be transcribed quickly, you not only make the message more effective by getting it to the recipient within a short time but you also help to reduce the cost.

Careful dictation increases the accuracy of transcription as well as the speed. Just as the message is of no value until it is delivered, it is of no value if it contains certain types of errors.

A special period for dictation each day increases efficiency.

In fact, some errors can cause a message to be a liability rather than an asset. Errors in amounts and dates often lead to confusion, embarrassment, and inconvenience. Incorrect spellings and improper choices or words that may have similar sounds sometimes create comical situations. Perhaps such situations could be tolerated and even appreciated if they did not necessitate further correspondence, thus leading to greater expense for both the sender and the receiver.

Dictating efficiency can be enhanced greatly by giving due consideration to such matters as handling names and addresses, handling numbers, and giving special instructions. The transcriber's knowledge of terms and her understanding of the content of the message, and the dictator's enunciation and the speed at which he dictates also contribute to dictating efficiency.

NAMES AND ADDRESSES

Although many people dislike their first or middle names, almost everybody likes his last name; and he likes to hear it and to see it fairly often provided it is pronounced properly and spelled correctly. Many names that have identical pronunciations are spelled differently. Some examples follow:

Boling	Bowling
Clark	Clarke
DeMent	Dement
Gray	Grey
Lee	Leigh
Lewis	Louis
Liles	Lyles
McDonald	MacDonald
Myer	Meyer
Noles	Knowles
Reese	Reece
Way	Wey

Other names, although pronounced and spelled differently, have similar pronunciations. A few examples are in the following lists.

Daniel	Daniels
Herren	Herring
Moyer	Moyers
Roberson	Robertson
Woodard	Woodward

Still other names such as *Elise* and *Elsie* are spelled similarly but do not have similar pronunciations. Take special care to see that each name you dictate is spelled correctly by the person who transcribes your message.

When you dictate a reply to a letter, you can be certain that the transcriber knows the correct spelling of the addressee's name by handing her the letter to which you are replying so that she can copy the name and the address from that letter. This practice of letting the typist copy from the letter you received not only helps to insure accuracy in typewriting the name and the address, but it also speeds up the transcription process. A typist can typewrite much more rapidly and accurately from typewritten or printed copy than from dictation that has been recorded manually or by machine. The time required for dictating a letter is greatly reduced when the name and the inside address are not dictated but are copied from a letter.

A procedure that is highly recommended is scheduling most, or possibly all, of the day's dictation for a particular time. Perhaps the dictation period should begin as soon as the required information has been collected and the necessary decisions have been made for replying to the letters that were received in the current day's mail. Letters other than replies should be dictated during this same period. Often office work may necessitate that some other time during the day be scheduled for dictation; but the earlier the dictation can be given, the better the chances are of getting your letters in the mail that day.

A procedure that saves a great deal of dictation time is that of dictating all of the replies before dictating any other letters. Number your letters (1, 2, 3, and so on) in the upper left-hand corner as in the following illustration; and as you begin to dictate a reply, simply dictate the number you have assigned and follow that number by the salutation and then the message.

After you have dictated all of the replies, give the typist the letters you have numbered so that she can typewrite the names and the addresses from the letters.

When a typewritten or a printed copy of the name and address is not readily available for copying, you must dictate that information. Take special care to enunciate clearly and to dictate slowly enough so that, when a stenographer is recording the dictation, she will have adequate time to write the names in longhand. Whether you are dictating to a stenographer or to some type of recording machine, *spell* slowly any name that is spelled differently from the way the transcriber is accustomed to spelling an identical or similar-sounding name.

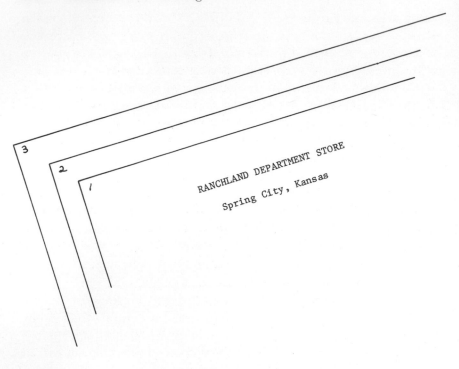

NUMBERS

Accuracy in handling numbers is extremely important for several reasons. Because transpositions and other types of errors can be made easily in dictating, in listening, and in typewriting, provisions should be made for the typist to copy numbers whenever copy is available from which she can read. An error in a ZIP code or in some other part of an address almost always leads to a delay in the letter's reaching its destination. Such errors may make the delivery of the letter impossible.

Numbers within the body of the message must be transcribed accurately to avoid confusion or an incorrect interpretation. A letter containing the date *Friday, April 27,* would certainly lead to confusion if the actual date is *Friday, April 26.* An error of this type may necessitate further correspondence or telephone calls; or because it may cause the addressee to believe the date under consideration conflicts with other plans, he may react entirely differently from the way he would react if the correct date were in the letter. *Verify all dates before dictating them*. Errors in amounts (money, time, supplies, and so on) can lead to loss of business or to a misunderstanding concerning some transaction.

Numbers within the body of the message usually have to be dictated rather than copied. The person dictating the numbers should be especially careful to read the numbers correctly, to enunciate clearly, and to dictate them slowly enough for the stenographer to write them clearly. Long numbers should be dictated *in groups* rather than *individually*. For example, the number 348672 should be dictated "three forty-eight, six seventy-two" or "Thirty-four, eighty-six, seventy-two" rather than "three, four, eight, six, seven, two." Numbers dictated in groups can be understood more easily and thus transcribed accurately.

SPECIAL INSTRUCTIONS

Although the transcriber can be expected to punctuate most of the sentences that are dictated, you—the person dictating the message—should indicate the punctuation marks for special or unusually difficult situations. You should ordinarily supply these marks during the dictating process. You should also designate the ends of paragraphs.

You are responsible for giving any special instructions, such as the need to send carbon copies to various persons, the method of mailing (airmail, special delivery, certified mail, or another), when it is anything other than first-class mail, and the need for "rush" handling of the message. Give these instructions *before* dictating the letter. By your giving them before dictating, the transcriber will know to prepare extra copies when they are needed; and she will know to typewrite any other special notation such as *airmail* near the top of the page. Having these instructions first, the transcriber can save transcription time.

To insure a high degree of accuracy and speed in the transcription of your messages, encourage the transcriber to ask any questions for which she cannot readily find answers in the dictionary, handbooks, directories, and other sources of information that she has been taught to use efficiently. You should instruct her to ask any necessary questions *after* you have finished dictating the message. Any interruption during the time you are dictating can disrupt your trend of thought and affect adversely your dictating efficiency.

When you dictate to a recording machine, follow the specific instructions that the manufacturer has prepared for operating that particular model. Following these instructions will help you to record your dictation clearly so that it can be transcribed easily and accurately. You should, before you dictate a message, indicate to the transcriber whether the message is a letter, a memorandum, a report, a speech, or some other type of message.

KNOWLEDGE OF CONTENT

The transcriber's knowledge of the terms that are used and her understanding of the content of the message and the events leading to the desirability of sending the message affect the manner in which dictating should be done. When the transcriber is familiar with these factors (terms, content, and background), the composer of the message can dictate rather fluently. Even if he should enunciate less clearly than usual, the transcriber could probably record the dictation and transcribe it accurately. When, on the other hand, the transcriber is not familiar with some of the terms or the content, the person dictating must take special care to enunciate clearly; and he should perhaps take the time to spell some of the more difficult, specialized terms.

One executive who was working to help eradicate mosquitoes from the geographic area in which he resided dictated in one of his letters, "We have had anopheles mosquitoes in this area for a long time." The transcriber, who had little knowledge of the problem, transcribed, "We have had enough of these mosquitoes in this area for a long time." While the word *anopheles* seemed to be an ordinary word to the executive, his assuming that it was familiar to the transcriber was the cause for the letter's having to be retypewritten.

A similar error was made when an executive dictated this sentence when sending some information about a speaker for a special occasion: "Last year he won the Pulitzer prize." Because the word *Pulitzer* was not a part of the transcriber's vocabulary, she transcribed, "Last year he won the pullet surprise." Fortunately for everyone concerned, the error was detected and then corrected before the letter was mailed.

A person who dictates messages *must* enunciate clearly and spell (and possibly even define) words that he suspects may be new to the transcriber.

The term "key-driven calculator," even though it seems to be easy to pronounce, is frequently transcribed "keyed-ribbon calculator," "frayed-ribbon calculator," and so on, by typists who are not familiar with this type of office machine.

The transcriber is, of course, expected to use a dictionary and other reference books and to make the necessary inquiries to the person dictating so that she can transcribe accurately; but the person who does the dictating must assume the responsibility for making his dictation clear.

SPEED

The speed of the dictation is obviously governed somewhat by the stenographer's ability to record the message accurately. Even though the stenographer may be an expert who can write faster than most people can speak clearly, the person dictating must vary his dictation speed, even within a sentence, so that each word is intelligible. He should talk loudly enough to be heard easily, but dictation which is unnecessarily loud seems faster and more difficult to write than that which is given in a natural tone of voice.

Most dictation—whether to a stenographer or to a machine recorder—should be given so that there is a *slight* pause after each small group of words. The word grouping that is illustrated in the following sentence would be appropriate. "I appreciate your writing to me / about the maintenance problem / in your factory in Chicago." Other groupings could be just as effective. The dictation should be given, though, in a manner that will seem like natural talking and will enable the transcriber to understand the content of the message as well as the individual words.

Dictate as if you were talking with the person to whom you are sending the message.

Kinds of dictation

Your dictation should be of the same quality for a machine as it would be if it were to a stenographer. Clear enunciation and a pleasant, self-confident, cordial tone of voice contribute to the success of any successful communicator. These characteristics should be a part of all well-organized, carefully planned dictation for letters, memorandums, speeches, and reports.

Questions for discussion

1. What steps can an administrative manager take to stimulate the other executives in his organization to improve their ability to dictate business messages?
2. What steps can an executive take to improve his ability to dictate effectively?
3. What are some advantages of dictating to a machine rather than to a stenographer?
4. What are some advantages of dictating to a stenographer rather than to a machine?
5. What are some of the modern technological developments that enable transcribers to transcribe dictated material faster than was possible earlier?

Exercises

Improve the following sentences that were taken from business letters.

1. I believe the book will prove to be a good reference.
2. I should like to thank you for recommending me for the job of accounting clerk.
3. My check in the amount of $16.00 is enclosed.
4. This morning I mailed the brochure you requested in your recent letter.
5. The truck will depart at 4 P.M. this afternoon.
6. Enclosed is a copy of the pamphlet for your files.
7. The elimination of Form A should be considered.
8. A word-processing center will be opened in the near future.
9. Please do not forget the date of the sale.
10. They improved the appearance of the place by the addition of a fence along the south side of the lot.

Problems

1. Dictate replies to the two letters that follow. Grant the requests.

243 East Seventh Street
Delaware, Indiana
April 19, 1974

Rodgers Book Store
P. O. Box 1223
San Mano, California

Gentlemen:

Please send a gift wrapped copy of LITTLE PEOPLE by Scarlet Hale to my niece, Betty Starnes, whose address is 509 North Whiteoak Street, Dover, New Mexico. I should like for her to receive it for her birthday, which is on April 26. A check for $8.17 to cover the cost of the book and postage is enclosed.

Please send me more information about the book TREES OF THE SOUTH, the title of which is included in the list that you mailed to me last week.

Cordially yours,

Elizabeth Whaley

Enclosure

* * *

414 White Avenue
Knoxville, Georgia
April 18, 1974

Rodgers Book Store
P. O. Box 1223
San Mano, California

Gentlemen:

Will you please suggest the names of three books that would be appropriate gifts for two small boys who are very much interested in camping. One is twelve years old; the other, ten.

I should like to present three books to these little boys before their summer vacation begins next month.

Sincerely yours,

Mrs. James W. Driver

2. You are the personnel manager of a large department store. Thomas A. Armstrong has applied for a job as salesman in your furniture department. Dictate a letter to him inviting him to come for a personal interview. His address is P. O. Box 1216, Southern State University, Sparta, South Carolina.

13

Communicating orally

SOME MESSAGES are transmitted by *writing to readers;* others are transmitted by *speaking to listeners.* The principles involved are the same for written and for oral communication. These two processes are so closely related that any attempt to separate them completely would seldom occur under ordinary circumstances. As examples of the close relationship that exists between the two, many letters are dictated (spoken) before they are written; and quite often parts of the letters are written in longhand even before they are dictated for transcription. Also, many speeches are written, at least partially, before they are delivered orally.

The information in the preceding chapters is devoted primarily to the transmitting part of communicating by writing letters. In this chapter the transmitting aspect of communicating by speaking is emphasized.

To transmit an oral message effectively, the speaker must exercise special care to pronounce words correctly, to enunciate clearly, to use good grammar, to modulate his voice so that it is pleasant, to use gestures appropriately, and to present his ideas in the proper order. At the same time he must be perceptive to the reactions of his listeners. Excellence in these qualities helps the speaker to win the confidence and the respect of his listeners, and it enables him to present his message in such a way that the listeners concentrate on the content rather than on the manner in which it is presented. Creating a receptive mood for the receiver of a message and thereby causing him to share the information and emotions that are transmitted is the aim of every writer or speaker.

Many occasions arise daily that require employees at all levels of the organizational structure to communicate orally. Conversing with other employees and with customers or clients, talking on the telephone, giving instructions or explanations, and seeking information are among these routine activities. Some of the other oral communication activities in which many workers engage are giving oral reports, conducting demonstrations, presiding at meetings, leading discussions, and making speeches.

Conversations and interviews

When conversing with any other person (employer, prospective customer, client, colleague, and so on), you have, in addition to your well–chosen words that are pronounced properly and enunciated clearly, other valuable mediums such as smiles, winks, and tone of voice to enhance your ability to communicate effectively. Use them advantageously. Use the mediums that help you to project *your* personality.

A smile—provided it is genuine—is a great asset; but a fake smile can hamper your communication effectiveness and can even cause the person with whom you are conversing to develop a feeling of distrust for you. While everyone should strive constantly to improve his own personality and to be as cheerful as he can be under existing circumstances, he must maintain a quality of naturalness. If you are the type of person who can display a cheerful outlook without smiling very much, do not spoil your good trait by trying to fake smiles. Sincerity is the key to success with any communication medium. Be sincere; *be yourself.*

Modulate your voice so that it is pleasant to your listeners. If you have a high-pitched voice, lower it. Whether your voice is shrill, soft, or harsh, you can modulate it so that it will be pleasant to your listeners and will still be distinctively yours. Regulating the speed with which you speak can do much to improve the quality of your speaking. Controlling the volume so that your speech is loud enough to be heard easily but not so loud that it will cause your listeners to be uncomfortable or to believe that *you* are uncomfortable also contributes to the effectiveness of your communication. Just as a communicator chooses *words* that suit his particular personality, he also uses a tone of voice, facial expressions, and other gestures that suit his particular nature.

Voice inflection, talking speed, and proper pronunciation contribute a great deal to the effectiveness of your speaking ability. For the many words that have more than one correct pronunciation, choose the pronunciation that seems natural for you. Almost always the pronunciation you use is the one that is used by the people with whom you associate. The tendency to imitate seems to be innate. Perhaps the reason anyone uses the same pronunciation his associates use is the natural inclination to avoid conspicuousness, which would cause the listener to be aware of the manner of speaking, thus detracting from concentrating on the message.

Even though the desire to imitate to some degree is commendable, you must keep alert to the need for deviating from the frequently heard incorrect pronunciations. Make needed corrections in pronunciations when you recognize them.

Important for every participant (speaker and listener) in oral communication is the practice of looking into the eyes of the person with whom he is conversing. Looking directly at the other person *throughout* the conversation is not necessary. On some occasions there will be very little opportunity for you to look directly at the other person. For example, when you are giving or receiving instructions or when you are conducting or observing a demonstration, you must pay close attention to the object or the materials that are being used.

Cultivate the habit of looking, at least part of the time, at the person with whom you are communicating. This practice is evidence of good character, and it lets him know that you are interested in talking with him.

Telephone calls

When you talk on the telephone, your voice and the words you use represent you. Facial expressions and gestures that help you to communicate effectively in a person-to-person conversation help you in telephone conversations only to the extent that they enable you to project the proper tone of voice. A person who smiles while talking on the telephone is more likely to project a good image of himself than is the person who frowns or holds a "deadpan" expression. Modulate your voice to help you create the kind of impression that you wish to make on the person with whom you are talking.

An important step in communicating effectively on the telephone is to visualize the person with whom you are talking and to talk *with him* rather than *at the telephone transmitter*. Speak at a normal rate and with the same low-pitched tone that you would use when conversing in a person-to-person situation. Use your voice inflections to eliminate monotony.

Because you have immediate feedback or response to your comments, you should use the same words and sentence fragments that are natural for person-to-person communication but that are inappropriate for written communication. When you transmit a message by writing, you have the privilege and the responsibility of editing. The necessary delay in response to written messages requires a more carefully planned type of presentation for your message. Telephone calls, as well as person-to-person conversations can be easy and very effective.

When there is some type of mechanical interference that causes your listener to have difficulty in hearing your voice clearly, you may need to talk somewhat louder, and possibly a bit more deliberately than usual, especially when you must use some word such as a proper name that is not familiar to him. For words that are difficult to understand (an example is the proper name Luigs), you should spell the word in this manner: L for *Lincoln,* U for *United,* I for *Iceland,* G for *Gertrude,* S for *Samuel.* For each letter in a hard-to-hear word, use a word that is familiar to the listener.

Numbers, too, are sometimes difficult to understand. When your listener has difficulty understanding a number, you should pronounce each digit rather slowly and enunciate just as clearly as you can. A further suggestion for making clear the number you are pronouncing is to give the two or three numbers that normally precede it. For example, if the listener has difficulty understanding the number *eight,* you may say, "six seven, *eight"* with emphasis on the last digit.

Always use a tone of voice that will help you transmit the information and the feeling that you wish the listener to receive.

Reports

A business report may be defined as a presentation of information that pertains to some element of business. That information can be presented orally or in writing. The business reports that are presented orally are discussed in this chapter.

The person who collects information, analyzes and classifies it, and organizes it so that it can be presented clearly and meaningfully to the listeners is usually the person who is most familiar with the particular matter being reported. He may report to one person or to many persons. His job is to make a thorough study of the business matter under consideration and to present the results of his study *so clearly to his listeners that the report cannot be misunderstood.* To achieve this goal, he must maintain the listeners' attention throughout the report. To maintain the listeners' attention, the reporter must present his information interestingly.

Because no two identical oral reports are made to one audience, the reporter obviously has to have some leeway in his manner of presentation. He does, though, need some guides in preparing and presenting his reports. These ten suggestions should help you to give oral reports effectively.

1. Simplify the data.
2. Make the report concise.
3. Get the listeners' attention early.
4. Present the information in a logical order.
5. Use visual aids effectively.
6. Choose your words carefully.

7. Enunciate clearly and naturally.
8. Give easiest–to–understand information first.
9. Exhibit self–confidence.
10. Talk to your listeners.

This list of suggestions is not exhaustive. A study of them will, however, assist you in laying the groundwork for preparing and presenting good oral reports.

SIMPLIFY THE DATA.   You, the reporter, are responsible for collecting, organizing, and interpreting all information pertaining to your report before you present it. By studying thoroughly the matter under consideration, you will gain an understanding of the problem and the facts you gather to reach a solution. You will, perhaps, have clerical and/or computer assistance in analyzing your data so that you can reach valid decisions. Because in most instances your listeners' backgrounds for this particular report will be significantly more limited than yours, you must do all that you can to simplify the data you present.

Your goal is to make certain that your listeners understand your report. You can take various steps to simplify your data. These steps will be determined by you, the type of report involved, the nature of the information available, and the interests and backgrounds of your listeners.

MAKE THE REPORT CONCISE.   The cost of the time involved for the reporter and the listeners places restrictions on the amount of time that can be allowed for oral reporting. Another factor governing the time that you can afford to use for an oral report is the limited span of concentration of any listener or group. For your report to be effective, therefore, it must be concise. You should present all significant facts so that your listeners understand them, but you must omit nonessential details that do not enhance the clarity or interest of the necessary information. Perhaps you should in most instances be prepared to discuss additional information that one or more of your listeners may wish to have; and you must include all information that is needed for a clear, accurate presentation.

Remember that conciseness and brevity are not the same. Conciseness means that all necessary information is presented and that no unnecessary information is included. Brevity means that only the major points are presented but that more information is needed for a thorough understanding of the full report.

Give *concise* reports. Make them long enough to be complete, yet short enough to be interesting.

GET THE LISTENERS' ATTENTION EARLY.   So that the listeners clearly understand your report, you must get their attention at the beginning of your presentation. The technique you use to get their attention will be governed by many possible factors. Some of these factors are your personality, the personalities of your listeners, and the nature of your report and the exact findings of your study.

Sometimes an appropriate way to get the attention of your listeners is to ask a question that will cause them to begin thinking about your topic. Pause long enough to allow them to do some initial thinking, but do not give them enough time to "set their minds" and be reluctant to accept the report you have carefully prepared.

Another way to cause your listeners to concentrate on the beginning of your report is to make a statement that surprises or startles them.

A third type of beginning that is frequently effective is that of identifying the solution you have reached for the problem and following this statement with your reasons for choosing this solution.

Any beginning must be followed by appropriate comments to create the desired effect and to maintain the listeners' attention.

PRESENT THE INFORMATION IN A LOGICAL ORDER.   A logical order for one report would not necessarily be logical for another. Some information can be presented best in chronological order; some should begin with the *cause* and proceed to the *effect*. Other information may be presented in any one of many other arrangements. Choose the sequence that you believe will seem to be logical to your listeners.

Use visual aids effectively. Visual aids (graphs, charts, tables, maps, and so on,) can be used advantageously in many oral reports. These items provide variety in your presentation, and they present some types of information much more clearly than do words alone. When you use a visual aid, use it in a manner that will cause the listeners to focus their attention *on one spot*. Some of the easy-to-use methods are these:

1. *Illustrations.* Tables, charts, and similar devices can be drawn on a large piece of cardboard or construction paper. Each illustration must be large enough to be seen clearly by each listener.
2. *Screens.* Information can be projected onto the screen by overhead projectors and transparencies, opaque projectors, slide projectors, and movie projectors.
3. *Flip charts.* Illustrations prepared for use as a flip chart can be presented efficiently. The action involved in *efficient* handling of the materials helps to maintain the attention of the listeners.
4. *Flannel boards.* A great deal of flexibility is an attribute of flannel board presentations. Small bits of information can be shown at one time. Parts can be added at appropriate times, and items can be rearranged easily.

Getting everyone in the group to look at a specific item is much easier when their vision is focused on one spot than when they are looking at identical information in different locations, as when reading pages that have been duplicated. Perhaps the presentation that causes the most difficulty in getting all listeners to concentrate on the item on which the reporter is commenting is that of allowing small groups to share one piece of paper containing a visual aid. This situation leads to discussion within the small group, thus causing the participants to miss the points being discussed by the reporter.

Use visual aids when doing so will enable you to present your information more clearly and in less time. Whenever possible, use some type of visual aid that causes the listeners to focus their *attention on one spot*.

CHOOSE YOUR WORDS CAREFULLY. A good vocabulary is a genuine asset to you in any type of communication. Using a good vocabulary does not necessarily mean using a large number of polysyllable words, but it does mean your using the words that help you most to convey or to comprehend messages transmitted through spoken or written words. Continue to enlarge your vocabulary and at the same time practice using the words that seem to be the best for whatever occasion arises.

When you are giving an oral report, you must choose words that will be readily understood by each of your listeners. The words you choose should fit *your* personality and should help you to make your report interesting. Use verbs liberally, and use appropriate descriptive words—adjectives and adverbs—that contribute to the clarity of your report.

Your carefully chosen words should be connected grammatically for clear, easy-to-follow reporting.

ENUNCIATE CLEARLY AND NATURALLY. For any message that you transmit orally, your objective should be that of causing the listener to concentrate on the content and meaning of your message rather than on the manner in which it is presented. Clear enunciation and natural pronunciation are requirements for achieving this objective. Mumbled words cause the listeners to exert so much effort to determine what words have been spoken that they cannot concentrate adequately on the message itself.

Speaking in an unnatural voice or pronouncing words in a manner that suggests affectation causes the listeners to lose interest in the report and to perhaps form an unfavorable impression of the reporter. If the people in your area say "ēither," do not say "īther." Be consistent throughout your report. If you say "prēsentation" one time, do not say "presentation" at some other time in your report. Maintain the respect of your listeners by pronouncing all of your words correctly, clearly, and naturally.

Speak loudly enough to be heard easily, yet quietly enough to make your voice pleasant for the people to whom you are talking.

GIVE EASY–TO–UNDERSTAND INFORMATION FIRST. Even though you do all that you can to simplify your information and to present it as effectively as you can, some parts of your oral report may be easier than others. Try to present the easiest-to-understand information first. This pattern may not be feasible because another arrangement seems to be the most logical for organizing your report. For some reports, however, the presentation of the easiest-to-understand information first may be the report characteristic that enables you to determine the logical approach to use.

Easy-to-understand information encourages your listeners, whereas difficult information early in your report tires them and may cause them to feel that the entire report is difficult to comprehend. Give due consideration to your listeners.

EXHIBIT SELF–CONFIDENCE.   Exhibit self-confidence in making your oral reports. You can develop this needed self-confidence by preparing adequately for your report presentation. Your preparation should include thorough study of the information you collect, careful organization and preparation of visual aids, and a detailed outline for the entire report. Good grooming will also help you to feel self-confident. Wear clothes that fit you comfortably and that cause you to feel that you make a good appearance.

People tend to believe in you as much as you believe in yourself —provided, of course, you do not appear to be cockey or a "smart aleck."

TALK TO YOUR LISTENERS.   Look at the people in your group as you give your oral report. Learn to look directly into the eyes of each listener at various times during your report and avoid looking at one or a few individuals more than at the other listeners. When you are not looking directly at an individual and are not looking at a visual aid you are presenting, look at the group as a whole. Your vision span can include several people at one glance.

The person who looks at the ceiling or into space rather than at his listeners as he makes an oral presentation cannot expect to make that presentation effectively. Looking at your listeners enhances the effectiveness of your reports as much as does your well-modulated voice, self-confidence, command of the language, clear enunciation, or any other characteristic of your oral presentation.

Demonstrations and instructions

Oral communication includes demonstrations of various types. Salesmen frequently demonstrate the uses or the operation of the products, appliances, and machines that they sell. Employees give similar demonstrations for understudies, new employees, and visitors to their offices. Before you begin a demonstration of any type, make sure that you are thoroughly familiar with the items you are to handle and that you have all of the necessary supplies (electrical outlets, and so on) required for an efficient demonstration.

Move through the various steps quickly enough to make it obvious that you are well qualified for your task, but move slowly enough to permit your observers to understand each step. Even though you must spend a good portion of your time looking at the items you are demonstrating, look directly into the eyes of your observers during each pause and while you are answering questions that they ask.

Because you cannot face your audience all of the time during the demonstration, be especially careful to enunciate clearly and to talk loudly enough to be heard easily.

You can enhance the effectiveness of your demonstration by telling your observers what to expect before you actually begin the demonstration. A quick review after the demonstration has been completed increases the effectiveness of that demonstration still further. Allowing an interested observer to go through each step under your supervision oftentimes pays rich dividends when you have finished a demonstration for the purpose of making a sale or of teaching an employee to perform a certain task.

As is true with all other situations involving oral communication, making it easy for the listeners to leave after completing your demonstration helps them to maintain a good attitude toward your work. Do not, therefore, deliberately detain any listener beyond the time that is absolutely necessary to terminate your demonstration.

Meetings

As a dynamic worker, you will perhaps have numerous occasions to preside over meetings. A meeting, such as an interview, may be for two people only; it may be for a large group to whom you will introduce a person who will give an oral report; it may be a company-sponsored club or civic club; or it may be a meeting of members of management with union officials. Regardless of the nature of the meeting or the size of the group, you will want to make a favorable impression on all of those who attend.

Adequate preparation is a prerequisite for success in presiding over any group. Be sure that you know the purpose of the meeting, the organizational structure of the group, and the background for any anticipated business that will require action at the meeting. Knowledge of the organizational structure will help you to determine the degree of formality by which the proceedings should be conducted.

Exhibiting your self-confidence helps the participants to relax and to believe that the leadership of the group is in capable hands. The suggestions for the oral communications (reports, demonstrations, and so on) discussed in the preceding section of this chapter are equally important to your success as a presiding officer. A list of some of those previously discussed suggestions follows:

1. Dress appropriately for the occasion.
2. Choose your words carefully.
3. Pronounce words correctly and naturally.
4. Enunciate clearly.
5. Use good grammar.
6. Modulate your voice so that it is pleasant and easy to listen to.
7. Use gestures appropriately.
8. Be perceptive to the reactions of your listeners.
9. Look into the eyes of your listeners.

For a club meeting or any other group meeting for which formal parliamentary procedures are to be used, follow those in *Robert's Rules of Order Newly Revised* or those that may have been previously adopted for your particular group. Be thoroughly familiar with the rules that are to be followed. The ability to conduct the meeting according to the adopted rules without having to consult the printed source during the proceedings contributes much to your success as a presiding officer.

Discussions

Whether or not you are the presiding officer for the entire meeting, you may be responsible for leading a discussion on a particular topic or for a smaller number from the entire group. Enticing people to discuss the matters that are to be handled can be a challenge. Following a set of "hard-and-fast" rules will tend to formalize the discussion and therefore discourage some people who might participate if an informal atmosphere prevailed. No set of rules can be formulated for leading a discussion. Some suggestions that are usually effective, however, in stimulating participation are:

1. Help the group members to relax.
2. Ask for specific questions.
3. Avoid the trite, "Are there any questions?"

This list is by no means all inclusive, but a study of these suggestions will help you obtain the type of participation you desire.

1. HELP THE GROUP MEMBERS TO RELAX. One way to help members of a group to relax is to direct a question to someone who does not hesitate to talk when he has something that he believes is worth saying. Be sure that the question you ask him is one that he can answer and that his answer will require more than one or two short, simple sentences. Continue this procedure until you have several members of the group involved in the discussion. Their participation will help to relax not only themselves but also the other members of the group. All of them will then be more inclined to continue with comments that will bring out the necessary discussion.

2. ASK FOR SPECIFIC QUESTIONS. After a topic has been discussed by you or someone else and you believe that it should be discussed further, one way to get the members of the group to ask questions for discussion is to call on someone by his name and

say, "What questions do you have about . . .?" Such a question as this tends to cause the person you have addressed to feel that you actually expect him to ask a question; and he will, in most instances, feel free to ask whatever question that comes to his mind.

So that all of the members of the group have an opportunity to ask questions, you may, after you have asked specific persons what questions they have, direct the same statement, "What questions do you have about . . . ," to the entire group rather than to an individual.

3. Avoid the trite "are there any questions?" A poor way to stimulate discussion is to ask the trite question "Are there any questions?" This wording tends to inhibit the listeners. They feel that the person presiding does not actually wish them to participate, but that he merely asked this question to conform to a procedure that is followed by many other people. Only those who are somewhat outspoken or those who have a question that they consider to be of extreme importance will respond to "Are there any questions?" *Do not use this trite question.*

Once the topic has been discussed to the extent you and the other participants feel desirable or the time allotted for the discussion has passed, you must terminate the discussion. You should make a few cordial statements (perhaps express appreciation to the group for their participation) to let them know that the objective of the discussion has been reached. Do not, however, belabor the point. When members of the group realize that the objective has been achieved, they will be ready to leave the meeting. Allow them to leave promptly and gracefully.

Speeches

The person who invites you to speak to a group pays you a compliment by inviting you. He extends the invitation because he and the others in charge of planning the meeting have confidence in your ability to speak. They respect you. They believe that you have something appropriate to say for the occasion, and they believe that you can present your information well. Maintain their respect by preparing adequately for your speech and by presenting it well.

Long before the time you are to speak, do whatever research is needed to collect the desired information. Organize that information so that your listeners can easily understand the points you wish to make. Whether you present your speech by following a set of notes, by reading the entire message, or by speaking without notes but from a careful study of the materials, you should consider the possibility of organizing your speech into these three parts:

1. Tell what you are going to tell.
2. Tell.
3. Tell what you have told.

The title of your speech will have been given to the listeners through means of a printed program or by the person who introduces you, or you will have mentioned the topic before proceeding with your speech. An acceptable way to lead in to a speech is to acknowledge the comments made by the person who introduced you and perhaps to add some humorous comments. Humorous comments are not essential and are not usually included merely to entertain. They are made frequently to get the listeners' attention and to help *them* and the *speaker* to relax.

1. TELL WHAT YOU ARE GOING TO TELL. An effective way to begin is to announce the subtopics of your speech. Through these subtopics you tell the listeners what you are going to tell them. If the points to be covered can be easily separated from one another, you may wish to mention the *number* of suptopics in addition to identifying them. Whether or not you mention the number, you should identify the subtopics. Identify them in the order in which you will discuss them in your speech.

2. TELL. Having told your listeners what you are going to tell, you are ready to proceed with telling them the information that you have prepared. The manner in which you present that information cannot be standardized. The style of your presentation will be governed by many factors. Among them are your personality and manner of speaking, your listeners' interests and

backgrounds, the nature of the information you are presenting, and the occasion for the meeting. Simply presenting facts is seldom a good way to present a speech. You should almost always use illustrations to help clarify or to emphasize the facts you present. These illustrations may be stories (real or fictitious) that relate to your speech, or they may be visual aids of various types. Still other types of illustrations may be used not only to help you to clarify or to emphasize the information you present but also to entertain your listeners.

Listeners have to be entertained. Entertainment may be provided through humor, though using humor is by no means the only way to entertain. Information presented clearly with appropriate illustrations to relate that information to the listeners often provides sufficient entertainment to maintain the listeners' attention throughout your speech.

All of the suggestions for effective oral transmission of messages that have been discussed, and in some instances repeated, throughout the preceding sections of this chapter apply to making speeches. Some of those suggestions are repeated here:

a. Exhibit self–confidence.
b. Dress appropriately for the occasion.
c. Choose your words carefully.
d. Pronounce words correctly and naturally.
e. Enunciate clearly.
f. Use good grammar.
g. Modulate your voice so that it is pleasant and easy to listen to.
h. Use gestures appropriately.
i. Be perceptive to the reactions of your listeners.
j. Look into the eyes of your listeners.

These ten suggestions cannot be overemphasized.

Another characteristic that should be stressed for an effective speaker is *enthusiasm*. Enthusiasm is contagious. The speaker who is enthusiastic about his subject can easily maintain the interest and the respect of his listeners.

3. TELL WHAT YOU HAVE TOLD. The conclusion of your speech should ordinarily be a summary of the main points you have stressed. *Retelling* would be boring. You can at this point, though,

profitably make a quick reference to the main points by mentioning key words that will help the listeners to recall those points and to readily understand how they relate to one another. Hopefully, the relationships will have been made clear as you presented your information; but reinforcing those relationships is usually appropriate at the end of a speech.

Keep your speeches as short as they can be to still cover your topic and subtopics adequately and interestingly enough to maintain the attention of your listeners throughout your speech.

Conclusion

Complete coverage of all the principles that pertain to oral communication is obviously beyond the scope of any one chapter of a book. The suggestions offered in this chapter will, nevertheless, serve as a framework on which you can build your skills for more effective oral communication. Study these suggestions carefully.

Questions for discussion

1. Why should a speaker look at the people in his audience as he delivers a speech?
2. What can an inexperienced speaker do to help himself relax before his audience?
3. What are some of the visual aids besides those mentioned in this chapter that a speaker can use advantageously?
4. What are some of the characteristics of a good speaker? And what are some of the characteristics of a poor speaker?
5. What are some of the factors that a person can utilize to improve the delivery of his well-prepared speech?

Exercises

Improve the following sentences.
1. Can you ship my order before the 21st of July?
2. You will eat Thursday at eleven o'clock.

3. On page 2 of the pamphlet, you will find a description of the new calculator.

4. Please inform us of the exact time of the interview.

5. You will find that brochure is full of many ideas for shortcuts.

6. I should like to take this opportunity to thank you for asking Clara and me to participate in the recruiting project May 17.

7. We cannot send the radio you ordered until January 23.

8. Any of our salesclerks will be glad to be of assistance to you in the selection of the furniture for your new office.

9. Why not mail your check today to take advantage of this special record offer?

10. Not more than thirty-two minutes will be required for the completion of this exercise.

Problems

1. Give a short demonstration (perhaps five minutes) of the use of some small appliance such as an adding machine, a copying machine, an electric drill, a hot comb, a hair dryer, a food chopper, or a vacuum cleaner.

2. Give a short (three-minute) report on your first interview for a job. If you have had no job interview, report on the preparations you will make for the first interview that you will have.

3. Give a three-minute report on the characteristics of a good manager of an office, a department, a factory, or some other unit.

4. Give a three- to five-minute report on the qualifications necessary for some particular job (door-to-door salesman, accountant, secretary, receptionist, grocer, or other).

14

Informal reports

As was stated in the preceding chapter, a business report may be defined as a presentation of information that pertains to some element of business. That information can be presented orally or in writing. Written reports play a vital role in the conduct of business affairs. Some of the reports are written for individuals or groups outside the organization in which they are written; others are written for internal use. Intra-organizational reports flow in upward, downward, or lateral fashion and affect personnel in all levels of the organizational structure.

So that the objective of a report can be reached readily, the report must be written clearly, accurately, and in an appropriate style. Some reports should be presented in an informal manner, though others should be presented formally. Informal business reports are discussed in this chapter; formal business reports are discussed in Chapters 15, 16, and 17.

The objective of the report, the circumstances surrounding it, the intended readers, and the characteristics of the writer are among the most important factors that determine the way information should be presented.

The report on the following page served adequately the purpose for which it was intended. The writer presented the desired information by writing with a pen on a 3 by 5-inch sheet of note paper. The chairman of a department of a university had asked the six other instructors in the department to give him a record of the enrollment for each course they were teaching. These reports were to be presented at the end of the first day classes met for a new term. After all classes had met that day, one instructor, Robert S. Morrison, took this short report to the chairman's office and placed it on his desk. Because this reporting procedure is routine for that department, the information was clearly understood by the receiver of the report. Adding other features (date, receiver's name, and so on) that are ordinarily essential for a good report would have been valueless for this occasion. In fact, additional details would have detracted from the readability of the report.

Such simple reports as this one merit very little space in a textbook that is designed for enhancing the quality of business writing. This report does, though, serve as an excellent example of appropriate presentation for a particular situation.

Frequently recurring types of informal reports that do merit considerable study are memorandums, letters, fill-in forms, and longer documents in which such features as headings and graphics can be combined with expository writing for effective reporting.

Memorandums

Memorandums are used extensively for intra-organizational communications. When the type of information normally transmitted by use of a memorandum is to be sent outside your organization, you should use a letter. Letter reports are discussed in the next division of this chapter.

Because memorandums are for internal usage, they are quite informal in both format and writing style.

FORMAT

When you prepare a memorandum, you should choose a format that contributes to easy reading of your message. Any one of the many existing formats may be appropriate; but to minimize mechanical details in this chapter, only one format is illustrated. Other formats are shown on page 458 in the reference section of this book.

With circulation limited to individuals within your organization, no identifying information such as that for a letterhead is needed. Plain stationery, therefore, should be used. In addition to the word *memorandum*, which is usually centered horizontally about one inch from the top of the page, the guide words *from, to, date,* and *subject* are generally used, as in the illustration on the following page.

Type the guide words in all capitals to make them stand out from the rest of the wording. Triple space between the word *memorandum* and the guide words, which are double spaced, and then triple space between the final guide word and the first line of the message. Single spacing is usually preferred for the message, though double spacing may be used.

Beginning the names, date, and subject lines two spaces beyond the colon that follows the word *subject* makes these items easy to read and simplifies the mechanics of typewriting the memorandum. As the memorandum is to be used inside your organization, it should be characterized by informality in format as well as in writing style. Starting each memorandum about one inch from the top of the page, therefore, is an appropriate placement and is easier to typewrite than if you center it on the page.

Because of the extensive use of the memorandum as an internal communication medium, many organizations use stationery that has the word *memorandum* and the four usual guide words printed on it. This practice saves a considerable amount of time that is required for typewriting, and it obviously governs the

MEMORANDUM

TO: Mr. James E. Miller, Production Manager

FROM: Harold L. Rogers *H.L.R.*

DATE: March 16, 1973

SUBJECT: Materials Handling in The Warehouse

The new procedure you recommended for handling materials in the warehouse
has been approved. I appreciate your studying this problem so thoroughly
and outlining a procedure that seems to have several advantages over the
present one.

Please have the equipment in the warehouse rearranged so that you can begin
the new procedure for handling materials on April 1.

/fgh

placement on the page. As is true for business letters, the second
and succeeding pages of multiple-page memorandums are typewritten on plain stationery.

The appearance, although informal, must be neat, as neatness
contributes to easy reading and thus to good communication.

You may or may not sign the memorandum. To indicate that you have read it after it was typewritten, you may place your initials beside your name, which is typewritten.

WRITING STYLE

Informal, conversational tone should characterize the memorandum. Contractions are appropriate for these internal messages. Clarity, completeness, and accuracy are just as important for internal messages as they are for those that go outside your organization. Always cast your sentences so carefully that ambiguity will be eliminated and proofread carefully to make sure that the figures you use are correct and that your words are spelled correctly so that the ideas you intend to convey are properly interpreted.

Use good grammar; it contributes to good communication. Organize the content of your message in a memorandum, as well as in any other communication medium, to help insure that the information and the emotions you transmit will be "shared" by the reader.

Present your ideas in a logical order. The order in which you present them will be determined by such factors as the circumstances involved, the reader's knowledge of the situation, and your individual writing style.

The subject line should be worded carefully so that a person who reads it will have a reasonably good idea of the major points that are covered in the message. No part of the body of the memorandum should be dependent on the subject line. The message should be written in such a manner that if a reader should overlook the subject line and should read only the body of the memorandum, he would receive the entire message. The subject line is to be used as an introduction only or as a means of locating the desired message at a later time when several memorandums may be filed together. The memorandum body should always be independent of the subject line.

Informal as the memorandum is, good business etiquette requires that the receiver be given a courtesy title—Mr., Miss, or other. A man who sends a message (memorandum, letter, or other medium) always omits his courtesy title (see page 296 and page 458).

Letters

A letter is usually the medium that is used to transmit a short (one- or two-page) business report to someone outside the organization in which that report is prepared. The formats illus-

---

WATERTOWN INTERIOR DECORATORS

Watertown, Maine

March 19, 1973

Mr. George L. Maxwell, Manager
Ranch and Farm Insurance Company
1182 Main Street
Lawrenceburg, Maine

Dear Mr. Maxwell:

Subject: Office Interior Decorating

Here is the report you requested on the work we have contracted
to do for you:

1. The lighting fixtures are in our warehouse and
    can be installed the day your electrical con-
    tractor completes the rewiring of your building.

2. The carpets you selected are being shipped from
    the supplier in Kansas City on March 29. We can
    lay the carpets on the 31st.

3. All of the draperies have been completed and are
    ready to be installed as soon as the carpets have
    been laid. Installing them will require only
    about three hours.

When I drove by your office building yesterday afternoon, I was
very much impressed by the work your contractor has done to the
exterior of the building; and I am glad that we have an opportunity to contribute to the good appearance of the interior.

Please call me when the electrical contractor completes the re-
wiring of your offices.

Cordially yours,

John M. Reynolds

John M. Reynolds
Assistant Manager

/wyc

trated on page 298 and on pages 447 and 448 of the reference section of this book are appropriate for letter reports.

For a quick introduction to the contents of the letter and for easy reference after the letter has been placed among others, a subject line should be used for a letter report. This point is illustrated in the letter on page 298.

The content and the organization of the body of a report that is presented by means of a letter are the same as for a memorandum. The writing style should also be somewhat the same. Always strive to convey your ideas and feelings *so clearly and accurately that they cannot be misunderstood!*

Whether your report is directed to a person within your organization or to someone outside that group, you are trying to make a favorable impression by presenting your message in an *appropriate* manner.

Forms

Government and other external agencies require numerous reports from almost all types of organizations. Constant internal reporting is also taking place among departments, branches, and subsidiaries. Even though the preparation of many of these reports has been simplified by using printed forms, much time and energy is still necessary to furnish the vast amount of information that is called for. Although perhaps nothing can be done to reduce the work involved in reporting to outside agencies, further simplification is needed for internal reporting.

In many instances certain items of information are required for two or more reports. When you design the report forms for recording information, you should attempt to arrange them so that the person who receives your report can easily transfer the information from the form he receives to the one he must complete. For example, if three items on one page of one report can be transferred to one page of another rather than to three pages— one item to the page—of another report, the efficiency in reporting can be increased. The information can be transferred faster and more accurately.

The accompanying forms A and B were used for reporting to

Form A

SCHEDULE OF CLASSES

_____ Quarter, 19___

College of _____

List courses according to the course numbers (lowest number first).

Dept.	Course No.	Code No.	Course Title	Hrs. Cr.	Instructor	Room No.

Form B

SCHEDULE OF CLASSES

_____ Quarter, 19___

List courses according to departments within each college (alphabetical order for departments).

Code No.	Dept.	Course No.	Course Title	Hrs. Cr.	Room No.	Instructor

two offices within the same university. After Form A was revised so that the sequence of the items was the same as for Form B, the person who completed Form B each quarter by transferring information from the other form could complete the task in less time, with less effort, and with a higher degree of accuracy than before the form was revised.

Multiple-page reports

An informal report for any of the types that are discussed in the preceding divisions of this chapter may be longer than one page. Memorandums and letters are seldom two full pages, however. In most instances an informal report that is more than two pages should be written in a style similar to the one described in this division of this chapter. An example of a multi-page report begins on page 302.

As a general rule, busy executives and other employees will, with very little hesitation, spend the time necessary to read a well-written short memorandum or letter. No persuasion is generally required to get them to read the pertinent data contained in a routine form report. Reports of these types can usually be read so quickly that they can be finished without interruption for some other business activity.

The longer the report, the more persuasion is necessary to get the intended reader to read the entire report. Neatness, correctness in spelling and in expressing numbers and ideas, good grammar, logical organization, and interesting writing style are of utmost importance in encouraging people to read business reports. In addition to these features, which have already been discussed in this chapter, some other informal report characteristics that help to encourage people to read these multiple-page reports are discussed in this division. The features discussed are organizing, paragraphing, headings, spacing, illustrating, and footnoting.

ORGANIZING

Good organization is especially important for business reports that are several pages long. The ideas should be presented in a

CARTER HOTEL CONVENTION FACILITIES

Since our hotel was opened on November 15, 1972, we have hosted an average of two and one half conventions a month. The attendance for these meetings has ranged from 73 to 546. In addition to our almost ideal location, other carefully planned, efficiently operated facilities contribute to the unusual appeal that our hotel has for many groups.

Space and Services

Some of our specially planned convention facilities are meeting rooms, exhibit areas, and bedrooms and suites for overnight guests. The provision of outstanding catering service, recreational activities, a large variety of equipment and appliances, and expert handling of room reservations and registration activities enhance the appeal of our hotel as a convention site for a group of any size from *eight* to *eight hundred*.

Meeting Rooms

All of the meeting rooms are on the first floor of the east wing and have easy access to the corridors, the rest rooms, the exhibit area, the parking lot, and the registration area. Each of the *nine* meeting rooms is fully carpeted, well lighted, and expertly decorated. The electrical outlets are spaced so that any ordinary appliance or piece of equipment can be used in any section of the room.

Each room is equipped with a temperature control switch and a switch that permits the occupants to adjust the brightness of the lights to produce the desired effect for whatever activity is under way. The seating can be arranged for dining, and it can be arranged in auditorium style or in conference style. Some rooms are designed to be used individually; others can be combined.

Individual Usage.—Five of the meeting rooms are used individually. Each room will seat twenty persons in a conference room arrangement or forty persons when the chairs are arranged in auditorium style.

Meals are served in only one of these small rooms; twenty persons can be served in that room.

Combinations.—Four meeting rooms can be used individually, or any of them can be combined by opening the folding doors that separate them. Each of these rooms will seat seventy-five persons for dining or 150 persons by arranging the chairs in auditorium style.

Exhibit Area

A large exhibit area that is 120 by 130 feet is between the group of five small meeting rooms and the group of four large meeting rooms. This location is ideal for organizations meeting in any of these nine rooms. The electrical outlets are spaced 10 feet apart across the entire exhibit area.

Our sales manager will instruct Jason Decorators, a local organization, to provide any special items that you need for your convention exhibits.

Bedrooms and Suites

All of our 600 spacious guest rooms and suites have shag carpets and Mediterranean style furnishings. Each room is equipped with a color television, a radio, and a direct-dial telephone. Standard-size beds are in the 300 rooms that have two beds. Queen-size beds are in the 290 rooms that have one bed each.

The ten suites—each of which consists of a large parlor, a bedroom, two bathrooms, and two dressing rooms—have queen-size beds.

Catering

The banquets, luncheons, breakfasts, receptions, etc., at our hotel are catered by the Lacy Catering Service, a nationally known organization. Our sales manager can arrange an appointment for any group representative to discuss menus. For any menu that you choose, the food will be excellent; and the price will be reasonable.

Recreation

Our recreation manager will reserve tickets for you to take the regularly scheduled tours of the city, and he will arrange special tours for groups of four or more. He will also reserve tickets for you to any of the local theatres. We are within five blocks of the three leading theatres in the city. High-calibre music and floor shows are provided nightly in our main dining room.

Reservations

All you have to do to reserve bedrooms for your convention participants is to send us a list of their names and addresses. Or if you prefer that they make their own room reservations, we will send you a supply of forms that they may use. We will confirm each reservation within one week from the time we receive it.

Registration

We provide tables, typewriters, and any other equipment you may need to register those who attend your convention. An area in the main lobby is set aside for registration.

You may deposit the money you collect for registration fees in our safe for overnight protection.

Summary

The five small meeting rooms, the four large meeting rooms, the 600 bedrooms and suites—along with the ideally situated exhibit area—accommodate large conventions as well as small ones. These physical features; the recreation we provide; and such services as catering, handling the reservations, and handling the registration activities account for the fact that we have hosted an average of two and one half conventions a month since we opened our hotel on November 15, 1972.

logical order so that the readers can grasp them easily. The readers should know what to expect in the report.

These previously given three steps apply equally to written and to oral reports:

1. Tell what you are going to tell.
2. Tell.
3. Tell what you have told.

Following the title of your report, which should be typewritten in all capitals and centered horizontally near the top of the page, should be a few statements that will get the readers' attention and help to cause them to become interested in the content of your report. You are then ready to introduce the key ideas that are presented in the body of the report.

1. TELL WHAT YOU ARE GOING TO TELL. By introducing the topics that are covered in your report, you prepare the reader for the body of your report. You can introduce the topics in such a manner that the reader will be interested in reading them. This plan also helps you to present your message in a logical, well-organized way.

2. TELL. Having told your readers what you are going to tell, you are ready to present the information that you wish them to read. Discuss the topics in the order in which you introduced them. The degree of thoroughness with which you cover your topics should, of course, be determined by the purpose of the report and the other factors involved.

3. TELL WHAT YOU HAVE TOLD. Conclude your report by summarizing the key points you have presented in the body. A short summary of the topics you have discussed serves as a quick review and as a desirable reinforcement for the ideas. This type of ending also helps the readers to perceive the proper relationships that exist among the major points.

This plan of *tell what you are going to tell, tell,* and *tell what you have told* is almost always appropriate for a multiple–page report. This plan provides for flexibility. No two sets of circumstances from which reports arise are identical; therefore, no two reports should be identical..

PARAGRAPHING

A page of information that is divided into rather short paragraphs can be read much more easily than can the same information that is presented in what appears to be one very long paragraph. Careful paragraphing also encourages people to read the material you have written. Although the content of your report is the major factor in determining the division of your information into paragraphs, you can to some extent arbitrarily divide the information so that a logical arrangement allows you to use short paragraphs. Vary the lengths of your paragraphs. Some of them should be very short, while others should be somewhat longer. Excessive use of short paragraphs may cause the reader to think that the report is poorly constructed or that it contains only fragments of the information that it should contain.

You can also use paragraph lengths advantageously to emphasize certain points in your report. When you have used several fairly long paragraphs, you may use an extremely short one to emphasize an idea. You may, on the other hand, use a longer-than-usual paragraph to emphasize an idea. Some long paragraphs are necessary to permit you to include supporting facts or illustrations for the key ideas.

Appropriate paragraphing not only encourages the readers to read your report, but it also helps them to "grasp" more of the content of your report than they would if a less satisfactory paragraphing plan were used.

HEADINGS

When you are to write a report that is several pages long, you will be wise to remember the principle that length breeds length; that is, adding features such as headings that contribute to easy reading is essential. Such features encourage busy executives to read these longer reports immediately rather than to defer reading them until other shorter tasks have been completed.

Headings to indicate divisions of the information add significantly to the readability of the multiple-page report. When the reader can see at a glance that some plan was used to organize the information, he is encouraged to read the report. Use headings appropriately.

Use headings to highlight key points that are presented. By organizing your report well, you will probably have two or more paragraphs that follow each heading. In some cases, however, a heading may be needed for only one paragraph.

The content of a division must always be independent of the heading that it follows. The headings are included in the report to help portray the organization of the material, to encourage the receiver of the report to read it, and to provide stopping places if the reader must interrupt the reading of the report before completing it. Headings help him to locate the point at which he is to resume reading after the interruption. They also help him to locate specific sections that he wishes to *reread* later.

The person who reads the text of a report but skips the headings should obtain as thorough an understanding of the report content as he would if he were to read the headings as well as the text. This means that the heading must be restated or paraphrased in the body of the division or subdivision that follows the heading. This key word or phrase should be included in the topic sentence, which ordinarily comes early in the first paragraph, for that division. Although the topic sentence is often the first sentence of the paragraph, this arrangement should be varied to help provide variety in writing style and in the order of presentation that contribute to making the report interesting.

Use short headings that are indicative of the key ideas of the paragraphs that follow them. Use consistent, parallel styles for headings. Typewrite them so that they stand out from the text of the report and are easy to read. A good plan to follow is to typewrite the headings in upper- and lower-case letters and *underline* them. They may be centered horizontally or typewritten flush with the left margin. Both of these placements may be used—the center heading to indicate a division and the left-margin heading to indicate a subdivision. A third-level heading would begin at the paragraph indentation and would be *underlined* and followed by a period and two spaces, or it would be followed by a period and a dash. The first sentence of the paragraph follows on the same line. Merely *underlining* the key word or phrase in the first sentence of a paragraph would be proper for indicating a fourth-level heading.

The headings may be typewritten in red if the typewriter on which the report is typewritten is equipped with a two-color (black and red) ribbon. Whether you double space or single space the report, you should triple space before the heading and double space after it.

SPACING

Multiple-page reports may be single spaced or double spaced. Possibly your choice for spacing would be determined by the preference of your readers, if you know that they have a preference. Your choice of spacing may also be determined by the amount of space that is available or the number of pages you can afford to use if you are mailing copies to several people. Double spacing can cause the report to be a few pages longer than it would be if it were single spaced, thus leading to additional expense for postage as well as for stationery.

Parts of a report can be spaced in such a way that specific points are emphasized. For example, the information in one section can be highlighted by single spacing that part if the rest of the report is double spaced. Also, that special part can be typewritten with shorter lines than are used for the major portion of the report.

A major principle to remember is that the pages of a report should never be crowded. Alternating text and graphic illustrations helps to keep the pages "open" and causes them to appear to be easy to read. Leave ample margins. This practice helps to avoid a crowded appearance, and it provides space for readers to make short notations when they wish to do so.

ILLUSTRATING

Illustrations contribute a great deal to the clarity, interest, and readability of a report. Use illustrations that will help the readers to understand and to appreciate the ideas that you wish to convey.

You may use illustrations (analogies, stories, actual cases, and so on) in narrative style; and you may use such graphic aids as maps, tables, charts, graphs, drawings, and photographs. Graphic presentations are discussed in detail in Chapter 16.

FOOTNOTING

From time to time you may wish to use footnotes to indicate sources of information for your report. Footnote usage and preparation are discussed in Chapter 17. To illustrate a correct method of footnoting various types of sources of information, some examples are given on pages 428 and 429 of the reference section of this book. On pages 373 and 387, some footnotes are shown to illustrate the proper placement on the pages of a report.

Other informal reports

The instructions given in the preceding paragraphs for writing informal reports apply also to preparing leaflets, pamphlets, brochures, and other similar reports. For a report that is to be printed, you should consider the possibility of including color to enhance the appearance of the report and to help encourage people to read it. Colored headings, stationery, and illustrations of various types may be used. Appropriately used color is the characteristic that contributes most to wide readership of a long business report that is prepared for a large audience.

Questions for discussion

1. What are the advantages of using memorandums instead of letters for internal communication mediums?
2. How are headings in informal reports related to captions on file folders?
3. Why is a study of forms important for increasing the effectiveness of your communications?
4. What are some examples of informal reports that were not mentioned in this chapter?
5. How can you apply the *word-processing* concept to recurring types of informal reports?

Exercises

Improve the following sentences that were taken from business letters.

1. A description of the saw can be found on page 9 of the enclosed brochure.
2. The audit will require a short period of time.
3. I have received your check in the amount of $14.00.
4. My secretary will be more than happy to be of assistance to you.
5. Enclosed you will find a copy of the letter that I mailed to Mr. Ralph Ralston under the date of October 1.
6. We will be able to ship your order promptly.
7. Please return the enclosed form as soon as possible.
8. The president informed me that the group will meet January 30.
9. Your statement for the month of June is correct in every detail.
10. Why not use the self-addressed envelope for mailing your check in the amount of $15.00.

Problems

1. You are the administrative manager of a large organization. In the past the clerical employees were paid every other Friday. Beginning next month, they will be paid twice a month. They will be paid on the 15th, and they will be paid again on the last day of the month.

   In the past they have had to go to the payroll office to get their paychecks. All future paychecks will be delivered to them.

   Write a memorandum that can be duplicated and sent to each clerical worker in your organization.

2. The president of the large organization by whom you are employed asked you to find out how the office workers in your organization feel about the plans that have been used in the past to schedule vacations. As administrative manager, you have obtained that information. As you would expect, some of the employees like those plans; others do not like them. You should give the president some of the reasons for their preferences.

   Write a memorandum to the president and give him the information he should have.

3. The president of the large organization for whom you are doing some consulting work is considering the possibility of investing a

large sum of money in word-processing equipment. He has asked you to collect, as a preliminary part of the feasibility study that will be conducted, the following information: the number of employees who dictate at least ten letters a week, the number of people who transcribe at least ten letters a week, the number of typewriters in the offices, the number of individual dictating and transcribing machines in the offices, and the number of pages (letters, memorandums, and reports) that were typewritten last month.

Write a letter to the president and give him that information. Address the letter to T. Carroll Heilman, Southeast Insurance Company, P. O. Box 1722, Kingsville, Tennessee.

4. Write a complete, clear set of instructions for the operation, care and maintenance of some type of appliance or piece of equipment (an office machine, a household appliance, a lawn mower, or some other item). Use headings and *possibly* some type of graphic aid that would help the user of the item to follow the instructions that you write.

5. The manager of each department of the organization for whom you work has been asked· to prepare a procedures manual for his department. Assume that you are an office worker in the personnel office, the purchasing office, the printing office, or the mailing department. Write a detailed description of a procedure that you follow regularly to complete some particular task. Write the description so clearly that a new employee could follow the procedure you describe without further instructions.

This report will be combined with the others that are being prepared for the manual for your department.

15

Formal reports

CLARITY, completeness, conciseness, consideration for the reader, and other basic principles of writing apply to all written communication mediums—letters, memorandums, formal reports, and others. The principle that is perhaps most inclusive and therefore of first importance is that of appropriateness for the occasion.

The letter is obviously the appropriate medium for most short, written messages that are transmitted to individuals outside your organization. Likewise, the memorandum is the appropriate medium for most short, informal, written messages to personnel within your group. Some business conditions require extensive study that leads to the writing of rather long, detailed messages. Such messages are usually presented best by means of a formal report.

Formal reports may be directed to persons within the organization in which they are written or to persons outside that group. The reports that are prepared for internal use are almost always directed to an individual or a group on a level of the organizational structure that is higher than the level on which the report writer is employed. Whether the report is intended for external or for internal organizational use, the writer must exert special efforts to present his report in such a manner that the readers will be favorably impressed by it. Oftentimes the written messages are the only communication mediums that an employee can use to transmit messages to certain individuals either inside or outside his organization.

Prepare messages that represent you well. By doing so, you will have the personal satisfaction that comes from excellence in performance of your duties; and continued good reporting will help win for you the confidence of your superiors. The business employee who writes well has a distinct advantage over his peers who are equally well qualified except for the ability to write well. Always put your best foot forward when writing a message of any kind.

Before you decide on the type of medium you will use to present your message, you must have a thorough understanding of the use that is to be made of that message. By knowing that objective, you can determine the most appropriate medium to use and then begin preparing to write. For presenting some messages, the formal report is the medium that you should use.

In this chapter some of the ways of collecting and processing information and some of the ways of preparing outlines for formal business reports are discussed. Methods of presenting information by means of formal business reports are discussed in Chapters 16 and 17.

Collecting information

You should feel complimented when you are requested to write a report. The person who asks you to perform this task believes that you have the ability to study the conditions adequately and to submit a report that is clear and will help him to reach the decisions that he must make.

Whether you have been assigned the task of writing a formal report or whether you have chosen to write it on your own initiative, you will have some valuable information that you have accumulated through your experiences. Otherwise you would not have been asked to write the report; neither would you feel competent to initiate the writing project. You will, in almost all instances, though, recognize the need to obtain additional data.

Numerous sources of information are available for business reports. A thorough understanding of the objective to be achieved by your report will help you to determine whether to collect primary data, secondary data, or some of both types.

Primary data

Primary data are usually collected by observing, interrogating, or experimenting. You may need to use a combination of two or three of these methods for obtaining primary data for some business reports.

Observing.   Much valuable information can be obtained by observing certain activities. Office consultants or other personnel may observe the work of office employees when a systems and procedures study is under way. Marketing analysts sometimes study the traffic flows inside a specific store, among stores within a specified section of a city, or along the sidewalks.

Helpful data can be collected by observing numerous other activities. The two examples mentioned here are only representative of the types of studies that may include data that are collected by this means of research.

One person may make all of the observations, observers may work in pairs or in possibly larger groups, or they may alternate so that one person or a group of people would work during certain hours or days and others would work at other times. The observers may use a prepared checklist for recording the data they collect, or they may jot down notes about the activities they see without using a prepared list of items. The objective of the study, the types of activities to be observed, and the work habits of the researchers are some of the factors that determine the procedures that should be followed when collecting information by this method of research.

Interrogating.   Interrogating is a popular method of collecting data for some types of business reports. Questions may be asked orally during personal interviews or telephone interviews, or they may be submitted in writing.

Some advantages of asking the questions during a personal *interview* are these:

1. You have an opportunity to explain fully the reason for asking the questions, and you therefore usually obtain full cooperation from the interviewee.
2. You have an opportunity to explain the meaning of any question that may possibly contain some element of ambiguity.
3. You get immediate responses to your questions, thus expediting the process of collecting information.
4. Through this method of asking questions, you frequently obtain valuable data that you are not actively seeking.

A major disadvantage of collecting information by means of a personal interview is the expense involved. The time required for conducting the interview (time for both the interviewer and the interviewee) and the time required for traveling make this method too expensive for use when a large number of people are to be interrogated and when they are scattered over a wide geographic area. The expense then places restrictions on the number of people who can be interviewed and the geographic area that can be included in your study.

When you collect information through personal interviews, you should prepare a list of questions to take with you. This list will enable you to make sure that you ask the same questions to all interviewees. These questions should be arranged in a logical order and should be arranged in such a way that will permit you to record your answers rapidly and accurately.

Answers to questions such as the following can be recorded easily:

1. How many office employees do you have?
   _____ Women
   _____ Men
2. What factors do you consider in selecting office employees?
   _____ Appearance
   _____ Letter of application
   _____ Personal recommendations
   _____ Scholastic average
   _____ Voice
   _____ Work experience
   _____ Other _____

Other arrangements for prepared questions and answers are also appropriate for the interview method of collecting information.

Some interviews can be conducted by telephone. Use the same type of list of questions for telephone interviews that you use for personal interviews. You can obtain some types of information more readily when talking with the interviewee in person than on the telephone, but you can interview many more people and cover a much larger geographic area by telephone than through personal interviews. When comparing these two methods of interviewing, the telephone method is obviously less expensive.

A major portion of the business information that is collected by interrogating is obtained by mailing lists of questions. When only a few questions are asked (one to five perhaps), a return postal card or a letter in which the questions are numbered is probably the best way of presenting them. The illustration on this page is an example of a postal card that contains five questions.

```
1.  How many people five years old or older reside
    in your home? _____

2.  What type of TV set do you own?
    _____color      _____black and white

3.  What style TV set do you own?
    _____console    _____portable

4.  How old is your TV set?
    _____0-3 yrs.    _____3-6 yrs.    _____6 yrs. or
                                                 older
5.  Have you ever had TV cable service?
    _____yes      _____no
```

A postal card questionnaire

When you use a letter to collect data, you should enclose an addressed, postage-paid envelope for the addressee to use when sending the answers to you. The return portion of the postal card will, of course, have adequate postage and must include the name and address of the person who is to receive the answers that have been requested. The principles that you should follow in constructing the questions and in explaining your reason for asking them are the same as the principles you should follow when preparing a questionnaire. Study the following paragraphs before you construct a questionnaire.

To collect a sufficient quantity of reliable data by the use of a *questionnaire,* you must construct your questionnaire carefully. Among the most important points to be followed in preparing a questionnaire are these:

1. State each question clearly—*so clearly that it cannot be misunderstood!* To write that clearly, you must use only the words with which each reader is familiar. Each word in your questionnaire must be used in such a way that each reader will interpret its meaning the same way that you interpret it in the context in which it is used. Word the question carefully so that each reader will interpret the question in the way you intend for him to interpret it.

2. Ask only those questions that the recipients will be willing to answer. Omit those questions that the recipients hesitate to answer because of their religious, political, or personal views. Many people will not answer questions pertaining to ages, income, or financial status.

3. Arrange the questions in a logical order with the easy–to–answer questions first. This arrangement encourages recipients to complete the questionnaire. After they have answered almost all of the questions, they will be more likely to answer one or more hard–to–answer questions near the end of the list than they would if the more difficult questions were asked early in the list. When a person is confronted with a difficult–to–answer question near the beginning of a questionnaire, he tends to believe that a major portion of the questions are difficult to answer and therefore is inclined to discard the questionnaire rather than complete it and return it to you. Many questionnaire recipients have to refer to their records for answers to some of the questions in a list. They are often not willing to do this extra work unless they have already answered a major portion of the questions on your list.

4. Make it easy for the recipient to record his answer to each question. When you can supply several possible answers so that the recipient can specify his answer by merely placing a check mark by one of the answers you have supplied, you should use this arrangement. When there is a possibility that his answer would not be one of those you have supplied, provide a space for him to write his short answer to the question as in the following example:

What was your job title on your most recent full-time job?

_____ Accountant	_____ Stenographer
_____ File Clerk	_____ Typist
_____ Secretary	_____ Other (specify) _____

When a check mark can be placed by a range such as those in the example that follows, people are more inclined to supply the desired information than if you ask for a specific figure.

What is your age?

_____ 16–18 (years)	_____ 39–48
_____ 19–28	_____ 49 or older
_____ 29–38	

When a question cannot be answered by using a simple check mark, ask for some other very short answer. People hesitate to write long answers. A question that requires a long answer causes some recipients to omit that particular question or to give an incomplete answer; it causes others to decline to complete any part of the questionnaire.

5. Provide an open-ended question. After you have listed all of the questions you wish to obtain answers for, end your question series by including a question that permits the questionnaire recipient to write whatever he wishes to add. Some recipients like to use this space to provide additional information that they believe is pertinent to the study. Some of them like to use the space to give reasons for the answers they have recorded to the other questions.

Restrict the length of your questionnaire. When you can limit it to one page and still maintain an attractive arrangement that is easy to read, you should limit it to one page. Attractiveness and an arrangement that helps the recipient to realize that the questionnaire is short and easy to fill out encourages him to comply with your request to complete the questionnaire and return it to you.

Your questionnaire must be duplicated well on good quality paper. Expensive bond paper is not necessary, but some grade of stationery on which the recipient can write easily and clearly is essential.

Clearly written, concise instructions for answering should precede the list of questions. The instructions may also include a statement that the recipient need not identify himself unless he wishes to receive a summary of the findings of your research. He should be assured that whether or not he gives his name and address, he will not be identified in the report that will be written as a result of your questionnaire study. Instructions for returning

BRADLEY MANUFACTURING COMPANY
Waterford, NJ 08099

_____

_____
_____
_____

_____:

To complete the information that we must have to decide whether
to open a branch office in Sidney, will you please fill out the
enclosed questionnaire?

We were pleased to learn from your local employment office that
you are available for office work. If we decide to open an
office in Sidney, we will send you an application form by May 1.

The addressed, postage-paid envelope that is enclosed is for
your use in returning the questionnaire, which will require only
a few minutes of your time to complete. Your returning the completed questionnaire by March 10 will be very much appreciated.

                    Cordially yours,

                    Ellis G. Graham

                    Ellis G. Graham
                    Personnel Manager

msb

Enclosures 2

the completed questionnaire may be included on the same page as the questions, though this is not absolutely necessary when the transmittal letter gives these complete instructions.

You should send a letter of transmittal with your questionnaire. That letter should cause the recipient to develop an interest in

---

BRADLEY MANUFACTURING COMPANY
Waterford, NJ 08099

AVAILABILITY OF OFFICE WORKERS IN SIDNEY

Please answer the following nine questions by placing check marks in the appropriate spaces and by writing in the answer to question 5. You may need to write in answers to questions 2 and 3.

1. How many years have you worked full time?
    _____ 1-3   _____ 10-12   _____ 19-21
    _____ 4-6   _____ 13-15   _____ 22-24
    _____ 7-9   _____ 16-18   _____ 25 or more

2. For what type(s) of organization(s) have you worked full time?
    _____ Banking   _____ Retailing
    _____ Educational   _____ Service
    _____ Manufacturing   _____ Other (specify)_____

3. What was your job title on your most recent full-time job?
    _____ Accountant   _____ Stenographer
    _____ File Clerk   _____ Typist
    _____ Secretary   _____ Other (specify)_____

4. What was your monthly salary the last year you worked full time?
    _____ 201-300 (dollars)   _____ 501-600
    _____ 301-400   _____ 601 or more
    _____ 401-500

5. What was the most recent year that you worked full time?_____

6. What is the highest level of education you have attained?
    _____ High School Diploma _____ Two years of college
    _____ Business College   _____ Three years of college
    _____ One year of college _____ Bachelor's Degree

7. What is your marital status?
    _____ Single   _____ Separated
    _____ Married   _____ Divorced
    _____ Widowed

8. What is your age?
    _____ 16-18 (years)   _____ 39-48
    _____ 19-28   _____ 49 or older
    _____ 29-38

9. Specify the type of office work for which you are best qualified. Use the back of this sheet if you need to.

your questionnaire survey and should tell him how he can benefit by participating in it. When the study pertains to some element of business that affects him, your offering to send him a summary of your findings may very well be the best thing you could offer to do for him to show your appreciation for his help. For some studies your offer to reciprocate may be the best way for you to show appreciation for his responding to your questionnaire. In some instances you may offer to send a small gift to each recipient who returns a completed questionnaire. The conditions that apply to your survey and to the recipients' interest in it will, of course, help you to determine an appropriate offer to make in response to the recipients' assistance.

You should assure the recipient of your questionnaire that his answers will be treated confidentially. Do enclose an addressed, postage-paid envelope for his use in returning the completed questionnaire. Refer to this enclosure, of course, and make a courteous request for him to provide the desired information.

Study the transmittal letter and the questionnaire on pages 319 and 320.

EXPERIMENTING. Some business information can be obtained through experimenting; however, this method, which is highly important in the physical sciences field, is used much less frequently than observing and interrogating in business research.

As a business report writer, you should consider the possibilities of using any one or a combination of any of these three methods—observing, interrogating, and experimenting—of collecting primary data when you begin the task of collecting the information necessary to write a report.

SECONDARY DATA

Various sources of secondary data, those data that have been collected by someone else, are available to you. Books, periodicals, directories, letters, business reports, financial statements, and other records are among these sources.

As a writer of business reports, you should become familiar with more and more publications that are in the reference departments of libraries. The more you know about the types of information that are available, the more thoroughly you can study the conditions on which you must report. The records of your own organization as well as those of other groups contain much valuable information for your use. Sometimes you must write a report that is identical in purpose and design to one that has been written in another organization.

By studying the completed report, you can write your own report, which will be different so far as facts and figures are concerned, much easier than you can by having to determine your own procedures and to construct your own research instruments (questionnaires, formulas, experimental designs, and so on). When using secondary data in this manner, you are of course bound by ethics to give credit to the assistance you received by referring to these documents. Footnotes are used to give proper credit for this help. Footnote usage is discussed on page 364.

Processing information

Once the information needed for a business report has been collected, it must be tabulated, analyzed, and organized for presenting it appropriately to the intended readers.

TABULATING

Tabulating may be required for some secondary data. The major tabulating task, however, is in the processing of primary data. With the widespread use of computers, the tabulating task can usually be performed in a computing center. This facility saves a tremendous amount of time, and it provides for a high degree of accuracy. Even with this help, the report writer is sometimes responsible for coding the information that he records on a check list or that he receives in answer to the questions he asked in a letter, a postal card message, or a questionnaire. He may even be required to transfer the coded data from the original source document (letter, questionnaire, and others) to the input medium (tape, punched card, or other) for the computer. The report writer who must perform these tabulating tasks should consult an operator in the particular computing center in which the data will be processed for specific instructions for performing the coding function.

The report writer is usually responsible for tabulating small quantities of data. He may actually perform this detailed task, or he may instruct clerical workers to do the tabulating. For quick and easy tabulation and analysis of the small quantity of data that were obtained by the postal card questionnaire on page 316, which was completed by fifteen recipients, the information may be coded and tabulated in the form that is in the following illustration.

Answers to postal card questionnaire (fifteen responses)

	Question number							Question number			
	1	*2*	*3*	*4*	*5*			*1*	*2*	*3*	*4*	*5*
1.	5	c	c	0	n		9.	3	c	p	3	n
2.	3	c	c	3	n		10.	3	c	p	3	n
3.	2	c	p	3	n		11.	4	b	c	6	y
4.	2	c	p	3	n		12.	6	c	c	3	y
5.	3	c	c	3	y		13.	2	c	p	3	n
6.	2	c	c	3	n		14.	3	c	p	3	y
7.	5	b	c	6	n		15.	4	c	p	6	n
8.	4	b	c	6	y							

Key to answers to questions:
1. actual number given
2. c = color; b = black and white
3. c = console; p = portable
4. 0 = 0–3 yrs.; 3 = 3–6 yrs.; 6 = 6 yrs. or older
5. y = yes; n = no

By studying this tabulation, you can see that respondent No. 8, for example, had four people five years old or older residing in his home; he had a black and white TV; the TV was a console model; the TV was six years old or older; and the respondent had had TV cable service.

From this type of tabulation, you can make whatever cross tabulations you wish to make. For example, you may like to show how many people who had color TV have had TV cable service. You can obtain that information by cross tabulating the "c" answers to question 2 with the "y" answers to question 5.

ANALYZING

By cross tabulating the answers to the questions you have asked, you can see relationships that exist between answers to any two questions. By studying an analysis of this type, you can see that some relationships are *meaningful* while others are *meaningless*. Those relationships that have no value can usually be omitted from the report. Because some readers would believe that such an analysis would reveal significant findings, however, some of them should be presented. By referring to them in the proper place in the report body, you may appropriately include the detailed analysis that seemed to be of little significance in the appendix of the report. Further discussion of the report appendix section and its use begins on page 358.

Organizing

Data that have a significant bearing on your business report may be presented through exposition or by using graphic aids along with expository writing. These methods of presenting data are discussed in Chapters 16 and 17.

Outlining

A good outline helps the writer to present his information in proper order, and it helps make the writing task easy. The alphanumeric (or alphameric style that is illustrated in the following skeleton outline is only one of several correct styles, but it is popular and is easy to use:

        I.
            A.
            B.
    II.
            A.
                    1.
                    2.
                    3.
            B.
    III.
            A.
            B.
            C.

IV.
  A.
  B.
    1.
    2.
      a.
      b.
      c.
    3.
V.
VI.
  A.
  B.
  C.
    1.
      a.
      b.
        (1)
        (2)
    2.
VII.
  A.
    1.
      a.
        (1)
          (*a*)
          (*b*)
        (2)
      b.
    2.
  B.

An obvious fact that is sometimes overlooked when an outline is being constructed is that at least two parts are created when an item is divided. For example, when the information for a Roman numeral is divided, at least two letters (A and B) must follow. The information for either letter can then be further divided into two or more parts.

As is illustrated in the foregoing skeleton outline, dividing any one part does not necessitate dividing any other part of equal rank.

You may use this alphanumeric style for either a topic outline or a detailed outline. The topic outline, which includes only a word or a short phrase for each division, is usually sufficient for a simple report, for a recurring type of report, or for even the more involved reports that are written by experienced writers. An example of a topic outline follows:

ESTABLISHING A SALES AND SERVICE OFFICE

    I. Introduction
        A. Purpose of the study
        B. Research method
        C. Limitations of the study
        D. Sales and service facilities
        E. Expected growth in city, businesses, and schools
    II. Calculators and adding machines
        A. Calculators in schools
            1. Rotary
                a. Electric
                b. Manual
            2. Printing
            3. Key-driven
        B. Calculators in offices
        C. Adding machines in offices and schools
    III. Dictating and transcribing machines
        A. Age
        B. Extent of usage
    IV. Duplicators
    V. Other appliances
        A. Typewriters
        B. Posting machines
    VI. Conclusion
        A. Summary
        B. Conclusions
        C. Recommendations

A topic outline is sometimes expanded into a detailed outline, which is a step nearer the completed copy of the report. A detailed outline such as the following example is especially helpful for an inexperienced report writer and for an experienced writer of some types of reports that are new to him:

ESTABLISHING A SALES AND SERVICE CENTER

   I. For an organization to operate most efficiently, its facilities should be located near the sites at which services are required.

      A. This study of office machines was made to secure information needed to determine whether or not Office Equipment, Inc., should establish a sales and service office in Scioto Falls, Ohio.

      B. A questionnaire survey was conducted to determine the status of existing services and facilities.

      C. The schools and the offices that employed at least ten persons were included in this survey.

      D. Only one office machines company has a sales office in Scioto Falls. The nearest service organization is 65 miles away.

      E. An additional high school is to be built within the next two years. With two large manufacturing concerns building plants in Scioto Falls within the next three years, the city population is expected to increase from 33,000 to some 41,000 by 1977.

  II. The three city high schools and the 21 offices included in the survey own a variety of brands of calculators and adding machines.

      A. Each high school offers an office machines course.

          1. The schools have four brands of rotary calculators.

             a. Almost all of the rotary calculators are electric models.

             b. Two schools still have a few old models of manual calculators.

          2. More printing calculators than any other kind have been purchased during the past three years.

          3. The key–driven calculators are used for demonstrations only.

      B. All of the offices have some printing and some rotary calculators.

      C. The offices and the schools have both ten-key and full-keyboard adding machines that are in good condition.

 III. The offices and the schools have only a limited number of dictating and transcribing machines.

      A. Most of the dictating and transcribing machines are old.

B.   The dictating and transcribing machines are not used extensively in Scioto Falls.

IV.   One high school and seven large offices have offset duplicators as well as stencil and spirit duplicators; the two other schools and the small offices have spirit duplicators only.

V.   The other machines that are used extensively are typewriters and posting machines.

A.   About 80 percent of the typewriters are electric models; the schools still have some manual typewriters.

B.   Three brands of posting machines are used in the small offices only.

Questions for discussion

1.   What are some types of business data that can be gathered by experimenting?

2.   Why should you prepare an outline of your report before you begin writing it?

3.   Why might a business report writer need to be familiar with more than one outlining scheme?

4.   What steps can you take to eliminate ambiguity from the questions that you include in a questionnaire?

5.   What factors must you consider when determining the format that you will use for a questionnaire that you will prepare?

Exercises

Improve the following sentences that were taken from business letters.

1.   Installation of the equipment will require about eight minutes.

2.   In order to collect the desired information, I shall use a questionnaire.

3.   We are collecting the information for the purpose of being prepared to make a sound decision.

4.   I believe that this guide will prove to be helpful to you in outlining.

5.   A copy of the report that you requested in your recent letter is enclosed herewith.

6.   I am sending you a copy of the report under separate cover.

7. I want to thank you for sending me a copy of the report.

8. Why not consider the possibilities of the installation of a larger computer than the one you are now using?

9. Due to the fact that the schedule was changed, we will be able to attend the meeting.

10. If I can be of further assistance to you, please do not hesitate to contact me.

Problems

1. You are the director of student employment on your campus. During the past six years your students have worked during the summer vacations for a large number of organizations throughout your region. So that you can learn more about the way the students have performed and so that you will be better prepared to help students obtain summer jobs in the future, prepare a postal card questionnaire for mailing.

2. You are planning to invite seniors from a large number of high schools to come to your campus to compete in a typewriting contest. Write a letter that you can mail to the typewriting teachers in the high schools to collect information that will help you to determine the type of contest to conduct. Ask a minimum of five questions in your letter.

   You can obtain valuable information by mailing these letters. After all, the primary purpose of the contest is to encourage high school students to visit your campus. Hopefully, this visit will encourage them to enroll in your college next year. You will not, of course, mention this objective in your letter.

3. You have decided to open a variety store in a small college town. The two suitable places that are available for rent are just about equal so far as size, appearance, layout, and general condition are concerned. You are trying to decide which of the two places to choose. They are in separate sections of the downtown area.

   You have decided to collect information about pedestrian traffic in the two areas. This information may be what you need to choose between the two available places. Prepare the checklist that you will have duplicated for use by the people who will observe the traffic flows for you.

4. You are the director of student employment on your campus. So that you will be better prepared to help students secure part-time

jobs, you will interview the personnel managers of several large local organizations. Prepare the checklist that you will duplicate and use during these interviews.

5. You are the director of the co-op program for the business students in your school. The students in this program work full time one year between each two years of college. They work in various types of organizations in several states. Some of them hope to continue on a full–time basis with their employers after graduation from college.

    This co-op program is gaining in popularity with the students. You need to know about more opportunities for them. Prepare a questionnaire to be duplicated and mailed to organizations that may be interested in participating in this co-op program. Also, write the transmittal letter with which you will mail the questionnaire.

16

Using graphic aids

AFTER collecting, tabulating, and studying the information for your report and after preparing an outline, you are ready to decide which ways are best for presenting the information to your readers. You will obviously use expository writing for at least part of the presentation. You can use various types of graphic aids to enhance the clarity, the interest, and the readability of some of your reports.

At least *three* items are required for a graphic aid of any type. When only two items are to be presented, a compound subject, a compound object, or a compound sentence is the best device to use for presenting them.

A very useful device for presenting simple data is the informal table (sometimes referred to as a *text table* because it is presented as a part of the text to which it is connected). An informal table may consist of a simple list of items, or it may have two or more columns. While such a table may have column headings and column totals, it has no table number or title; and it is not ruled. This type of table is preceded by a lead–in sentence that is usually followed by a colon. Some examples follow.

The agent handles these four types of insurance policies:

collision
fire
life
medical

The brands studied and the number of employees who preferred each brand follow:

Royal............................. 27
Olivetti.......................... 16
Smith-Corona.................... 11

The replies are shown by the employee classifications as follows:

Classification	Yes	No
Typist......................	26	17
File clerk...................	21	11
Stenographer...............	12	23
Secretary...................	5	8
Totals................	64	59

Seldom does an informal table consist of more than three columns. Data that require more than three columns can usually be presented more effectively by use of some other type of graphic aid. Among the most frequently used graphics are *formal tables, pie charts, bar charts, pictograms, line graphs,* and *maps.* The best way to choose the type of graphic aid that will serve best as a supplement to your expository writing is to consider the nature of the information you are presenting, the purpose for which you are presenting that information, and the characteristics of the intended readers of your report.

To use graphic aids effectively, you must have a thorough understanding of how they are constructed, the kinds of information that can be depicted clearly through them, and how they should be interpreted.

Constructing

The six graphic aids (formal tables, pie charts, bar charts, and the others) that are discussed in this section have these common characteristics of construction: (1) number, (2) title, (3) footnotes, and (4) source notation.

1. Number.   Graphics contain especially important information to which reference will be made before, during, and after the first reading of the entire business report. They should, therefore, be numbered so that they can be referred to easily.

When formal tables and other graphics (pie charts, line graphs, and others) are used in one report, two sequences of numbers are required. One sequence is required for the formal tables; the other sequence, for all other graphics. For example, if a report contains two formal tables, one pie chart, and one bar chart, the formal tables should be numbered Table 1 and Table 2; and the pie chart and the bar chart should be numbered Figure 1 and Figure 2.

Formal tables and other graphics may be intermixed; for example, Table 2 of four tables may be presented between Figure 3 and Figure 4. Tables and other graphics are intermixed in the skeleton report that is appended to Chapter 17.

Arabic numerals should ordinarily be used for each sequence. Roman numerals may, however, be used for formal tables, provided only a few such tables are used. High Roman numerals cannot be read so easily as Arabic numerals; therefore, Roman numerals should not be used for a large number of tables.

2. Title.   Each graphic must be given a title. The title should be concisely and carefully worded to indicate the nature of the information that the graphic contains. The questions *what, when, where,* and *how classified* should usually be answered by the carefully worded title. The title should be typewritten in upper-case letters 2 spaces below the graphic number. The double ruling at the top of the formal table should be typed two spaces below the title. Titles for charts or graphs should be 2 spaces above the chart or graph. (See Table 1 on page 377 and Figure 2 on page 338.

Even though information that is typewritten in all upper–case letters is more difficult to read than that which is typewritten in upper– and lower–case style, titles for graphics are emphasized when they are typewritten in upper–case style and are easily recognized as a part of the graphic instead of part of the exposition when graphics and expository writing are presented on the same page.

To facilitate the reading of these upper-case words, the titles should be arranged in short lines of varying lengths. The in-

verted pyramid arrangement as in the following illustration
should be used when practicable:

PRINTING AND ROTARY CALCULATORS IN OFFICES
IN SCIOTO FALLS, OHIO
JUNE, 1973

When this arrangement is not practicable, normal pyramid
style or an arrangement that would permit the alternating of
longer and shorter lines should be used. Examples of each of
these two arrangements follow:

REPAIR OF CALCULATORS AND TYPEWRITERS
IN SCIOTO FALLS OFFICES AND SCHOOLS IN 1973

LETTER STYLES USED MOST OFTEN
BY SELECTED ORGANIZATIONS IN TENNESSEE
IN 1973

3. FOOTNOTES. The meaning of some information that is included in a graphic aid is clear to the report readers only when
it is explained by a footnote. Use a footnote, therefore, to clarify
such information. The footnotes should be typewritten two spaces
below the body of the graphic. Single space footnotes that are
longer than one line and double space between the footnotes
when two or more are used for one graphic aid. The line length
of the footnote should be approximately the same as the width of
the graphic aid. The first line of each footnote should be indented.

A footnote may be indicated by using an asterisk, a number, or
a letter of the alphabet. An asterisk may be used with words or
figures and *should be used* when both *figures* and *ideas expressed
by words* are to be explained. Asterisks may be used for all footnotes unless the number of footnotes that are used is rather large.

When several footnotes are used to explain figures, letters of
the alphabet should be used as superscripts. When several footnotes are used to explain information expressed in words, figures
should be used as superscripts. Figures and letters as superscripts
(footnote indicators) should not be intermixed, however, for any
graphic aid.

Footnotes are numbered consecutively for each graphic aid.

Any symbol (asterisk, letter, or number) may be used once, therefore, for each graphic aid.

4. SOURCE NOTATION.   Ordinarily, a notation should be made about two spaces below the body of the graphic (or two spaces below the final footnote when footnotes are used) to specify the source of the information that is presented in the graphic (see the source notation for Figure 2 on the following page). If the information for *all* of the graphics in one business report came from one source and that fact is explained in the introductory section of the business report, the source notation may be omitted from *all* of the graphics in that report.

In the following paragraphs *special characteristics* are presented for each of the six graphics—formal tables, pie charts, bar charts, pictograms, line graphs, and maps—that are discussed in this chapter.

FORMAL TABLE

A formal table is perhaps the most frequently used graphic (or visual aid) for business reports. This table can be used to show large quantities of data, and it can be used to present data that are more specific than can be presented by the use of any other graphic aid.

Columns can be arranged to show percentages as well as figures for various items. Percentages can be carried several places beyond the decimal point. When the percentages are obtained from a sampling, however, one or two places beyond the decimal would be adequate to show meaningful calculations.

Columns can be arranged in the formal table to show comparisons very clearly. The table should have fewer columns than items that are shown under the first column heading for the body of the table.

Each formal table should begin with a double line and end with a double line. Single lines are used (1) to separate a spanner heading from the column headings, (2) to separate column headings from the body of the table, (3) to indicate that the table is continued on the following page, and (4) to separate the body of the table from the totals (when totals are included). The ruling and careful spacing of the parts of a formal table contribute a great deal to the clarity of the information that is presented by this popular type of graphic (or visual aid). Study the format of the table on this page. Other mechanical details that help to make the table easy to read are illustrated in the four tables that are in the skeleton report, which begins on page 367.

The mechanical details presented in the four tables in the skeleton report are as follows:

Table 1 on page 377
1. A spanner heading over column headings.
2. Lengthwise arrangement on the page when the table is too wide to be typewritten across the page.
3. Insertion so that the *top* of the table is toward the binding when the table is arranged lengthwise on the page.
4. Items grouped in threes with double spacing between each two groups.
5. Ruling for a table more than one page long (a single line at the bottom of the page with a double ruling at the beginning of the following page).
6. Inclusion of the table number but not the title on the second and succeeding pages for a table more than one page long.
7. Spacing of part of a table that does not fill a whole page.
8. Alphabetic listing of items.

TABLE 1. Foreign Automobiles owned by students in nine Northwestern Universities, Summer, 1973

| | *Number* | | *Percent* | |
Make	*Men*	*Women*	*Men*	*Women*
Marc......................	187	176	18.0	18.7
Super-A...................	185	161	17.8	17.1
Jaurez....................	165	159	15.9	16.9
Karato...................	157	150	15.1	15.9
Toyette..................	153	139	14.8	14.8
Le Oui...................	98	76	9.4	8.1
MacKelsy.................	67	58	6.4	6.1
Other*...................	23	19	2.2	2.0
Totals.............	1,035	938	99.6	99.6

* No more than six people owned any one of the eight makes included in this classification.

Source: Campus automobile registration offices.

Table 2 on page 379

1. Placing short tables within the text material on a page.
2. Spacing between first double ruling and single ruling under column heads when only one line is required for column heads.
3. Double spacing of table items when only a few items are included.

Table 3 on page 381

1. Two spanner headings and two columns for percentages.
2. Grouping items in fives with double spacing between each two groups.
3. Descending order for listing of items (except "other," which was listed last) .
4. More than one footnote for the table.
5. Placing a large table on a page separate from the exposition.

Table 4 on page 385

1. Column heading designating "dollar" entries.
2. No total line at the bottom of the table.
3. Double spacing of items when only a few items are included.
4. One footnote for the table.
5. Placing a table at the bottom of the page.

The only time you can begin a table on a page that contains expository writing or another graphic aid is when you can complete that table on the page on which you begin it.

PIE CHART

A pie chart is a helpful device for presenting simple data. This graphic, which is given a number and a title and may contain a source notation and footnotes, has those four characteristics of a formal table; but the simplicity of the data it contains is characteristic of an informal table.

A pie chart is used for presenting 100 percent of the data that are concerned. This type of chart helps the report reader to see at a glance (1) the relationship of each part of the chart to the whole and (2) the relationship of each part to each of the other parts. This colorful graphic aid gets the readers' attention, adds to the attractiveness of the report, and provides a "change of pace" that is desirable for long reports.

So that a pie chart can be read easily, the following mechanical details, which are illustrated in the example on the next page, should be observed when you construct this type of graphic aid.

1.   The first and largest section of the pie should begin at the "twelve o'clock" position, and the sections should be shown in descending order. When several figures are combined to form a section labeled "other" or "miscellaneous," that section should be last in the sequence even though it is larger than some of the other sections. This arrangement is followed because no individual group of figures in the "other" or

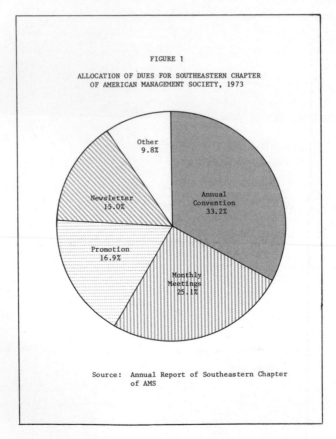

FIGURE 1

ALLOCATION OF DUES FOR SOUTHEASTERN CHAPTER
OF AMERICAN MANAGEMENT SOCIETY, 1973

Other
9.8%

Annual
Convention
33.2%

Newsletter
15.0%

Promotion
16.9%

Monthly
Meetings
25.1%

Source: Annual Report of Southeastern Chapter
of AMS

"miscellaneous" section would constitute a section as large as the smallest section that is in the pie chart.

2. A minimum of three sections should be in each chart.

3. The number of sections should be limited to perhaps five or six. When more divisions are needed, another type of graphic aid should be used instead of the pie chart.

4. Each section should be colored or shaded, and each section should have a color or shading pattern different from all other sections.

5. Areas immediately surrounding the section designations should not be colored.

6. The section designations must be typewritten in *one* reading position; that is, the reader must not be required to adjust the page as he reads the various section designations.

7. The outside line should be heavier than the lines that separate the sections.

8. When a section is too small to accommodate the necessary designation, that designation should be placed outside the pie with an arrow pointed to the section to which it pertains.

FIGURE 2

DISTRIBUTION OF MONTHLY INCOME FOR FAMILY A
JANUARY, 1973

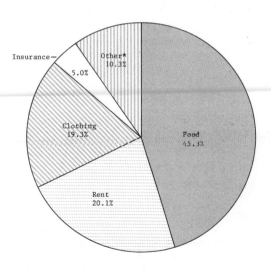

*No item in this classification amounted to more than 3.0 percent.

Source: Interview with husband and wife of Family A

Lines at the usual page margins (as on the preceding page) may add to the attractiveness of the page. Such lines are not *required,* however.

LINE GRAPH

A line graph is a useful device for presenting data that represent a time span. Trends for a limited number of items can be depicted quite well with this graphic aid. The number of items that can be included depends somewhat on the figures that the lines represent; for example, if two or more lines should follow the same path, confusion would result. Another type of graphic should be used, therefore, for that body of data. The lines may *cross,* however, without causing any difficulty in interpreting the data that are presented. A line that represents a particular item should be of a color or pattern that is different from any other line in the line graph.

To show the true relationships that exist among the data that the lines represent, draw those lines on paper that has been ruled in *squares* rather than in *rectangles.*

The base of the graph should represent times (years, months,

FIGURE 3

PIANO PURCHASES BY TYPES OF CUSTOMERS
IN SHADES VALLEY, WEST VIRGINIA
1969-1973

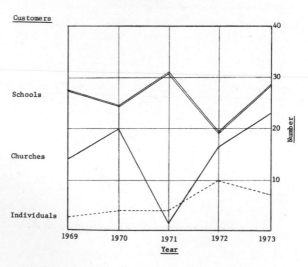

Source: Records of Pianos, Inc.

weeks, days, hours, and so on) ; the side should represent the other measures (dollars, pounds, bushels, and so on) that you wish to depict.

For easy reading, the lines that represent the data should be heavier than the lines that form the squares of the graph. Study the construction of the line graph on the next page.

BAR CHART

Comparisons and relationships that exist among figures can be shown by a bar chart. To show these comparisons and relationships properly, the bars that represent the variables should be the same width; and they should be of the same color or shading pattern. The *lengths* should be drawn to indicate the figures that the bars represent (see Figure 4 below).

Because the readers' attention is directed to the bars, each bar should be wider than the space between any two bars.

The base should represent one set of variables such as dates, classes, states, or others; the side should represent another set of variables such as dollars, tons, or gallons.

FIGURE 4

DAILY AVERAGE TEMPERATURES IN WOLF CITY, VERMONT
FEBRUARY 1-7, 1973

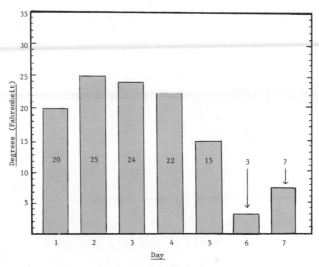

Source: Wolf City Weather Station Records

Several items can be shown in one bar chart. When the number of items that are included requires the use of a large chart, very light leader lines such as those in the chart on the preceding page can be used to contribute to easy reading. Whether the chart is large or small, entering within the bars the figures that the bars represent helps the readers to see at a glance the actual figures as well as the relationships that are shown by the bar lengths. When the bars are too short to accommodate the figures, you should write the figures above the bars and draw an arrow pointing to the bar to which the figure belongs (see Figure 4 on page 341.

The bars can be single or double. Double bars, which should be drawn side by side as in the example on the following page, are very useful for showing two classes of data such as those data for the two sexes, for two periods, or for two departments. A legend is frequently needed to explain what each part of the double bar represents. This legend should be drawn the same width as the bars of the chart and should be presented within the lines that surround the body of the chart.

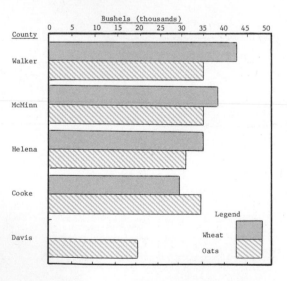

FIGURE 5

GRAIN PRODUCTION IN A FIVE-COUNTY AREA
OF SOUTHEAST KANSAS, 1973

Source: Agricultural Extension Service Records

The bars may be drawn vertically or horizontally. Vertical bars help to show clearly the types of figures that rise and fall such as prices, temperatures, and production. Horizontal bars are often used to represent items that expand and contract such as concrete and metal. For some charts the direction in which the bars should be drawn would be determined by the amount of space needed and the amount available for the chart.

The bars should be shown in a logical arrangement. Descending order is often the most logical arrangement. For some charts, however, alphabetical order, chronological order, or some other arrangement may be most logical and therefore most easily interpreted by the readers of your report.

PICTOGRAM

A pictogram is essentially the same as the bar chart; that is, these two graphic aids are used to present the same types of data. The mechanics of construction are the same for both of them with one exception: in the pictogram the data are presented by means of simply drawn pictures rather than by means of bars. With this construction the information presented in the pictogram is somewhat less specific than that presented in a bar chart.

FIGURE 6

THREE-BEDROOM HOUSES CONSTRUCTED
BY H & H CONSTRUCTION COMPANY
1969-1973

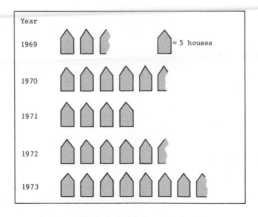

Source: Files of H & H Construction Company

One advantage of using the pictogram, however, is that it attracts attention more readily, especially by readers who may have only a casual interest in the report; that is, they are interested in seeing the information but are not required to make a major business decision based on that information.

Pictograms are used more frequently perhaps in reports that are directed to the general public than in those that go to a small group of readers inside the organization for which the business report was written.

An example of a pictogram is on page 343.

MAP

A map is a useful device for showing some types of information. The map may cover a large area such as the United States; or it may cover smaller areas such as a region, a state, a county, a city, or a city block. The information can be presented in a variety of ways. Some examples of the ways in which information can be shown on a map follow:

1. *Dots* can be placed on the map so that each dot shows the location of a particular type of business establishment, and so forth.

FIGURE 7

STATES REPRESENTED BY REPRESENTATIVE B
OF SCOFIELD PAPER COMPANY
1973

Source: Sales Manager's Files

2. A part of the map can be *shaded or colored* to indicate the geographic area that is served by a particular office, representative, and so on.

3. *Lines* can be drawn to indicate routes of various types.

The shaded part of the map on the preceding page represents the geographic area that is assigned to a sales representative for a large distributor of paper products.

Interpreting

Even though you can use graphic aids to present information in an easy-to-read manner for most readers, some of the readers of your report will probably need some assistance in interpreting part of that information. As an effective communicator, you must provide through expository writing the statements that will enable the readers to interpret properly the information you present. Without your comments the readers may not recognize some significant meanings that your data provide.

Another reason for interpreting your graphic aids through expository writing is that some readers of business reports do not pay close attention to graphic aids, and some of them have difficulty interpreting information that is presented in this manner. Too, some of the readers know so little about the particular data your report contains, you must give them some interpretative comments so that they see the information in its true perspective. For these reasons you must write an interpretation of each formal table, chart, or graph that you include in your formal business report.

Some readers like to refer to a graphic aid as they read your interpretation of it. You should, therefore, place the graphic aid within the text of the report; and you should place it near the expository writing that you include as an interpretation. Each graphic aid must be introduced *before* it is discussed. Some of the effective ways by which a graphic aid may be introduced are illustrated in the examples that follow:

> The brands of rotary calculators purchased by Scioto Falls schools in 1973 are shown in Figure 1 on page 4.

Calculators in Scioto Falls offices are classified by age in Table 1 on page 6.

The data in Table 4 indicate that 66 of the posting machines have a trade-in value of $500 or more each. (In this case the table is on the same page with the introduction; therefore, the page number is omitted.)

A glance at Figure 3 reveals a steady increase in the number of purchases of ten-key electric adding machines from 1969 through 1972. (Figure 2 is on the same page as the introduction.)

Use variety in introducing the graphic aids in your formal business reports.

When the spacing permits, the sequence of introducing the graphic aid, presenting it, and then interpreting it is the preferred order to follow. Because of spacing limitations, however, this order has to be adjusted in many reports. *Without exception,* though, the graphic aid is always introduced before it is presented or interpreted.

When space permits, place a small graphic aid on the same page with its interpretation. This arrangement enables the reader to refer to it easily as he reads your interpretation. When a graphic aid cannot be placed on the page with its introduction, it must be placed on the following page. In such a case the graphic aid has to follow your interpretation, or it has to be placed within the text of your interpretation.

Various arrangements (presenting the graphic before interpreting it, presenting the graphic within the interpretative comments, and presenting the graphic after it is interpreted) are depicted in the skeleton report that is appended to Chapter 17. (See pages 374, 376, and 379 for examples of the arrangements that are described in this paragraph.)

Because of the varying types of information depicted in graphic aids, because of the different objectives of the reports in which graphic aids are used, and because of differences in reactions among readers of formal business reports, no set of strict instructions can be given for interpreting the information that is presented in a graphic aid.

The report situation will govern the report writer's task of interpreting. Some factors that you should ordinarily consider when starting to interpret a graphic aid are these:

extremes
high and low figures
second to high and second to low figures
similarities
mean
median
mode
total number of items
number of classifications in the graphic aid

Never would the inclusion of all of these nine suggested factors be appropriate for the interpretation of any one graphic aid. The ones that should be included are those that seem to be most significant for the particular report that you are writing. In your interpretation point the readers' attention to the most significant items in such a manner that your interpretation will help him to see the proper significance of the information that is presented.

Specific figures should be shown in tables, charts, and graphics; though restating these *specifics* in the interpretation should be avoided in nontechnical data. Unless a survey included 100 percent of the population of the universe studied, the data could be no more than an approximation, anyway. The readers of nontechnical data are ordinarily more concerned with close approximations than with specifics. Therefore, instead of stating "The product was used by 31.2 percent of the townspeople," write such statements as, "The product was used by slightly more than 30 percent of the townspeople." You may convert such percentages to fractions for readers who would probably grasp the meaning more easily and quickly by reading fractions; for example, "The product was used by almost one third of the townspeople."

Approximations that are used appropriately help readers to understand and to remember proper relationships and meanings of data.

In some reports approximations must *not* be used; for example, a packer is planning to ship frozen foods by refrigerated trucks or railway cars. The foods must be transported in compartments in which the temperature never exceeds 32°F. You must not, in this situation, tell the representatives of the firm contracting for the transportation that the temperature in the refrigerated compartments ranges from 25°F to approximately 30°F when the high is actually 33°F. Such a statement could cause the reader to make a decision that would be very costly. If he should note this fallacy as he studies the graphic aid as well as your interpretative comments, he would probably lose faith in your reporting.

The unbiased writer can help make the meaning of data immediately apparent by using interpretative comments. For example, he could write, "Only 18 calculators were sold in Athens in 1972," rather than merely stating the fact, "Eighteen calculators were sold in Athens in 1972." By including the word *only,* the unbiased writer would be telling the readers that eighteen is a small figure in comparison to expectations, in comparison to other periods, or in comparison to other items that were sold.

Instead of stating, "Fifteen calculators were purchased by schools in May," the writer could state, "Surprisingly, fifteen calculators were purchased by schools in May." The second statement would not only serve as an interpretative comment; it would also present the fact more interestingly than would the first statement.

Interpretative comments such as these must, of course, be used judiciously. Remember that the purpose of your interpretation of a graphic aid is to cause the readers of your report to understand quickly the significance or proper meaning of the information that you have studied very carefully.

Questions for discussion

1. What are some graphic aids not mentioned in this chapter that can be used advantageously to depict information in some formal reports?
2. In what ways does the inclusion of visual aids encourage many readers to read a long formal report?
3. Why should an interpretation be written for each visual aid that you present in a formal business report?
4. What are some of the advantages of coloring rather than shading the various segments of pie charts and bar charts?

5. What are some of the advantages of shading rather than coloring the various segments of pie charts and bar charts?

Exercises

Improve the following sentences that were taken from business letters.
1. You are justified in making a complaint about the defective fountain pen you purchased at our store recently.
2. Please correct an error of $25.00 in my account.
3. The letter was mailed May 18.
4. In reply to your recent letter, I am enclosing a copy of our catalog.
5. Enclosed herewith is a check in the amount of $27.00.
6. A statement for the month of April is enclosed under separate cover.
7. Please return the completed form as soon as possible.
8. I believe the suggestions on page 4 will be of benefit to you.
9. Being an outstanding businessman, I shall appreciate your advice on which stocks I should purchase.
10. The chairman asked Sam, Harold, and myself to study the situation.

Problems

1. Prepare a line graph to show the enrollment trends for three colleges of the Western State University, Omaha, Oregon, from 1969 to 1974. You received the following enrollment figures from the records in the registrar's office:

> College of Business Administration—700 students in 1969; 1000, 1970; 1300, 1971; 2800, 1972; 4,000, 1973; 5000, 1974
>
> College of Home Economics—200 students in 1969; 200, 1970; 1000, 1971; 1500, 1972; 1500, 1973; 1500, 1974
>
> College of Liberal Arts—2100 students in 1969; 2200, 1970; 2600, 1971; 2600, 1972; 2600, 1973; 2000, 1974

2. Prepare a line graph to show the figures for grain production in White County, Oklahoma, for the years 1930, 1940, 1950, 1960, and

1970. The following figures were obtained from the White County Department of Statistics:

Corn—2800 bushels in 1930; 2800, 1940; 3200, 1950; 3600, 1960; 4000, 1970

Wheat—2000 bushels in 1930; 2500, 1940; 2500, 1950; 3000, 1960; 4000, 1970

Oats—1400 bushels in 1930; 1500, 1940; 1900, 1950; 1000, 1960; 700, 1970

3. You learned from the 1973 edition of *Producer's Almanac* that our country produced coal and steel in the following quantities for the period 1968 through 1972:

Year	Coal	Steel
1968	5 tons	10 tons
1969	10 tons	12 tons
1970	12 tons	12 tons
1971	17 tons	12 tons
1972	19 tons	25 tons

Present this information in a bar chart.

4. According to the following figures that you obtained from records in the admissions office of your school, the total enrollment has increased almost every year since 1967:

In 1967 the total enrollment was 1700; in 1968, 1850; in 1969, 1951; in 1970, 2250; in 1971, 2100; in 1972, 2300.

Present this information in a bar chart.

5. If you do not know the amount of money you spent for school expenses last year, estimate the amount. Estimate the percentage of that sum that was spent for each of the following items: rent, books, clothing, recreation, transportation, and meals at school. Present this information in a pie chart.

6. By studying the personnel records of the Thomas Manufacturing Company last week, you learned the length of service each employee had with that company. Those who had worked less than 5 years were 18 men and 31 women; 5–10 years, 23 men and 28 women; 10–15 years, 37 men and 21 women; 15–20 years, 41 men and 17 women; 20–25 years, 17 men and 3 women; 25–30 years, 8 men and 4 women; 35 or more years, 10 men and 2 women.

Present this information in a formal table. Show not only the *number* of men and women in each classification of length of service but also the *percentage* of men and women in each classification of length of service.

7. Write an introduction and an interpretation for the line graph that you prepared for Problem 1.

8. Write an introduction and an interpretation for the formal table that you prepared for Problem 6.

17

Writing a formal report

WHETHER OR NOT you use graphic aids to supplement the expository writing in a formal business report, you must give careful consideration to your writing style. You must strive to present your information in an interesting, easy-to-read, and easy-to-understand form for your readers.

Remember that your report represents you. You should also remember that because the internal formal report goes to someone on a higher level of the organizational structure than you are on, he is a person whose salary is higher than yours. The organization for which you work cannot afford to pay him to decipher facts and figures that it pays you to present clearly to him and to other readers. Almost without an exception a formal business report is read by several readers, and it is read more than once by some of them. Some readers read only parts of the report, and some of those who read the entire report also reread parts of it from time to time. Knowing that parts of your report will be read at various times helps you to realize the importance of having the finished copy properly organized and clearly and interestingly written.

To present your report in the most effective manner possible, you must give careful consideration to the design or organization, the methods of presenting the information, and the format and appearance of the finished copy.

Organization

A formal business report consists of four major parts: preliminary pages, introductory section, presentation of the data, and reference materials. These major parts may typically include the elements listed in the following outline.

I. Preliminary pages
    A. Letter of transmittal
    B. Title page
    C. Table of contents
    D. List of tables and/or illustrations*
    E. Summary
    F. Conclusions
    G. Recommendations
II. Introductory section
    A. Statement of the purpose *or* objective of the study
    B. Description of the research method
    C. Other introductory information
III. Presentation of the data†
    A. Exposition
    B. Graphics
IV. Reference materials
    A. Bibliography
    B. Appendix

The report elements presented in the preceding outline are discussed in the order in which they would probably be written. Then at the end of this chapter a skeleton report is presented to illustrate the organization and the format of a formal business report that contains the elements discussed in this chapter.

---

* Frequently omitted.

† May be presented in one or more major divisions.

Introductory section

An introductory section containing background information should precede the body (presentation of data section) of a formal business report. The usual subdivisions of this introductory section are a statement of the purpose *or* the objective of the report and a description of the research method. The other subdivisions that are used vary somewhat among reports.

STATEMENT OF THE PURPOSE OR OBJECTIVE OF THE REPORT. The first item to be prepared for the introductory section of a nonroutine formal business report prepared for management or for an outside agency should be a clear, concise statement of the purpose *or* the objective of the report. One well-constructed sentence is ordinarily best for this particular subdivision. In a few instances more than one sentence may be needed.

DESCRIPTION OF THE RESEARCH METHOD. Ordinarily the statement of the purpose of the report should be followed by a description of the research method used for that report. For simple routine reports the description may be condensed to a very brief statement. When very complex methods of research are used for a report, the research method may be described in detail in the appendix with a summarized description in the introductory section. In such a case the summarized description must include a statement referring to the details in the appendix.

For nonroutine reports the research method should be so clearly described that a reader could redo the research if he should choose to do so. Such a detailed description will help him to evaluate the validity of your research findings.

Only in the *simplest routine* reports can the description of the research method be omitted, and only in *rare* instances should the research method be described in the appendix.

OTHER INTRODUCTORY INFORMATION. At some point in the introductory section, information that tells who authorized the report should be included. This information, which is sometimes included in the transmittal letter when the letter is bound with the report, causes some readers to pay more careful or prompt attention to the report than they would if it were omitted.

In many reports you may need to call certain limitations of the report to the readers' attention. You may need to define terms that are used with special meanings for the report, and you may need to review some history of the events that preceded the report. If other research has been done that relates to that which you have done for your report, you may need to refer to that research. Such references may be the type of recognition you should give for help you have obtained; or if the results of that work are not applicable to your report, you may wish to use this reference to let your readers know that you have examined the results of the other research and that they were of no value for your report.

Omitting this reference could cause some reader to believe that you could have benefitted by studying the other research findings as well as the methods that were used for it.

Headings indicating some types of background information that may be appropriate in a formal business report are included in the skeleton report that begins on page 367. You should never include in any section any information that does not contribute in some way to the effectiveness of your report.

PRESENTATION OF THE DATA

You should present the findings of your study in the order of their importance. Sometimes the order of importance is the same order that you followed in listing the questions for a report that is based on a questionnaire study or on an interview method of research. Even though the findings may be presented in the order in which the questions were asked, you should not ordinarily re-state the questions in the text of the report. Often, replies to two or more questions can be combined under one heading in the text.

As a reference must be made in the body of the report to each exhibit in the appendix, the readers will know that the questionnaire is included in the appendix and can, if they desire, refer to the questionnaire for the exact wording of the questions.

As has been stated earlier, you may present the data through exposition entirely or through a combination of expository writing and graphics.

PRELIMINARY PAGES

After you complete the body of your report, you are ready to prepare the preliminary pages. These pages often include the summary, the conclusions, the recommendations, a table of contents, a list of graphics, a title page, and a letter of transmittal.

SUMMARY. All of the significant findings of the study should be summarized and placed on a page or on as many pages as are needed following the table of contents or the list of figures, if such a list is included in the report. The summary, like all other elements of the report, must be presented as concisely as possible and in a clear, interesting, and easy–to–read style. The summary should include a restatement of the purpose of the report and of any of the significant facts that are in the body of the report. The summary must not contain any information that is not presented in the report body.

To make the summary appear to be short and therefore to encourage people to read it, you should single space it even though you may have used double spacing for the report text.

CONCLUSIONS. Unless otherwise directed, the report writer is expected to draw conclusions and to make recommendations. By summarizing all of the significant findings, you can base your conclusions on the information in the summary section. Analyze each finding thoroughly and study all possible relationships that may exist among them. On the basis of this thorough study, draw conclusions that are not only logical but are also valid.

Number the conclusions and state them in such a way that the readers can easily understand their meanings. When a conclusion is based on more than one finding, you may also number the findings and place in parentheses beside the conclusion the numbers of the findings on which the conclusion is based.

RECOMMENDATIONS. Any recommendations that you make should be based on the conclusions, and obviously on the findings, drawn from your study. When you make alternate recommendations, you should present them in the order of feasibility according to your best judgment. Number the recommendations.

The summary, the conclusions, and the recommendations (all of which should be single spaced) may be presented on one page when space permits.

TABLE OF CONTENTS AND LISTS OF FIGURES. A table of contents showing the page number for each organizational heading and each first–degree subject–matter heading should precede the introductory section of the report. Third-degree headings are usually omitted from the table of contents.

Frequently, neither a list of tables nor a list of figures is needed in the report. However, for long reports that contain numerous graphics to which frequent references will likely be made after the first reading of the report, such lists may be desirable. When such lists are included, they should be placed on the page with the table of contents if space permits. A list of tables and a list of figures have been included in the skeleton report on page 369 to illustrate the format that should be used when these lists are included.

TITLE PAGE.   A title page containing the report title, the date on which the report was submitted, the name of the report writer, and the name of the principal reader or department for which the report was written should precede the summary page. These *four* items of information plus any other items that may be specified by the person authorizing the study should be arranged in a manner that will produce an attractive, easy-to-read title page. The title, which should be typewritten in all capitals, should be concise and descriptive of the report contents. The report title and the statement of the purpose *or* objective of the report should contain the same information. These two items will, however, differ in wording. The title should, in most instances, be a phrase; the statement of the purpose of the report should be a complete sentence.

LETTER OF TRANSMITTAL.   Use a letter of transmittal to submit the report to the person for whom you prepare it. When the letter contains information that should be transmitted to only the person who authorized the report or some other person who is to be the principal reader of the report, the letter should be attached to the report title page by means of a paper clip. That letter should contain sufficient reference to the report to make it easy for anyone who reads the letter after it has been detached to identify the report to which it was originally attached.

When the letter contains information that should be available to all readers, it should be placed immediately behind the title page and bound with the report.

Although you should not include your *opinions* in the body of the formal report, you may include them in the transmittal letter. Your specific assignment, your knowledge of the situation, and your relationships with the readers should enable you to determine the extent to which you should include your opinions.

Depending upon the existing circumstances, other types of information may be included in the transmittal letter, which should we written according to the letter-writing principles presented earlier in this book.

REFERENCE MATERIALS

Reference materials, which may include a bibliography and an appendix, follow the body of a formal business report.

BIBLIOGRAPHY.   The bibliography should follow the last page of the body of the report. Printed and duplicated works cited by footnotes in the body of the report should be listed in alphabetical order in the bibliography. Additional references that you wish to call to the readers' attention *may* also be included in this alphabetical list, though including these additional references in the bibliography of a formal report is rarely necessary.

A bibliography that includes a proper presentation of various types of sources of information is shown in the skeleton report on page 388.

APPENDIX.   Instruments (questionnaires, checklists, and so on) used in collecting data for the report should be presented in the appendix, which follows the bibliography. Items such as formulas, illustrations, and other details not absolutely essential to the report text may be shown in the appendix. When several items are included, they should be lettered (Appendix A, Appendix B, and so on).

Presenting the information

The good organization of a report must be supported by other characteristics that make the report clear, interesting, and easy to read. Some of the features that contribute to this type of presentation are headings, writing style, emphasizing techniques, and footnotes.

HEADINGS

Headings contribute a great deal to the readability of a formal business report. They help to show the organization plan that was used in presenting the information, and they help the readers to locate specific sections of the report. The organizational headings *Introduction, Summary,* and so forth are essential in a good report ten pages or longer; they are helpful in many shorter reports.

Upper- and lower-case letters underlined make a simple, appropriate style for typewriting organizational headings. This style is recommended for most reports. The organizational headings should be centered horizontally between the side margins of the page and should be placed 3 spaces below the last line of the preceding paragraph and 2 spaces above the first line of the following paragraph. This heading style is illustrated in the skeleton report which begins on page 367. That skeleton report is presented primarily as an illustration of a good format, though it also contains reminders of the nature of the information that would be presented in each section.

When an organizational heading is the first item following a page number, it should be typewritten three spaces below that number, which is on the sixth space from the top of the page. The organizational heading *Introduction,* which is on a page that contains no number, is 9 spaces from the top of the page (3 spaces below the usual place for a page number).

Subject-matter headings are also desirable features of a report. Appropriate headings that are used freely help the report writer organize the report, and they help the readers understand the report organization. The readers can, by glancing at the organizational and the subject-matter headings, get a good idea of what information the report contains. Headings enable the readers to make quick references to particular parts of the report.

When one subject-matter heading is used under an organizational heading, at least two such subject-matter headings must be shown. *Any division of a report obviously creates at least two parts.*

Provided the organizational headings are referred to as first–degree headings, the two or more subject-matter headings that would be necessary when dividing the information under an organizational heading would be referred to as second-degree (or second-level) headings. These *second-degree* headings are typewritten flush with the left margin of the text and three spaces below the last line of the preceding paragraph and two spaces above the first line of the following paragraph. Often, the first letter of the first and the last words as well as all nouns, pronouns, adjectives, verbs, and interjections are capitalized in headings (see the skeleton report on page 367) . According to one style, the first letter of a preposition of five letters or more is also capitalized. Articles and conjunctions are usually not capitalized.

When the text under a second-degree heading is divided, at least two third-degree headings must be used. *Third-degree* headings are indented the same number of spaces as other paragraphs of the report. Usually, only the first letter of the first word of third-degree headings (except proper nouns) is capitalized. These headings are typewritten two spaces below the last line of the preceding paragraph. They are underlined and are followed by a period and two spaces or a dash. The first sentence of this subdivision of the text follows on the same line with the third-degree heading. Third-degree headings are illustrated in the skeleton report on page 374.

Fourth-degree headings can be shown by underlining the key word of the paragraph. The paragraph should be constructed so that the key word appears early in the first sentence. In the first illustration of a fourth-degree heading in the skeleton report on page 374, the key word *electric* is the third word in the sentence. In the second illustration (also on page 374) , the key word *manual* is the first word of the sentence.

Single words or phrases are preferred for organizational and subject-matter headings; yet occasional use of short declarative sentences or questions may be made. Consistency is necessary, however, within each division or subdivision of the report. Short words and phrases may be used under one organizational heading, as is illustrated in the skeleton report on page 374; and short declarative sentences and/or questions as illustrated on page 383 may be used under another organizational heading within one report.

WRITING STYLE

Correctness, as well as the other fundamental principles of writing any type of business message, is of major importance in your formal business reports. Some writing style characteristics that are quite good for informal messages should be omitted from formal reports. Some of the style characteristics that merit discussion as they pertain to formal business reports are personal pronouns, voice, tense, and contractions. Accuracy in punctuating, in expressing numbers, in constructing sentences, and in paragraphing is essential for any effective business report.

PERSONAL PRONOUNS. First- and second-person pronouns (I, we, me, us, our, ours, you, your, and yours) should be used discreetly if at all in a formal business report. This treatment of pronouns is perhaps the biggest difference between the writing styles for formal reports and for other written communication mediums. Some readers prefer that the writer use these pronouns. Try to find out how the readers of your report react to this usage. If one or more readers object to their usage, use only third-person pronouns (he, she, her, they, them, their, and others).

With some practice, you can limit your pronoun usage to those of third person and still write in a style that does not seem stilted. This formal style requires you to use more passive voice construction than is necessary with informal style; but these sentences can be cast in such a manner that they seem strong, alive, and natural.

Natural expression contributes to the interest and readability features of your writing style.

VOICE. Use active voice (the subject of the verb does the acting) more extensively than passive voice (the subject of the verb receives the action). Using active voice enables you to present information concisely and in a lively style. Sometimes, of course, you should use passive voice because it is the natural style for certain instances; and you should use it occasionally to add variety to sentence structure. Sometimes, too, there is a psychological advantage to using passive voice when, if you used active voice, your statements might be interpreted as an attempt to place blame on a specific individual. To illustrate this point, the following two sentences are given:

> The machine is out of order because the operator left the motor running overnight. (Active voice for the subordinate clause.)

> The machine is out of order because it was left running overnight. (Passive voice for the subordinate clause.)

Use verbs appropriately to help you achieve the objective of the report.

TENSE. For many formal reports you must use past, present, and future tenses. Ordinarily you should use present-tense verbs in presenting research data, as the data are current at the time the report is used. The use of present tense tends to make the report information more dynamic and interesting than would be the case if you used past tense.

For those reports that will probably be read for some specific purpose after the data are outdated, you should use past tense for the sentences that refer to those data. Use present tense for any sentence that will be true at any time in the future. For example, "A description of the motor is on page 8." (The description will remain on page 8 as long as the report is intact.)

CONTRACTIONS. Use contractions in informal communication mediums only. In a formal report write "The report is interesting, and it is concise" instead of writing "The report is interesting, and it's concise."

NUMBERS AND PUNCTUATION. Accuracy in expressing numbers and in punctuating sentences is essential for clear, easy-to-read reports. Some rules for writing numbers and some rules for punctuating are presented in the reference section of this book. Study them carefully.

SENTENCE AND PARAGRAPH STRUCTURE. Cast each sentence so that it can be read easily and will be interpreted properly. Short sentences can be read more easily than long, involved sentences. An entire report made up exclusively of short, simple sentences would be monotonous reading, however; and the contents would be difficult to comprehend. Vary the lengths and the types of sentences in your reports. You should ordinarily include simple, complex, and compound (and possibly some compound-complex) sentences in long reports. You should use some short and some longer, carefully worded sentences so that the *average* sentence length will probably be from fifteen to twenty words. A majority of the sentences should be simple and short.

Paragraphs must be constructed so that they are clear and coherent. A majority of the paragraphs of a report should be short. To help make the report interesting and readable and to emphasize certain items, vary the lengths of your paragraphs. Long paragraphs and short ones should be intermixed in the report. The *average* length of paragraphs may well be from four to eight lines.

EMPHASIZING TECHNIQUES

While useless repetition must be eliminated, some repetition gives needed emphasis to particular facts and figures. Following the frequently used organization of *tell what you are going to tell, tell,* and *tell what you have told* is an example of purposeful repetition. Discussing graphics that are presented in your report is another example of the appropriate ways that you may repeat to emphasize facts, figures, or ideas.

You may also use some mechanical techniques to emphasize specific points in your report. Some of the mechanical techniques that are used most frequently are underlining, indenting, spacing, and numbering.

UNDERLINING.   Words, phrases, clauses, and short sentences that are underlined attract the readers' attention, provided the number of items underlined is limited. The underlining technique would lose its effectiveness if it were used excessively, and such practice would make the report difficult to read. For greatest effectiveness, underlining should be limited to short areas at infrequent intervals in a report.

Examples of the underlining technique for emphasizing are shown in the summary section of the skeleton report on page 371.

INDENTING.   You can emphasize certain facts, figures, or ideas by presenting them in lines that are indented from both side margins of the report. This technique is illustrated in the skeleton report on page 376. You can single space these lines for perhaps even greater emphasis. When several quotations are single spaced and indented in one report, however, the practice of single spacing and indenting from both margins to emphasize a point should be avoided. Because this format is the same as that used for long quotations, readers would tend to think of this material as a quotation rather than as a point that you have emphasized.

NUMBERING.   Numbering and listing items within the text is another mechanical technique that you may use for emphasizing. This technique is illustrated by one spacing arrangement on page 371 and by another spacing arrangement on page 372.

Numbering and listing items provides for easy reference and easy reading as well as for emphasizing.

FOOTNOTES

When you use secondary information, you should use footnotes of some conventional form to cite the sources of your information. You should number the footnotes consecutively throughout the report.

To illustrate a correct method of footnoting various types of sources of information, some examples are given in the reference section of this book. On pages 373 and 387, some footnotes are shown to illustrate the proper placement on the pages of a report.

Footnotes for tables and other graphics were discussed in Chapter 16.

Illustrations of paraphrasing and using direct quotations (both short and long) are in the reference section.

Format and appearance

The report should be planned carefully. A good format not only provides for attractive appearance but it also contributes to readability. Although any one of several formats is appropriate for a formal business report, only one format is described in this book.

For the finished copy of your report, you should give due consideration to the stationery, spacing, pagination, color, duplicating, and binding.

STATIONERY

Typewrite your report on a good quality of 8½ by 11-inch white bond paper. Paper of 20-pound weight and 25 percent rag content is excellent. Good quality stationery enhances the appearance and the durability of the completed report.

Use a typewriter that has clean type keys and is equipped with a dark ribbon. Correct all typewriting errors by erasing and then striking the proper keys. A well-written report that is carefully typewritten on high-quality stationery will represent you well.

SPACING

The report text should be double spaced with one-inch margins at the top, bottom, and right-hand side of each page. Use a 1½-inch left margin so that when the report is bound, the lines will appear to be centered horizontally on the page.

Indent the first line of each paragraph 7 spaces.

PAGINATION

Number each page of the report except the title page and the first page of the introductory section. While no page number should appear on the title page or on the first page of the introductory section, numbers should be assigned to them. Use lowercase Roman numerals for preliminary pages; use Arabic numerals for the text and the closing pages.

Typewrite the page number in the upper right-hand corner 6 spaces from the top and *one inch* from the right edge of the paper. Type the page numbers without using punctuation marks. Punctuation marks would cause the page numbers to be hard to read.

COLOR

You can use color to enhance the attractiveness of your report. Colored graphics help to get the desired attention from the intended readers of your report; and by using color, you can complete this detailed task of preparing graphics in much less time than is required if you shade them. If your report is to be duplicated, make certain that the duplicator will reproduce the colors you wish to use. Otherwise you should shade the areas instead of coloring them.

You may also use a special color for the headings or for under-lining if your typewriter is equipped with a two-color ribbon.

DUPLICATING AND BINDING

You may use any available duplicating method that produces neat, clear copies on a good-quality paper. You may place the finished copies in simple, inexpensive paper or plastic covers. A cover that provides for loose-leaf binding or requires stapling is suitable for formal business reports. If facilities for spiral bind-ing are available, though, you should use spiral binding. A re-port that is spiral bound can be handled easily, and it can be opened so that the minimum of space is required for displaying any page.

Skeleton report

To illustrate the format features that are described in this chapter and to show the order in which the various parts of a formal business report should perhaps be presented, a skeleton report begins on the next page.

ESTABLISHING A SALES AND SERVICE OFFICE
FOR OFFICE EQUIPMENT, INC.
IN S̶C̶I̶O̶T̶O̶ ̶F̶A̶L̶L̶S̶, OHIO
J̶U̶N̶E̶,̶ ̶1̶9̶7̶3̶

A Report Prepared

for

The Sales and Service Department

by

R̶o̶b̶e̶r̶t̶ ̶W̶.̶ ̶H̶o̶l̶m̶e̶s

J̶u̶n̶e̶ ̶3̶0̶,̶ 1973

ii

OFFICE EQUIPMENT, INC.

Calcutta, Ohio

June 30, 1973

Mr. James L. Gordon, Director
Sales and Service Department
Office Equipment, Inc.
Calcutta, Ohio

Dear Mr. Gordon:

. . . .
. . . .
. . . .

. . . .
. . . . (For this particular report the . . . .
. . . . transmittal letter would be bound . . . . .
. . . . with the report.) . . . .
. . . .
. . . .

. . . .
. . . .
. . . .

. . . .
. . . .
. . . .

                              Cordially yours,

                              Robert W. Holmes
                              Analyst

prh

iii

CONTENTS

Page

TABLES

Number

iv

v

Summary

 This study of office machines was made to secure information needed to determine whether or not Office Equipment, Inc., should establish a sales and service office in Scioto Falls, Ohio.

. . . . . <u>calculators and adding machines</u> . . . .
. . . .
. . . .

. . . <u>dictating and transcribing machines</u> . . . .
. . . .
. . . .
. . . .

. . . . <u>duplicators</u> . . . . .
. . . .
. . . .

. . . . <u>other appliances</u> . . . .
. . . .
. . . .

Conclusions

. . . .
. . . .
. . . .

1. . . . .
. . . .

2. . . . .
. . . .

Recommendations

. . . .
. . . .

1. . . . .
. . . .
. . . .

2. . . . .
. . . .
. . . .

Introduction

Purpose of the Study

      This study of office machines was made to secure information needed to determine whether or not Office Equipment, Inc., should establish a sales and service office in Scioto Falls, Ohio.

Research Method

    . . . .

. . . . . (The research method for this study of office machines . . .
      would be described accurately in this section.)
. . . .

Limitations of the Study

    . . . .

. . . .

. . . . . (The limitations of the study may or may not be . . . . .
      tabulated as illustrated here.)
. . . .

      1. . . . .

        . . . .

      2. . . . .

        . . . .

      3. . . . .

        . . . .

. . . .

. . . . (At some point in the introductory section, information . .
      telling who authorized the study should be included.)
. . . .

. . . .

2

Sales and Service Facilities in Scioto Falls

. . . .

. . . . . . (This section would include background information . . . .
          pertinent to the study.)

. . . .

Expected Growth of City, Businesses, and Schools

. . . .

. . . .

. . . . . (This section would include background information   . . .
          pertinent to the study.)

. . . . According to Poe:

      . . . .
      . . . .
      . . . .
      . . . . (A quotation of three lines or more) . . . .
      .¹. . . . . .

      . . . .

. . . . , ". . (A short direct quotation   . . . ."² . . .
                       from the source quoted in
. . . .   the preceding paragraph) . . . .

. . . .

      . . . .

. . . . (Information in this paragraph taken from a . .
                    book but not quoted directly)

. . . .

. . . . .³

-----

¹Ralph Edward Poe, <u>Scioto Falls in Transition</u> (New York: Irwin
Publishing Company, Inc., 1972), p. 38.

²<u>Ibid</u>., p. 61.

³Mary Ellen Holt, <u>Growth of Secondary Schools</u> (Boston: McKinley
Press, 1972), pp. 68-72.

3

. . . .
. . . .

<u>Calculators and Adding Machines</u>

. . . .
. . . . . (This paragraph would include an introduction to the . . . .
topics which follow in this division of the report.)
. . . .

<u>Calculators in Schools</u>

. . . .
. . . .

    <u>Rotary</u>.--. . . . . , ...
. . . .
. . . . The brands of rotary calculators purchased by Scioto Falls schools in 1973 are shown in Figure 1
on page 4.

. . . .
. . . . . (As insufficient space is available for presenting . . . .
Figure 1 here, the discussion of Figure 1 would be
. . . . . presented here.) . . . .
. . . .

    By using <u>electric</u> calculators, the operators . . . .
. . . .

    <u>Manual</u> calculators cost less than . . . .
. . . .
. . . .

    <u>Printing</u>.--. . . . .
. . . .

FIGURE 1

ROTARY CALCULATORS PURCHASED BY SCHOOLS
IN SCIOTO FALLS, OHIO
1973

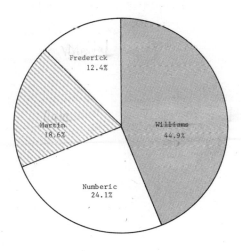

Source: City School Superintendent's Record

5

Key-Driven.--. . . . .
. . . .
. . . .
. . . .

. . . .
. . . .

. . (This mechanical technique for emphasizing . .
    --indenting from both margins--may be used
. . in various sections of the report.) . . . . .

. . . .
. . . .
. . . .
. . . .
. . . .

Calculators in Offices

. . . .
. . . .
. . . .
. . . .
. . . .

Calculators in Scioto Falls offices are classified by age in
Table 1 on page 6.

. . . .
. . . . (This first paragraph of the discussion of Table 1 . . . . . .
    would be presented here; the discussion would be
. . . . continued on page 8.) . . . .
. . . .
. . . .

6

TABLE 1

**CALCULATORS CLASSIFIED BY AGE
IN OFFICES IN SCIOTO FALLS, OHIO
JUNE, 1975**

Brand	Age (years)					
	0-3	3-6	6-8	8-10	10 or over	Total
Add-X	3	2	1	3	5	14
Allison	3	1	4	2	5	15
Buford	1	3	3	3	2	12
Burton	2	2	1	3	1	9
Cal-Q-Late	2	4	5	1	1	13
Clarifier	1	3	1	1	7	13
Countometer	2	1	2	1	5	11
Dividend	1	1	2	2	3	9
Figurefinder	2	2	3	1	2	10
Frederick	1	2	1	4	1	9
Martin	2	2	1	1	1	7
Math-O-Matic	5	3	2	8	1	19
Math-X	2	1	3	1	2	9
Numberic	1	2	2	2	2	9
Observer	2	1	1	1	1	6
Oliver	1	2	3	4	5	15
Plus-Key	1	2	1	3	1	8
Retriever	2	1	3	1	2	9

7

TABLE 1 (continued)

Brand	Age (years)					Total
	0-3	3-6	6-8	8-10	10 or over	
Statistic	3	1	1	1	2	8
Williams	2	2	1	3	1	9
Totals	39	38	41	46	50	214

8

. . . .
. . . .
. . . .
. . . .
. . . . . . The distribution by brand of printing and rotary calculators
in ~~Scioto Falls~~ offices is shown in Table 2.

TABLE 2

PRINTING AND ROTARY CALCULATORS IN OFFICES
~~IN SCIOTO FALLS, OHIO~~
~~JUNE, 1973~~

Brand	Printing	Rotary	Total
Cal-Q-Late	14	12	26
Countometer	14	10	24
Plus-Key	12	11	23
Martin	9	9	18
Oliver	8	1	9
Totals	57	43	100

. . . .
. . . . (The discussion of Table 2 would be presented here.) . .
. . . .

Adding Machines in Offices and Schools

. . . .
. . . .

9

. . . .
. . . .
. . . .
. . . .
. . . .
. . . .
. . . .
. . . .
. . . .
. . . .
. . . .
. . . .
. . . .
. . . .

. . . . Brands of calculators less than ten
years old·are shown in Table 3 on page 10.

. . . .
. . . .
. . . .

. . . . . . (A table or a chart which is only one page or less in . . .
          length must be presented on one page; that is, part
. . . . . . of the table cannot be presented on one page and   . . . .
          part on another page. Because Table 3 is so long,
. . . . . . it is presented on a page by itself; no text material . .
          is presented on that page. This plan is used even
. . . . . . though the discussion of Table 3 was completed in . . . .
          this paragraph.)
. . . .
. . . .
. . . .

10

TABLE 3

ADDING MACHINES LESS THAN TEN YEARS OLD
IN OFFICES AND SCHOOLS IN SCIOTO FALLS, OHIO
JUNE, 1973

Brand	Number		Percent	
	Offices	Schools	Offices	Schools
Frederick	300	100	15.9	12.4
Martin	300	90	15.9	11.2
Math-X	250	100	13.2	12.4
Plus-Key	225	90	11.9	11.2
Numberic	200	80	10.6	9.9
Cal-Q-Late	150*	75	7.9	9.3
Oliver	125	70	6.6	8.7
Williams	125	65	6.6	8.0
Burton	100	60	5.3	7.4
Dividend	90	60	4.8	7.4
Math-O-Matic	5	5	.2	.6
Other**	10	8	.5	.9
Totals	1880	803	99.4	99.4

*This figure includes five 10-key machines; all other machines were full-keyboard models.

**This classification includes no more than two machines of one brand.

382   *Better business writing*

. . . . The types of adding machines purchased by offices and
schools for the five-year period 1969-1973 are shown in Figure 2.

FIGURE 2

ADDING MACHINES PURCHASED BY OFFICES AND SCHOOLS
IN SCIOTO FALLS, OHIO
1969-1973

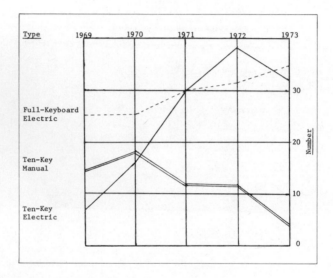

. . . .
. . . . . (The discussion for Figure 2 would be started here . . . . .
and would be continued on page 12.)
. . . .

12

<u>Dictating and Transcribing Machines</u>

. . . .
. . . .
. . . .

<u>The Machines Are Old</u>.

. . . .
. . . . . . (Short sentences and/or questions may be used for . . . . .
          subject-matter headings. Short phrase or one-word
. . . . . . headings are usually preferred, however.) . . . .

. . . .

<u>To What Extent Are Dictating Machines Used</u>?

. . . .
. . . .

<u>Duplicators</u>

. . . .
. . . .
. . . .

<u>Other Appliances</u>

. . . .
. . . .

<u>Typewriters</u>

. . . .
. . . .
. . . .
. . . .

13

Posting Machines

. . . . The brands and number of
each brand of posting machines in Scioto Falls offices are shown as
follows:

Monroe	36
Burroughs	18
Friden	9

. . . .
. . . .

        The yearly purchases of posting machines for Scioto Falls offices
for 1968–1973 are depicted in Figure 3.

POSTING MACHINES PURCHASED BY OFFICES
IN SCIOTO FALLS, OHIO
1968–1973

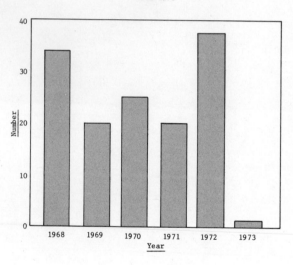

14

. . . .
. . . .
. . . . (Figure 3 would be discussed here.) . . . .
. . . .
. . . .
      . . . .
. . . .
. . . .
. . . .
. . . .
. . . . The data in Table 4 indicate that 66 of the posting machines have
a trade-in value of $500 or more each.

TABLE 4

TRADE-IN VALUE OF POSTING MACHINES IN OFFICES AND SCHOOLS
IN SCIOTO FALLS, OHIO, JUNE, 1973

Trade-In Value (Dollars)	Offices	Schools	Total
0-100	4	1	5
100-200	17	3	20
200-300	15	14	29
300-400	9	21*	30
400-500	5	51	56
500 or more	4	62	66

*One machine has been reconditioned.

15

. . . .
. . . . (The discussion of Table 4 would be presented here.) . .
. . . .

A glance at Figure 4 reveals the brands of posting machines purchased by schools in Scioto Falls in 1973.

FIGURE 4

POSTING MACHINES PURCHASED BY OFFICES AND SCHOOLS
IN SCIOTO FALLS, OHIO, IN 1973

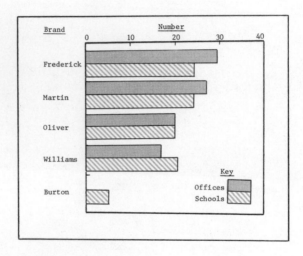

. . . .
. . . (The discussion of Figure 4 would be started here.) . . . .
. . . .

16

. . . .
. . . (The discussion of Figure 4 would be continued here.) . . . . . .
. . . .
. . . .
. . . . (In this paragraph information from an interview is used.) . . .
. . . .
. . . .[4]

---

[4]Interview with Roger Rahe, President, AMS, Scioto Falls Chapter,
May 31, 1973.

17

Bibliography

Accountants' Association. <u>Annual Report of the Planning Committee for
    the Year Ending June 30, 1972</u>. St. Louis: St. Louis Publishing
    Company, 1961.

Bates, Ruby L., and Clark, Marie S. <u>Today's Clerical Workers</u>. 2d ed.
    Hastings: The South-Western Press, 1970.

<u>Cookeville Gazette</u>. June 3, 1972.

Hanson, John W. (ed.). <u>Office Procedures</u>. New York: Irwin Publishing
    Company, Inc., 1970.

Hines, Howard E. "Office Equipment Repairs." Brunswick, Ohio: AMS
    Committee on Maintenance Contracts, 1972. (Mimeographed.)

Holt, Mary Ellen. <u>Preparing for Office Work</u>. 2d ed. Boston: McKinley
    Press, 1972.

Hughes, Harold J., Puett, John W., and Victor, Paul M. <u>Office Organiza-
    tion and Management</u>. Seattle: Prentice Publishing Company, 1969.

"Maintenance of Office Equipment," <u>Equipment Journal</u>, June 14, 1972.

_____. <u>Office Automation</u>. Dallas: Rinehart Publishing Company, Inc.,
    1970.

Poe, Ralph Edward. <u>Scioto Falls in Transition</u>. New York: Irwin Pub-
    lishing Company, Inc., 1972.

Sloan, Walter E. <u>Clerical Workers and Automation</u>. A Report to the
    Second National Conference of the Accountants' Association,
    Kansas City, April 29 to May 1, 1973. Prepared by the Committee
    on Maintenance Contracts. Kansas City, 1973.

Smith, Lynn D. "Office Equipment Problems," <u>Machine Accountants'
    Journal</u>, June, 1972.

Yates, Charles E., and Others. <u>Office Management</u>. 2d ed. Chicago:
    The Macmillan Press, 1970.

18

Appendix

. . . .

. . . .

. . . . . (Such items as instruments used in collecting . . . .
data for the report would be presented in this
. . . . . division of the report.) . . . .

. . . .

. . . .

Questions for discussion

1. Why should the summary section be placed *before* rather than *after* the body of the formal report?
2. What are the advantages of placing visual aids on separate pages rather than on the same pages with the report text?
3. What are the advantages of placing the visual aids on the same pages as the text of a business report?
4. The skeleton report that is appended to this chapter was written from data that were collected by making a survey. What are some other types of situations that would call for a formal report?
5. What are some appropriate ways of including definitions of specialized terms in a formal business report?

Exercises

Improve the following sentences that were taken from business letters.

1. It is the purpose of this letter to inform you of the date of the meeting which will be held in Kansas City on December 11.
2. I should like to thank you for sending the merchandise so promptly.
3. Please correct your error of $25.00 in my account.
4. Please send me a report for the month of September.
5. Enclosed with this letter is a check in the amount of $36.00.
6. In the event that some of the questionnaires are not completed properly, we will have to mail copies to other people.
7. In order to improve the working conditions in the factory, we have appointed a committee to make recommendations.
8. The report will be available in the near future.
9. Do not forget the meeting October 12.
10. I shall appreciate your sending me a confirmation of my reservation by October 11.

Problems

1. Having collected the information that you need to determine the availability of employment opportunities for the co–op students in your business program (see Problem 5, Chapter 15) present

that information in formal report form for the dean of your school. He will appreciate your recommendations for this program that is increasing in popularity among your business students. Use a variety of graphic aids in your report.

2. The chairman of the office administration department of your school is eager to do all that he can to help the students in his department to secure good jobs. He knows that the first impressions that applicants make are important. He has, therefore, asked you to study the procedures that are followed in employing office workers (secretaries, accountants, clerks, and so on) in various types of organizations in your locality.

Collect whatever information you will need and present it in the form of a formal report to the chairman of your office administration department. Use a variety of graphic aids in your report.

Reference section

You SHOULD present your business message in such a manner that the receiver will pay more attention to the content than to any other feature. To present your message that effectively, you must give due consideration to the tone, format, appearance, style of expression, and usage of mechanical details. The information in the preceding chapters is presented to help you enhance the effectiveness of your business messages. To supplement the information that is presented in the text and in the illustrations of this book, this reference section is appended.

The supplementary aids in this section are presented under the following topics:

Punctuating

PERIOD

1. END OF SENTENCE

Use a period at the end of a declarative or an imperative sentence.
Examples:

Examples are given to illustrate the principles.
Illustrate each principle that is presented.

2. ABBREVIATIONS

Use a period to indicate that a letter or group of letters represent a word that is not spelled in full.
Examples:

Mr., Mrs., Dr., No., a.m., p.m., Ph.D., Co., C.O.D., f.o.b.

When several initial letters are used together as an abbreviation for a group of words, such abbreviations can be typewritten in all capitals without periods.
Examples:

ABCA (American Business Communication Association)
ROTC (Reserve Officer Training Corp), AMS (Administrative Management Society)

3. DECIMAL POINT

Use a period to separate dollars from cents in sums of money that are expressed in figures.
Examples:

$7.21, $8.05, $117.32.

4. AFTER A FIGURE

Use a period after a figure that is used to enumerate items.
Examples:

The three letter styles that are illustrated in the reference section of this book are these:

1. Modified block.
2. Extreme block.
3. AMS simplified.

Exclamation point

1. ### Exclamatory remark

    Use an exclamation point after a *strong* exclamatory word, phrase, clause, or sentence.
    Examples:

    Stop!
    Run! The machine is afire!

2. ### Mild exclamation

    Unless the exclamation is very *strong,* use a comma after the word, phrase, or clause and a period at the end of the sentence.
    Examples:

    Well, you have solved the problem.
    You cannot afford to miss the wonderful opportunity.

Comma

1. ### Introductory subordinate clause

    When a sentence begins with a subordinate clause, use a comma to separate the subordinate clause from the independent clause. Do not use a comma to separate the clauses when the independent clause precedes the subordinate clause.
    Examples:

    If the price is low, I will purchase the land.
    I will purchase the land if the price is low.

2. ### Compound sentence

    Use a comma before the conjunction that joins the independent clauses of a compound sentence when a subject is expressed in each clause; but do not use a comma before

the conjunction when the subject is not expressed in the second independent clause.
Examples:

I have tried to state this principle simply, and I believe you can apply it easily.
I stated this principle simply and gave you this sentence as an illustration.

3. SERIES

Use commas to separate items in a series. Although the comma before the conjunction that precedes the final item is not absolutely necessary, including it often contributes to the clarity of the sentence.
Examples:

We have shipped the paper, the books, and the typewriters that you ordered last week.
The businessman may spend the day writing letters, talking with customers, and supervising office workers.

4. APPOSITIVES

Use commas to set off nonrestrictive appositives. Do not set off with commas appositives that are restrictive.
Examples:

Mr. John C. Smith, the company auditor, will present the report.
I believe you will be eager to learn more about the re-surfacing project, a matter of concern to almost all of the residents of our city.
I believe that your son Steve is heavier than his brother.

5. PARENTHETICAL EXPRESSIONS

Use commas to set off parenthetical expressions that tend to cause the reader to pause for that expression. No comma is absolutely necessary if the parenthetical expression would not tend to cause the reader to pause.
Examples:

However, the project will be supported by several civic groups.
A two-thirds majority of the residents, on the other hand, felt that the tax rate was too high.
The consultant is also of that opinion.

6. DIRECT ADDRESS

Use commas to set off a word that is used as a direct address.
Examples:

Sarah, will you please typewrite the letter for me?
I believe, Mr. Salem, that the batteries can be shipped on August 26.

7. INTRODUCTORY PHRASE CONTAINING A VERB FORM

Use a comma to set off an introductory phrase that contains a verb form.
Examples:

Having studied the assignment, he was ready to solve the problem.
To get the most out of your courses, you must study every day.

8. LONG INTRODUCTORY PHRASE

Use a comma to set off a long introductory phrase even though the phrase contains no verb.
Examples:

Within the next seven or eight weeks, we will make some major changes in our office procedures.
Throughout Mr. Charles C. Hamilton's childhood, he was influenced by the writings of his parents.

9. DATES

Use a comma to separate the day and the year when the month, day, and year are expressed. You may also use a comma after the year. Do not use a comma after the day or the year unless both are expressed except, of course, when the comma must follow the day because of some other punctuation principle that is involved.
Examples:

On January 26, 1973, the company adopted the new policy.
On January 26 the company adopted the new policy.
In 1973 the company adopted the new policy.
When you delivered the package to my home on January 26, I was attending a meeting in Philadelphia.

10. ADDRESSES

Use commas to separate parts of addresses that appear on the same line. When the city and the state are given, you may also use a comma after the state.
Examples:

His address is Box 1186, Pinehurst College, Carson, Alabama.
He moved from Hartsville, Kentucky, on September 15.

11. NONESSENTIAL CLAUSE

Use commas to set off a nonessential clause, a clause that is not needed to identify the noun it modifies but is included to give additional information that is perhaps of interest to the reader.
Examples:

The president, who lives three blocks from the office, walks to work each day.
The purchases journal, which is maintained by the assistant bookkeeper, has been misplaced.
The man who drove my tractor last year has accepted another job.

12. SHORT INFORMAL QUOTATIONS

Use commas to set off short informal quotations.
Examples:

The speaker said, "You are good listeners."
When the supervisor says, "I have news for you," we know what to expect.

13. COORDINATE ADJECTIVES

Use a comma to separate coordinate adjectives.
Examples:

He is a courteous, well-mannered young man.
The brightly colored, loosely woven materials are very popular.

14. DIRECT ANSWER

Use a comma to set off the direct answers *yes* and *no*.
Examples:

Yes, I shall be glad to serve on the committee.
No, you will not be required to pay the special fee.

15. TWO SERIES OF FIGURES

Use a comma to separate two series of figures when each figure is so large that it should be written as a figure rather than being spelled.
Examples:

In 1973, 1,818 people voted in favor of the bill.
For a circulation of 5,255, 267 carriers will be needed.

16. OMISSION OF COMMON ELEMENTS

Use commas to indicate the omission of common elements in the second and succeeding clauses of parallel structure.
Examples:

History had an enrollment of 76; English, 87.
Mr. Hartley coached baseball; Mr. Sams, football; and Mr. Holt, basketball.

17. SPECIAL OCCASIONS

Sometimes you will need to use a comma so that the meaning of the sentence can be grasped easily even though using the comma does not conform to any of the preceding sixteen rules.
Example:

Outside, the fresh air is stimulating.

SEMICOLON

1. COMPOUND SENTENCE CONTAINING A COMMA

Use a semicolon before the conjunction that joins the independent clauses of a compound sentence when a comma is used *within* one of the independent clauses.
Examples:

If you will learn punctuation principles, you will be prepared to punctuate accurately the sentences in your communication mediums; and you will also be prepared to help other writers who may seek help on this important aspect of effective writing.

A thorough understanding of the rules of proper punctuation contribute to your self-confidence; and it enhances your ability to write interesting, easy-to-read messages.

2. COMPOUND SENTENCE WITH NO COORDINATING CONJUNCTION

Use a semicolon to join the independent clauses of a compound sentence when no coordinating conjunction is used to join them.
Examples:

The writer applied the principles expertly; he had studied them thoroughly.
They prepared these examples for you; use them advantageously.

3. COMPOUND SENTENCE IN WHICH INDEPENDENT CLAUSES ARE JOINED BY A CONJUNCTIVE ADVERB

Use a semicolon to join the independent clauses of a compound sentence when a conjunctive adverb is used to introduce the second independent clause.
Examples:

He learned that the interest rate had been increased; consequently, he did not borrow the money.
We received the contract for supplying the maintenance services for the office machines; therefore, we must employ an additional serviceman.

4. SERIES

Use a semicolon to separate the items of a series when a comma is used *within* one of the items.
Examples:

The manager ordered two dozen No. 2 pencils; eight reams of 20-pound, 25 percent rag content paper; and two quarts of blue ink.
Within the next seven or eight weeks, the personnel manager will employ a receptionist; four file clerks; and six well–trained, experienced secretaries.

5.   ILLUSTRATION

Use a semicolon to introduce an illustration that is a complete sentence and is preceded by such expressions as *that is, namely, e.g., i.e.,* and *for example.*
Examples:

Each executive must be a good dictator; that is, he must be skilled in dictating well-organized letters in a minimum of time. John's assistant works efficiently; for example, he takes the initiative to make decisions when his superior is out of the office.

6.   ENUMERATION

Use a semicolon to introduce an enumeration in a sentence when that enumeration is preceded by such an expression as *namely, for example, i.e., e.g.,* and *that is.*
Examples:

The interior decorator emphasized the use of the warm colors; namely, red, orange, and yellow.
The speaker elaborated on the four management functions; that is, planning, organizing, coordinating, and controlling.

COLON

1.   SALUTATION

Use a colon after the salutation of a business letter.
Examples:

Dear Mrs. Gray:
Gentlemen:

2.   TIME

Use a colon to separate the hour from the minutes when you express time in figures.
Examples:

8:30 A.M.
4:45 P.M.

3.   QUOTATIONS

Use a colon to introduce a long formal quotation.
Examples:

The contract stated: "For all materials that are provided by the contractor, the owner will pay the purchase price plus 10 percent."

According to Brown:

Today's management trainee who can write clear, interesting, easy-to-read messages has a decided advantage over his peers who do not write well. The student who aspires to succeed in any business occupation must, therefore, spend sufficient time while in school to improve his writing ability.[1]

4. SERIES OF ITEMS

Use a colon to formally introduce a series of items.

Examples:

Please answer the three questions that follow:
1. How many women do you employ between the ages of 18 and 28?
2. What is the average weekly income of the high school graduates that you employ?
3. How many men received a promotion in your organization last year?

Some of the reasons that were given are these:
   Too much time is required to train them.
   A limited number of people applied for the job.
   Only six of the people who applied came for an interview.

5. EXPLANATIONS OR ILLUSTRATIONS

Use a colon to introduce an explanation or an illustration that is an independent clause.

Examples:

The reason for his great success is obvious: he works night and day.

He is an industrious young man: he works from 8 A.M. until 5 P.M. six days a week.

QUESTION MARK

1. DIRECT QUESTION

Use a question mark at the end of a direct question.

Examples:

Have you completed the report?
How much did the machine cost?

2.   COURTEOUS REQUEST

Do not use a question mark after a courteous request that is
stated as a question.
Examples:

Will you please reply before May 19.
Would you kindly send me a copy of the brochure you advertised in the *Cookeville Times.*

HYPHEN

1.   WORD DIVISION

Use a hyphen when dividing a word at the end of a line of
writing.
Examples:

work- ing
plan- ning
under- stand

2.   COMPOUND ADJECTIVES

Use a hyphen to form a compound adjective before a noun
that is modified by that compound adjective.
Examples:

the past-due account
the easy-to-read sentences
a two-week vacation

Note: Do not use a hyphen to join the words that form a
compound adjective preceding the noun it modifies when
one of the words is an adverb that ends with *ly.*
Examples:

the widely recognized authority (*Widely* is an adverb ending
with *ly.*)
a well-known speaker (*Well* is an adverb, but it does not end
with *ly.*)
the assembly-line techniques (*Assembly* ends with *ly,* but it is
not an adverb.)

Do not use a hyphen to join compound adjectives that appear *after* the noun they modify.
Examples:

The account is past due.
The speaker is well known.

3. COMMON ELEMENTS

Use a hyphen with each term for which a common element normally follows.
Examples:

two- and three-week vacations
six-, seven-, and eight-gallon cans

4. COMPOUND WORDS

Use a hyphen to join words that are used as a unit. (Consult an up-to-date dictionary when you question the use of a hyphen for these types of words.)
Examples:

sister-in-law
father-in-law
editor-in-chief

5. PREFIXES

Use a hyphen with some prefixes such as *self-, ex-,* and *re-* (consult an up-to-date dictionary when you question the use of a hyphen for these types of words) .
Examples:

self-confident person
ex-child actor
re-cover the chair (meaning to cover the chair again)

6. COMPOUND NUMBERS

Use a hyphen in compound numbers when they are written as words. (These numbers range from twenty-one through ninety-nine.)
Examples:

twenty-two
forty-seven
ninety-four

7. **FRACTIONS**

Use a hyphen in fractions that are compound adjectives that precede the nouns they modify.
Example:

a two-thirds majority

Do not use a hyphen in fractions that do not serve as adjectives that modify a following noun unless some special construction indicates the need for such usage.
Examples:

Two thirds of the members attended the meeting.
fifty one-thousandths

8. **CLARITY**

Use a hyphen when necessary to clarify the meaning you intend to convey.
Examples:

forty one-thousandths
forty-one thousandths
junior-college course
junior college course

APOSTROPHE

1. **INDIVIDUAL POSSESSION**

To show possession, use an apostrophe and an *s* with nouns that do not end with *s*.
Examples:

the man's car   one year's experience
the manager's office   men's clothing
Mrs. Jackson's assistant   women's apparel
children's playground

Also use an apostrophe and an *s* with pronouns—except possessive pronouns—to show possession.
Examples:

everybody's goals	everyone's desire
anybody's guess	somebody's book
anyone's opinion	someone's pen
one's ideas	nobody's fault

Do not use an apostrophe with possessive pronouns: *my, mine, our, ours, your, yours, their, theirs, his, her, hers, its.*

To show possession, add an apostrophe to plural common nouns that end with *s.*
Examples:

the ladies' lounge	the consultants' attitudes
the girls' typewriters	three years' experience
our boys' bicycles	

Use an apostrophe and *s* to show possession for one–syllable nouns that end with *s.*
Examples:

Moss's store
boss's desk

Use an apostrophe to show possession for words of more than one syllable that end with *s.*
Examples:

Mr. Childress' secretary
Lois' check

2. JOINT OWNERSHIP

Use an apostrophe with the final name only to signify joint ownership of an object or of objects.
Examples:

Harry and Mary's home
Wright and Childress' store

3. INDIVIDUAL POSSESSION

Use an apostrophe with each name to signify individual or private ownership.
Examples:

Harry's and Mary's homes
Wright's and Childress' wives

4. Contractions

Use an apostrophe to form contractions.
Examples:

can't for *cannot*
couldn't for *could not*
won't for *will not*
don't for *do not*

Parentheses

1. Supplementary or parenthetical elements

Use parentheses to set off elements that are included as parenthetical or as supplementary information that is not to be emphasized.
Examples:

In many instances polysyllabic words (including those of a specialized, technical nature) should be used.

When conversing with any other person (employer, prospective customer, client, or colleague), you may use several communication mediums.

A source notation should follow the final footnote (see Figure 3 on page 18).

He learned that one of the three vice presidents (he does not know which one) will attend the convention in Omaha next month.

Note: When a complete sentence is enclosed with parentheses within a sentence, the parenthetical sentence does not begin with a capital letter; and it does not end with a period.

2. Numbers or letters within a sentence

Use parentheses to enclose numbers or letters that introduce items that are given within a sentence.
Examples:

These three principles are emphasized: (1) Write promptly. (2) Determine the purpose of the letter. (3) Keep your reader in mind.

My suggestions are these: (a) Choose your words carefully. (b) Pronounce words correctly and naturally. (c) Enunciate clearly. (d) Use good grammar.

Dash

The most commonly used dash is known as the em dash—represented in typewritten copy by two hyphens.

1. ### Parenthetical elements that contain commas

   Use dashes to set off a parenthetical element that contains a comma.
   Examples:

   Miss Betsy Rayburn—frequently referred to as the most competent, most courteous, and most intelligent member of the staff—will represent us at the convention.

2. ### Abrupt element

   Use dashes to set off an element that is very abrupt.
   Example:

   Most dictation—whether it is to a stenographer or to a machine recorder—should be clear and well organized.

3. ### Appositive that contains commas

   Use dashes to set off a nonrestrictive appositive that contains commas.
   Examples:

   Mr. Kenneth Ross—an intelligent, energetic, conscientious young man who worked for us last summer—is the first person that I thought of as a candidate for the job.
   Those characteristics should be a part of all the well-organized, carefully planned dictation of business messages—letters, memorandums, speeches, and reports.

4. ### Sudden break in thought

   Use a dash to set off a sudden break in thought.
   Examples:

   The owner, the officers, or all of the employees of an organization—provided the total number is small—may sign the card.
   As is true with all other letters, the sentences that follow the beginning—the most important part of a letter—must be good.
   Casual as well as intimate friendships—both personal and business—are strengthened by good public relations experiences.

5. LARGE NUMBERS IN ADDRESSES

When two numbers appear together in the inside address of a letter, use a dash to separate the two.
Example:

126—26 Street

QUOTATION MARKS

1. DIRECT QUOTATION

Use a quotation mark at the beginning and at the end of a direct (verbatim) quotation whether it was originally spoken or written.
Examples:

The personnel manager said, "We need a person who is well trained for this particular job."
"You seem to be well qualified for the job," replied the correspondent.
The personnel manager wrote, "On November 8 we interviewed four men for the job of assistant production manager. Two of the interviewees are well qualified for the job."

When you interrupt a quotation by inserting words, use quotation marks to enclose each part of the quotation.
Example:

"We need a person," said the personnel manager, "who is well trained for this particular job."

When you quote more than one paragraph in a letter or a memorandum, use a quotation mark at the beginning of *each* paragraph and a quotation mark at the end of the *final* paragraph of the quotation.
Example:

Mr. Smallwood had this to say in his letter of April 6:
"We have spent a great deal of time preparing for this program, and we believe that the speakers we have chosen are the best that can be obtained.
"Please encourage the employees in your department to send their reservations before May 15. Cards that they may use to reserve rooms are enclosed."

Use single quotation marks to enclose a quotation within a quotation.
Example:

Mr. Smallwood wrote, "When Mr. Haley replied to my request of April 6, he said, 'Yes, you may use my name as a reference when you apply for employment with the J. C. Burns Company.' "

2. SPECIAL MEANINGS

Use quotation marks to enclose words that have special meanings in the context in which they were used.
Example:

The "Other" sector of the pie chart includes a collection of classifications each of which contains insufficient data to justify individual designations.

3. SUBDIVISIONS OF PUBLICATIONS

Use quotation marks to enclose the titles of articles that appear in a newspaper or a magazine and other divisions such as chapters, units, sections, and parts of other publications.
Examples:

Did you read the article entitled "The Immediate Outlook" in the latest edition of *Newsmonth?*
The June 8 edition of the *Cookeville Gazette* included a story entitled "Children's Outdoor Games."
"The Form Message" is one of the shortest chapters of this book.

ELLIPSES

Use ellipses with a direct quotation to indicate that one or more words have been omitted from the direct quotation. Ellipses can be used in these four ways:

1. *Three* periods at the beginning of a quotation signifies that the beginning of the quotation has been omitted.
   Example:
   The writer said, ". . . he will gladly make the adjustment for you."
2. *Three* periods within a quotation signifies that the beginning

and the end of the quotation are given but that some part of the statement is omitted.
Example:

> His letter stated, "October 28 was the announced deadline, but . . . we will accept the offer you made on October 30."

3. *Four* ellipses at the end of the sentence signifies that the final word or words of the quotation are omitted.
Example:

> He wrote, "Your check for $14 has been credited to your account. . . ."

4. A full line of ellipses signifies that an entire paragraph or more has been omitted from a long quotation.
Example:

> When discussing the problems of moving, Samuels concluded:
>
> Houses that are much larger than the one you described have been moved great distances at apparently economical rates. Two transportation firms would like to have the opportunity to move the house.
>
> . . . .
>
> Further study of the hazards involved should be made before a final decision is reached.[1]

BRACKETS

1. WITHIN PARENTHESES

Use brackets to enclose parenthetical expressions within material that is already enclosed with parentheses.
Example:

According to the representative, the message (we do not know what type of message [letter, telegram, or telephone call] he sent) contained an explanation of his plans.

2. IN QUOTATIONS

Use brackets to enclose statements within quoted material when the statements that are enclosed were not made by the person whose quotation is presented.
Example:

Mr. Ramsey replied, "I refuse to give an explanation for my actions [we do not know the reason for his refusal] in regard to that particular matter."

Spacing with punctuation marks

1. SEMICOLON AND COLON

   Always place the semicolon and the colon *outside* the quotation mark.
   Examples:

   When my administrative assistant was asked to comment, he said, "The problem was solved by our chief engineer"; and he handed the representative a copy of the report that described the solution.
   The names of the following senators were mentioned in the article "Today's Top Brass": Manning, Oliver, and White.

2. COMMA AND PERIOD

   Always place the comma and the period *inside* the quotation mark.
   Examples:

   When the prospect said, "I would have to see it to believe it," the salesman gave him an impressive demonstration of the machine.
   The secretary wrote, "My employer will be in his office again on Thursday morning."

3. QUESTION MARK AND EXCLAMATION MARK

   Place the question mark or the exclamation mark outside the quotation mark when the quotation is *not* a question or an exclamation. Place the punctuation mark *inside* the quotation mark when the quotation *is* a question or an exclamation.
   Examples:

   Did the executive say, "I must have the report before April 26"?
   The clerk replied, "Do you know his favorite letter style?"

I assure you that I did not say, "My secretary opened some of the bids before July 1"!

I heard the receptionist scream, "My typewriter is burning!"

4. **PERIOD WITHIN ABBREVIATION**

Never space after a period that is used within an abbreviation.

Examples:

He earned a Ph.D. Degree at a state university.
They open the office at 8 A.M. each day.

5. **PERIOD AFTER ABBREVIATION**

Space one time after a period that follows an abbreviation.
Examples:

Mr. Allen dictates rather rapidly.
Please send us two boxes of No. 2 pencils.

6. **PERIOD AFTER FIGURE**

Space two times after a period that follows a figure when numbering items.
Example:

The speaker elaborated on these three topics:
1. Profit sharing
2. Markup
3. Discounting

7. **DECIMALS**

Do not space after a decimal point.
Example:

Here is a check for $3.87.

8. **END OF SENTENCE**

Space two times after any punctuation mark at the end of a sentence.
Examples:

We received the order on Monday afternoon. We shipped the merchandise on the following day! I cannot understand why you have not received it. Could it be in your warehouse? I will call the freight line this afternoon.

9. COMMA

Space one time after a comma that follows a word, but do not space after a comma that is used within a group of figures.
Examples:

If you have completed a course in typewriting, you probably know these rules for spacing.
He mailed the check for $12,500 on May 16.

10. SEMICOLON

Space one time after a semicolon.
Example:

We received the order on Monday afternoon; we shipped the merchandise on the following day.

11. COLON

Space two times after a colon except when it is used within a group of figures.
Examples:

The names of the most popular letter styles follow: modified block, extreme block, and AMS simplified.
The plane will depart at 3:15 P.M.

12. DASH

Space one time *before* and one time *after* a dash that is made by striking the hyphen once. Do not space before or after a dash that is made by striking the hyphen twice.
Examples:

The personnel director discussed the problem with his three assistants - Mr. Rains, Mr. Sloan, and Miss Woods - on Thursday afternoon.
The personnel director discussed the problem with his three assistants—Mr. Rains, Mr. Sloan, and Miss Woods—on Thursday afternoon.

13. HYPHEN

Do not space before or after a hyphen.
Example:

Miss Hatmaker is a well-known writer.

14. APOSTROPHE

Space one time after an apostrophe that follows the last letter of a word. Do not space after an apostrophe that comes between two letters.
Examples:

He has had three years' experience in that type of work.
She has had only one year's experience in that type of work.

End-of-line divisions

1. BETWEEN SYLLABLES

Divide words between syllables only.
Example:

prob- lems

Note: Consult a dictionary when you need help to determine syllables. Words cannot be divided between some syllables, however, as is illustrated in the next two rules.

2. BETWEEN ONE-LETTER SYLLABLES

When 2 one-letter syllables come near the end of a line, divide between them.
Example:

situ- ation

3. AFTER A SINGLE ONE-LETTER SYLLABLE

Except for the exceptions that are illustrated next, divide a word immediately after a single one-letter syllable.
Example:

approxi- mate

Exceptions: Divide immediately *before* the single one-letter syllable *a, i,* or *u* when it is followed by the ending syllable *ble, bly, cal,* or *cle.*
Examples:

reli- able
prob- ably
cler- ical
mir- acle

4. MINIMUM OF TWO LETTERS AT THE END OF THE LINE

Leave a minimum of two letters on the line before a hyphen.
Examples:

re- ceive   *not*   a- vail

5. MINIMUM OF THREE LETTERS ON THE FOLLOWING LINE

Divide a word so that at least three letters are at the beginning of the next line.
Examples:

print- ing
print- ers   *not*   print- er

6. HYPHENATED WORDS

When a word is already hyphenated, divide only at the existing hyphen.
Examples:

sisters-in- law   *or*   sisters- in-law   *not*   sis- ters-in-law
self- confidence   *not*   self-con- fidence

7. BETWEEN DOUBLE CONSONANTS

Divide between double consonants except when the suffix *ing* follows a double consonant in the root word.
Examples:

com- merce
plan- ning
call- ing

8. PROPER NAMES

Avoid dividing a proper name; but when a name must be divided, divide only immediately before the last name.
Examples:

Mr. Leon J.	Henderson

not

Mr. Leon	J. Henderson
Mr.	Leon J. Henderson

9. DATES

Divide a date only immediately before the year.
Examples:

September 8,	1973

not

September	8, 1973
Sep-	tember 8, 1973

10. SUMS OF MONEY

Do not divide sums of money.
Examples:

$100,000
   not
$100,- 000

Capitalizing

1. SENTENCE BEGINNINGS

Capitalize the first word of a sentence.
Example:

Our representative will visit your store next week.

2. PROPER NOUNS

Capitalize all proper nouns.
Examples:

Jones, Steinway, Brown, Paz, Dietz

Capitalize words that form a part of a proper name even though these words would not be capitalized when used in other contexts.

Examples:

the Mississippi River	*but* river
the Comer Building	*but* building
Maple Avenue	*but* avenue

Capitalize a word when it is understood that the word refers to a proper name.

Examples:

We toured the University campus while we were in Lexington. (In this context the word *university* refers to a specific university, the University of Kentucky.)

He will enroll in a university next September. (In this context no specific university is designated.)

3. GEOGRAPHICAL AREA

Capitalize words that are used to designate a geographical area, but do not capitalize words that are used to designate directions.

Examples:

We will reside in the South.
They will drive south on Interstate 65.
His accent indicates that he is from the Middle East.
The house faces east and is well shaded by several large trees.

4. SPECIFIC COURSE TITLES

Capitalize specific course titles, but do not capitalize course titles of a general nature.

Examples:

Thirty students are enrolled in Typewriting 132 this term.
Thirty students are enrolled in typewriting this term.
Mary teaches accounting and economics.
Mildred's favorite course is Economics 213.

5. PERSONAL TITLES

Capitalize any title that immediately precedes the name of the person to whom the title refers.

Examples:

The letter was addressed to Mrs. Robert A. White.
The article was written by Professor May.
When Senator Ray spoke to our group on May 6, he outlined the plans for the project.

6. DAYS AND MONTHS

Capitalize the days of the week and the months of the year. Do not capitalize seasons of the year unless the name of the season is personified.
Examples:

They will meet on the first Thursday in October.
The group will meet sometime during the spring.
The winter snows were rather heavy.
When Spring lifts her head for a look at her surroundings, she will see that Old Man Winter has buried his head in the ground.

7. TITLES OF CHAPTERS, ARTICLES, BOOKS, AND PERIODICALS

Capitalize the principal words in titles of chapters, articles, books, magazines, newspapers, and other publications. Conjunctions, articles, and *short* prepositions are not usually capitalized. *Long* prepositions are usually capitalized.
Examples:

Did you read the chapter that is entitled "Safety in Investments"?
I enjoyed reading your second newspaper article, "Planning and Organizing for Purposes of Controlling."
When I read the magazine story "Poise Throughout the Crisis," I was reminded of the book that is entitled *A Crisis at the Office.*

Note: You may typewrite the title of a book in upper- and lower-case letters and underline them, or you may typewrite the book title in all capitals not underlined.
Examples:

J. Fred Rich wrote two books, *Investing in the Stock Market* and *The First Million.*
I read the book A CRISIS AT THE OFFICE last week.

Note: Do not use *both* styles within the same message or publication.

8. **DEITY**

Capitalize each noun or pronoun that refers to the Deity.
Examples:

He thanked the Lord for the many blessings.
The minister said, "Trust in the Lord and ask Him for His guidance."

9. **SALUTATIONS**

Capitalize the first word, as well as titles and proper nouns, in the salutation of a letter.
Examples:

Dear Mr. Haynes:
Gentlemen:
Dear Miss Roberts:

10. **COMPLIMENTARY CLOSINGS**

Capitalize the first word—the first word only—in the complimentary close of a letter.
Examples:

Sincerely yours,
Cordially yours,
Very sincerely yours,

11. **NUMBERS IN BUSINESS PAPERS AND LEGAL DOCUMENTS**

Capitalize numbers expressed in words in business papers and legal documents.
Examples:

Three Hundred Sixty-three Dollars
One Thousand Four Hundred Ninety-two Dollars

12. **QUOTATIONS**

Capitalize the first word of a quotation unless the beginning of the sentence is omitted from the quotation.
Examples:

Mrs. Allen wrote, "The stationery will be shipped on the 26th of June."
Mr. Hunter said, ". . . the merchandise is ready to be shipped."

13.   **PRONOUN I**

Capitalize the pronoun *I* in any context.
Examples:

I will let you know whether or not I can attend the meeting.

14.   **PARTS OF PUBLISHED WORKS**

Capitalize the major parts of books, volumes, documents, and plays.
Examples:

Chapter 3
Volume II
Unit 6
Act III, Scene II
Article V

Do not capitalize *page* when referring to a page number.
Example:

The illustration is on page 6.

15.   **SPECIAL ABBREVIATIONS**

Capitalize the abbreviation for the word *number* when it immediately precedes a figure, and capitalize the abbreviations for college degrees.
Examples:

Do you like item No. 4?
He earned a B.S. Degree at an accredited college.

Numbers

1.   **SENTENCE BEGINNING**

Always express a number as a word when it is used to begin a sentence.
Examples:

Eight players reported for practice on Tuesday afternoon.
Forty-three members voted for the change.

2.   LARGE ROUND NUMBERS

Express large round numbers in words.
Examples:

At least two thousand people attended the meeting.
Do you believe that property will sell for two million dollars?

3.   SMALL GENERAL NUMBERS

Use words to express numbers of a general nature one hundred and below.
Examples:

We ordered eighteen calculators last week.
My secretary transcribed twenty-three letters yesterday afternoon.

4.   STREETS AND AVENUES

Use words for street and avenue numbers that are ten or below.
Examples:

259 East Ninth Street
286 West 22 Street
2911 Tenth Avenue

5.   HOUSE NUMBERS, PAGE NUMBERS, MODEL NUMBERS, AND MEASURES

Use figures for house numbers—except *one*—page numbers, model numbers, and measures.
Examples:

12 Market Street
One Park Avenue
page 3
pages 22 and 23
Model 8
8 by 11 inches
6 feet
8 gallons
32°

6.   PERCENTAGES AND SUMS OF MONEY

Use figures as the preferred way to express numbers for percentages and for sums of money.
Examples:

At least 8 percent of the employees preferred the new model.
Eight percent of the employees preferred the new model. (*Always* express a number as a word at the beginning of a sentence.)
The pencils cost 10 cents each.
You may spend as much as $14 a night for a single room. (Omit the period and ciphers in even sums of money except in a series.)

7.   TIME

Use figures to express time except when the word *o'clock* follows the hour that is specified.
Examples:

The bus will arrive at 3:15 P.M.
He will open the office at 8 A.M.
He will close the office at twelve o'clock on Saturday.

8.   Use figures to express the day when the month precedes the day.
Example:

He will be graduated on June 8, 1977.

When the day precedes the month, use a figure with *st, nd, rd,* or *th;* or use words to express the day.
Examples:

1st of May
2nd of May
3rd of May
4th of May
twenty–second of May

9.   SEPARATE SERIES

When two small numbers appear together and represent different items, use a figure for one of the numbers and a word for the other.
Examples:

4 eight-cent stamps
four 8-cent stamps

Abbreviations

Only a few abbreviations are acceptable for business messages. Those that are acceptable are preferred over spelling in full. Use these abbreviations:

Mr.
Mrs.
No. (when it precedes a figure)
  I prefer style No. 16. *not* I prefer style number 16.
Co. and Inc. in an inside address when writing to an organization that abbreviates these words on its letterhead
The state name in an address when the ZIP Code follows (Only the two-letter abbreviations recommended by the post office are acceptable: AL, TN, TX, WV, etc. *not* Ala., Tenn., etc.)
YMCA, TVA, and other abbreviations for long names when the abbreviations and the names they represent are well known by the recipient of your message.

Spell in full days of the week; months of the year; and words in the inside address of letters such as *avenue, street, road,* and words that indicate direction.

126 North 18 Street

Quoting

In some of your formal business reports, you may wish to use information that has been written in another report or publication. You should in most instances present that information in your own wording. By following this practice, the information you take from another source can be presented in your own writing style; and it therefore enhances the readability of your report. This practice also is evidence that you have studied thoroughly the information that you include.

In some instances you may wish to quote verbatim the information that you take from another source. You should follow this procedure when your quoting in this manner would add strength to your report and when the quotation is especially well stated for your particular writing style.

Whether you paraphrase or quote verbatim, you must give credit to the source from which you have taken information. Give this credit by presenting the information appropriately in the text and by including footnotes in proper form at the bottom of your page. Some examples of paraphrasing and of leading in to quotations are shown next.

The paragraph that follows is an example of paraphrasing information that has been taken from a mimeographed report.

Because the average number of letters written each day by junior executives in the Southeast has risen from seven to eleven, an increase of slightly more than 36 percent, greater emphasis should be placed on dictating efficiency.[1]

A short quotation can be woven into your sentence in some such manner as this: When reporting on the effects of heat and humidity on the operating efficiency of electronic computers, Hayes and Ryan said, "You cannot expect your computer to operate with a high degree of accuracy when it is in a room where the temperature is higher than 80° or where the relative humidity is higher than 70 percent."[2]

The preceding quotation could be paraphrased. A verbatim quotation may, though, add strength to the point you wish to make if the readers of your report consider the authors of the quotation to be experts on the subject.

Quotations of three lines or more should be single spaced and indented from each margin of the page. With this spacing arrangement, no quotation marks are used.

Always introduce a quotation. You may also need to add some comments concerning the information in the quotation. When making these comments, avoid restating the detailed information that is in the quotation. Use variety in the ways you introduce quotations. Some examples of acceptable introductions follow.

---

[1] Talmadge A. Holtzman, "Increasing Correspondence Costs" (Athens: CPS Committee on Reducing Office Expenditures, 1973), p. 14. (Mimeographed.)

[2] Arthur T. Hayes and Leonard P. Ryan, "Housing the Computer Installation," *Machine Accountants' Journal,* April, 1973, p. 27.

When discussing the need for a systems study, Potter said:

The employees of the administrative services department of our organization are well trained. They are also intelligent, industrious, and cooperative; but they have been so closely related to their tasks so long that they naturally tend to think of the current systems and procedures as being the best that can be used.[3]

* * *

Yet, according to Raleigh:

The ideal systems and procedures are yet to be established. In some offices the routine paper work can be handled quite adequately by hand. In other offices the volume of routine work is so great that the use of electronic computers is obviously a *must.*[4]

Ramsey, author of one of the most widely used textbooks in office management, commented on the desirability of systems studies as follows:

Regardless of how intelligent, open–minded, and progressive an employee may be, he cannot possibly keep abreast of all of the technological changes that are taking place today. Employing experts to study the conditions is often necessary.[5]

When you indicate that any statement is a direct quotation, you must use the exact wording and punctuation that the author used.

The footnotes on pages 373, 387, and on this one are presented to illustrate the proper arrangement and the proper placement on the page. Examples of footnotes of various types of sources are presented in the following division of this reference section.

---

[3] Hobart N. Potter, *Office Systems and Procedures* (New Orleans: Wate Publishing Company, Inc., 1972), p. 87.

[4] Dwight O. Raleigh, *Information Handling Systems* (New York: Wilson Publishers, Inc., 1973), p. 281.

[5] John S. Ramsey, *Paperwork Simplification* (New York: Wilson Publishers, Inc., 1971), p. 186.

Footnotes

Some examples are given in this section to illustrate a correct method of footnoting various types of sources of information:

1. ONE AUTHOR:

[1] Ralph Edward Poe, *Scioto Falls in Transition* (New York: Williams Publishing Company, Inc., 1970), p. 38.

2. TWO AUTHORS:

[2] Ruby L. Bates and Marie S. Peters, *Today's Clerical Workers* (2d ed.; Hastings: The Western Press, 1970), pp. 37–38.

3. THREE AUTHORS:

[3] Harold H. Hughes, John W. Puett, and Paul M. Victor, *Office Organization and Management* (Seattle: Prentice Publishing Company, 1969), p. 38.

4. MORE THAN THREE AUTHORS:

[4] Charles E. Yates and Others. *Office Management* (2d ed.; Chicago: The MacDonald Press, 1970), p. 219.

5. NO AUTHOR GIVEN:

[5] *Office Automation* (Dallas: Hartwell Publishing Company, Inc., 1969), pp. 378–79.

6. EDITOR OF A COLLECTION:

[6] John W. Hanson (ed.), *Office Procedures* (New York: Williams Publishing Company, Inc., 1971), p. 416.

7. REPORT—NO AUTHOR GIVEN:

[7] *Annual Report of the Planning Committee of the Accountants' Association for the Year Ending June 30, 1971* (St. Louis: St. Louis Publishing Company, 1972), p. 19.

8. REPORT—AUTHOR GIVEN:

[8] Walter E. Sloan, *Clerical Workers and Automation*, A Report to the Second National Conference of the Accountants' Association, Kansas City, April 29 to May 1, 1972, Prepared by the Committee on Maintenance Contracts (Kansas City: The Conference, 1972), p. 4.

9. ARTICLE IN A PERIODICAL—NO AUTHOR GIVEN:

[9] "Maintenance of Office Equipment," *Equipment Journal,* June 14, 1971, p. 51.

10. ARTICLE IN A JOURNAL—AUTHOR GIVEN:

[10] Lynn D. Smith, "Office Equipment Problems," *Machine Accountants' Journal,* June, 1971, pp. 27–29.

11. ARTICLE IN A NEWSPAPER—NO AUTHOR GIVEN:

[11] News items in the *Cleveland Dispatch,* June 3, 1972, p. 3.

12. MIMEOGRAPHED ARTICLE:

[12] Howard E. Hines, "Office Equipment Repairs" (Brunswick: AMS Committee on Maintenance Contracts, 1972), p. 11. (Mimeographed.)

13. PERSONAL INTERVIEW:

[13] Interview with Roger Rahe, President, AMS, Scioto Falls Chapter, May 13, 1973.

14. SECOND REFERENCE TO A SOURCE:

[14] *Ibid.* [With no intervening reference, a second reference to the same volume and page of Holt's work requires only *ibid.*]

[15] *Ibid.,* p. 73. [Here reference is made to another page of Holt's work.]

[16] Poe, p. 78. [With an intervening reference or references, a second reference to the same volume of Poe's work (see footnote No. 1) must give the surname and the page number.]

State abbreviations to be used with ZIP Codes

Alabama	AL
Alaska	AK
Arizona	AZ
Arkansas	AR
California	CA
Colorado	CO
Connecticut	CT
Delaware	DE
District of Columbia	DC
Florida	FL
Georgia	GA

Hawaii	HI
Idaho	ID
Illinois	IL
Indiana	IN
Iowa	IA
Kansas	KS
Kentucky	KY
Louisiana	LA
Maine	ME
Maryland	MD
Massachusetts	MA
Michigan	MI
Minnesota	MN
Mississippi	MS
Missouri	MO
Montana	MT
Nebraska	NB
Nevada	NV
New Hampshire	NH
New Jersey	NJ
New Mexico	NM
New York	NY
North Carolina	NC
North Dakota	ND
Ohio	OH
Oklahoma	OK
Oregon	OR
Pennsylvania	PA
Puerto Rico	PR
Rhode Island	RI
South Carolina	SC
South Dakota	SD
Tennessee	TN
Texas	TX
Utah	UT
Vermont	VT
Virginia	VA
Washington	WA
West Virginia	WV
Wisconsin	WI
Wyoming	WY

Addresses and salutations for special correspondence

Although there is a trend toward informality in addressing government officials, military and naval personnel, and religious leaders, the forms of addresses and salutations that are used for those people are still somewhat different from those that are used for business personnel. Appropriate address forms and salutations for government officials, military and naval personnel, and religious leaders follow.

PRESIDENT OF THE UNITED STATES

The President   Sir:
The White House   Mr. President:
Washington, D.C.

The Honorable . . . (name in   My dear Mr. President:
full)   Dear Sir:
President of the United States   Dear Mr. President:
Washington, D.C.

VICE PRESIDENT OF THE UNITED STATES

The Vice President   Sir:
Washington, D.C.   Mr. Vice President

The Honorable . . . (name in   My dear Mr. Vice President:
full)   Dear Sir:
Vice President of the United   Dear Mr. Vice President:
    States
Washington, D.C.

CHIEF JUSTICE OF THE UNITED STATES

The Chief Justice of the United   Sir:
    States   Mr. Chief Justice:
The Supreme Court
Washington, D.C.

The Honorable . . . (name in   My dear Mr. Chief Justice:
full)   Dear Sir:
Chief Justice of the United   Dear Mr. Chief Justice:
    States
The Supreme Court
Washington, D.C.

OTHER FEDERAL, STATE, OR CITY OFFICIALS

For any of these officials, you may use The Honorable (name in full) followed by the title of the official.
Examples:

CABINET MEMBER

The Honorable . . . (name in full)
Secretary of . . . (office)
Washington, D.C.

Sir:
My dear Sir:
Dear Sir:
My dear Mr. . . . : (office)
Dear Mr. . . . : (office)

CONGRESSMAN

The Honorable . . . (name in full)
House of Representatives
Washington, D.C.

Dear Sir:
Dear Mr. . . . : (last name)

SENATOR

The Honorable . . . (name in full)
The United States Senate
Washington, D.C.

Sir:
My dear Sir:
Dear Sir:
My dear Mr. Senator:
My dear Senator:
Dear Senator:
My dear Senator . . . : (last name)
Dear Senator . . . : (last name)

GOVERNOR

The Honorable . . . (name in full)
Governor of . . . (name of state)
Capital city, State

Sir:
My dear Sir:
Dear Sir:
My dear Governor . . . : (last name)
Dear Governor . . . : (last name)
Dear Governor: (informal)

MAYOR

The Honorable . . . (name in full)	Sir:
	My dear Sir:
Mayor of the City of . . . (name of city)	Dear Sir:
	My dear Mr. Mayor:
City, State	Dear Mr. Mayor:
	My dear Mayor . . . : (last name)
	Dear Mayor . . . : (last name)

MILITARY AND NAVAL PERSONNEL

Include the following items in the addresses for both officers and enlisted men of the armed forces:

Full title of rank or rating (Colonel, Commander, Sergeant, and so on)

Branch of the service (Ordnance Department, and so on)

An abbreviation for the branch of the service (U.S.C.G. for United States Coast Guard, and so on)

Mailing address

Example:

Commander . . . (name in full)	Sir:
	Dear Sir:
Medical Corps, U.S.N.R. (address)	Dear . . . : (rank and last name)
	My dear . . . : (rank and last name)

RELIGIOUS LEADERS

POPE

His Holiness, the Pope State of Vatican City, Italy	Your Holiness: Most Holy Father:
His Holiness Pope . . . (name) State of Vatican City, Italy	Your Holiness: Most Holy Father:

CARDINAL

His Eminence (given name) Cardinal (surname) (address)	Your Eminence:

ARCHBISHOP OR BISHOP

The Most Reverend . . . (name in full) Archbishop of . . . (or Bishop of . . .) (address)	Your Excellency:

MONSIGNOR

The Right Reverend Monsignor . . . (name in full) (address)	My dear Monsignor:

PRIEST

The Reverend . . . (name in full) (address)	Reverend dear Father: (formal) Dear Father: (informal)

MOTHER SUPERIOR

The Reverend Mother . . . (address)	Reverend Mother: (formal) My dear Mother Superior: (informal)

SISTER

Sister . . . (name (address)	My dear Sister: Dear Sister: Dear Sister . . . : (name)

PROTESTANT EPISCOPAL BISHOP

The Right Reverend . . . (name in full) Bishop of . . . (place) (address)	Right Reverend: (formal) Dear Sir: (formal) My dear Bishop . . . : (last name) (informal)

PROTESTANT EPISCOPAL DEAN

The Very Reverend (name in full)
Dean of . . . (place)
(address)

My dear Dean:

METHODIST EPISCOPAL BISHOP

Bishop . . . (name in full)
Bishop of . . . (place)
(address)

My dear Bishop:

OTHER CLERGYMEN

The Reverend . . . (name in full)
(address)

Dear Mr. . . . : (last name)

WITH A DOCTOR'S DEGREE

Dr. . . . (name in full)
(address)

Dear Doctor . . . : (last name)

RABBI

Rabbi . . . (name in full)
(address)

My dear Rabbi:

For any salutation in this section, substitute *Madam* for *Sir* when writing to a woman.

Frequently misspelled words

Many of the two hundred words that are presented in alphabetical order in this division are frequently misspelled in business messages. None of these words are hyphenated except when they are divided at the end of a line. Although dictionaries separate all syllables, only those points at which the word may be divided at the end of a line are shown in this list.

ac–ci–den–tally
ac–com–mo–date
across
aisle
al–lot
among
ana–lyze
any time
ap–parel
ap–pear–ance
ap–pro–pri–ate
at–ten–dance

bank–ruptcy
ba–si–cally
bib–li–og–ra–phy
birth date
birth–place
busi–ness

cal–en–dar
can–di–date
cate–gory
choose
chose
chro–no–log–ical
col–lat–eral
col–lect–ible
col–umn
com–men–su–rate
com–mit–ment
com–mit–tee
com–pe–tent
com–peti–tive
con–gratu–late
con–science
con–sci–en–tious
con–spicu–ous
con–tin–gent
con–ve–nience
con–vey–ance
cor–po–ra–tion
cour–te–ous

dam–age
defi–cit
defi–nite
defi–ni–tion
de–lin–quent
de–pen–dent
de–scribe

de–sir–able
di–lemma
di–men–sions
dis–crep–ancy
divi–dend

ef–fi–cient
eighth
elec–tron–ics
eli–gi–ble
em–bar–rass
em–pha–sis
em–pha–size
en–thu–si–as–tic
en–velop
en–ve–lope
en–vi–ron–ment
equip–ment
ex–ceed
ex–ces–sive
ex–pe–ri–ence
ex–ten–sion
ex–tra–cur–ricu–lar
ex–traor–di–nary

fa–mil–iar
far–ther
fas–ci–nate
fea–si–ble
Feb–ru–ary
flex–ible
fluo–res–cent
fore–clo–sure
forty
fourth
fur–ther
fur–ther–more

gauge
genu–ine
ges–ture
gov–ern–ment
gram–mar
grate–ful
griev–ance
guar–an–tee

han–dling
height
hin–drance
hono–rarium

il–le–gal
il–leg–ible
il–lit–er–ate
in–ci–den–tally
in–del–ible
in–dis–pens–able
in–evi–ta–ble
in–ter–fered
in–ter–pret
in–ter–rupt
itin–er–ary

jeop–ar–dize

la–bel
labo–ra–tory
le–giti–mate
let–ter–head
li–brary
li–cense
lit–era–ture
loose
lose

main–te–nance
mari–tal
me–dio–cre
mim–eo–graph
mini–mize
mis–cel–la–neous
mis–spell
mo–rale
mort–gage

ne–ces–si–tate
ninety
ninth
no–tice–able

oc–ca–sion
oc–cur
oc–cur–rence

pam–phlet
par–al–lel
par–cel
par–tial
par–tici–pate
par–ticu–lar
per–se–ver–ance
per–sis–tent

per–son–nel
pre–cede
pre–ferred
pre–req–ui–site
pres–tige
pre–sump–tu–ous
preva–lent
privi–lege
prob–able
pro–ce–dure
pro–ceed
pro–fes–sor
prom–is–sory
pro–prie–tor

quan–tity
ques–tion–naire

re–ceive
re–cip–ro–cate
rec–og–nize
rec–om–mend

re–cur–rence
reg–is–tra–tion
re–im–burse–ment
re–mu–ner–ate
re–peti–tive
rep–re–sen–ta–tive
res–tau–rant
re–trieval
ro–tary

sales–clerk
sec–re–tary
seize
sepa–rate
ser–vice–able
simi–lar
sin–cerely
sopho–more
spe–cific
sta–tis–tics
study–ing
su–per–sede

sur–prise
syn–thet–ics

tar–iff
tem–pera–ment
tem–po–rary
ten–ta–tive
traf–fic
twelfth

unani–mous
un–doubt–edly
ut–most

va–can–cies
vacuum
va–ri–ety
vein
ver–ba–tim
vol–ume
vol–un–tary

Confusing terminology

Some words are spelled or pronounced in a manner similar, and in some instances identical, to other words; yet they have entirely different meanings. The wrong word, therefore, is sometimes used. A careful study of the words in the following list will help you to use the proper word for the occasion for which you are communicating. The definitions that are given here are obviously limited. Only enough information has been provided to help you make distinctions in meaning. For a complete definition of any word in this list, consult a dictionary.

This list, although extensive, is by no means exhaustive.

accede	to adhere to an agreement, to give consent	*ad*	advertisement
exceed	to go beyond, to be greater than	*add*	to join, to unite so as to increase
accept	to receive, to approve	*addition*	the result of adding
except	to exclude	*edition*	an issue of a publication
access	ability to enter, to approach		
excess	surpassing limits	*advice*	information
		advise	to give information

affect	to influence	*brunet*	masculine for dark coloring
effect	a result, to bring about	*brunette*	feminine for dark coloring
allowed	permitted		
aloud	with the speaking voice	*build*	(see billed)
		capital	assets, upper-case letter, city
altar	a place for worship		
alter	to change	*capitol*	a building
any way	any of several ways	*ceiling*	overhead part of a room
anyway	regardless	*sealing*	making secure
ask	to call for		
asked	past tense of ask	*cereal*	a grain product
		serial	arranged in a series
assistance	help that is given		
assistants	persons who help	*choose*	to select
		chose	past tense of choose
attendance	the act of attending		
attendants	persons who attend	*cite*	to refer to
		sight	something that is seen
bare	uncovered	*site*	a place
bear	an animal, to support, to produce		
		coarse	large, crude
berth	a bed, a place to rest	*course*	a path, a series of lectures
birth	beginning of life		
		coma	unconsciousness
billed	charged	*comma*	a punctuation mark
build	to construct		
		complementary	serving to complete
blond	masculine for light coloring	*complimentary*	flattering
blonde	feminine for light coloring	*continual*	occurring often but with interruptions
		continuous	without stopping
board	a piece of wood, a group of persons		
bored	affected by boredom, drilled	*conscience*	sense of moral goodness of one's own conduct
		conscious	mentally awake, active
born	brought into existence as if by birth		
borne	past tense of bear (support)	*cooperation*	working with another or others
brake	to retard, to stop	*corporation*	an organization
break	to separate parts		

correspondence	letters	*fiscal*	financial matters
correspondents	persons who write letters	*physical*	pertaining to the body or material
council	a group of persons	*flew*	past tense of fly
counsel	advice, one who gives legal advice	*flu*	short for influenza
		flue	an enclosed passage, a pipe
course	(see coarse)		
		formally	in a formal manner
device	something formed by design	*formerly*	at a time that has passed
devise	to form in the mind		
		forth	onward
die	to stop living	*fourth*	between the third and the fifth
dye	to color		
		foul	not favorable
disburse	to pay out	*fowl*	a bird
disperse	to scatter		
		further	(see farther)
discreet	showing good judgment in conduct		
discrete	individually distinct	*gesture*	a motion as a means of expression
		jester	a clown
disinterested	not affected by		
		hear	to perceive by the ear
disperse	(see disburse)	*here*	at this point
dye	(see die)	*holy*	sacred
		holey	having holes
uninterested	not interested	*wholly*	completely, fully
edition	(see addition)		
		incidence	act of falling upon or affecting
effect	(see affect)	*incidents*	subordinate actions or events
envelop	to wrap		
envelope	a folded paper to enclose a letter	*interoffice*	from one office to another
		intraoffice	within one office
exceed	(see accede)		
		it's	it is
except	(see accept)	*its*	of or belonging to it
excess	(see access)	*jester*	(see gesture)
fair	just, average, light in color		
fare	price of transportation	*lay*	to put something down, past tense of lie
farther	a greater distance		
further	additional		

lie	to recline, a false-hood	*passed*	having gone by, having completed a test successfully
lye	a strong solution	*past*	a former time
lead	to guide, a heavy metallic element	*patience*	a quality of being patient, forebearance
led	past tense of lead	*patients*	persons under a physician's care
lean	to incline so as to re-ceive support, thin		
lien	a claim against prop-erty because of a debt	*peace*	a state of tranquility
		piece	a part separated from the whole
leased	property contracted for use	*personal*	private
least	smallest	*personnel*	employees
lie	(see lay)	*physical*	(see fiscal)
lien	(see lean)	*piece*	(see peace)
loan	money lent or borrowed	*pole*	a long piece of wood
lone	situated apart from other things	*poll*	a questioning of per-sons, a place to vote
loose	free, unattached	*practicable*	possible but not fully tested
lose	to miss from one's possession	*practical*	useful
lye	(see lay)	*preceding*	going before
		proceeding	a transaction, continuing
marital	pertaining to marriage	*presence*	state of being present
martial	pertaining to war	*presents*	gifts
marshal	an officer		
martial	(see marital)	*quiet*	free from noise
		quit	to discontinue
may be	might be	*quite*	completely
maybe	perhaps		
		raise	to lift up
pain	distress	*raze*	to destroy
pane	a compartment of a window	*residence*	a place
		residents	persons who reside in a place
parcel	a package		
partial	a part only, inclined to favor one person or group	*respectfully*	marked by respect
		respectively	each in the order given

right	correct, direction	stationary	fixed, not moving
rite	a ceremonial act	stationery	letterheads, envelopes
wright	a workman		
write	to form words with a pen	suit	clothes
		suite	a set of rooms or furniture
role	a part taken by anyone		
roll	to turn over and over, a list, bread	sum	(see some)
		sweet	pleasing to the taste
sail	a part of a sailboat, to glide	their	possessive for they
sale	act of selling	there	at that point
sealing	(see ceiling)		
sell	to transfer property for a consideration	to	a preposition
		too	more than enough, also
serial	(see cereal)	two	a number
sight	(see cite)	track	a path, a mark left by something that has passed
site	(see cite)		
sole	fish, part of a shoe, the only one	tract	an area
soul	spirit	two	(see to)
some	unspecified amount		
sum	an amount of money, result of adding	uninterested	(see disinterested)
		waive	to forgo
some time	amount of time	wave	to sway
sometime	at some not specified time		
		wholly	(see holy)
stake	a marker, prize set in a contest	wright	(see right)
steak	meat	write	(see right)

Some other words that are frequently misused because of their similar meanings are in the following list:

among	use with three or more (The money was divided equally among the three heirs.)
between	Use with only two, but *at least two* (The money was divided equally between the two children.) NEVER write, "Place a marker between each page."

amount	use with things that cannot be counted (A large amount of water poured over the dam.)
quantity	use with things that cannot be counted (They bought a large quantity of sugar.)
number	use with things that can be counted (A large number of people attended the meeting.)
any	use with three or more (Any of the three salesmen will be glad to arrange a demonstration.)
either	use with only two (Either of the two salesmen will be glad to arrange a demonstration.)
balance	use with financial matters (The balance is due on December 1.)
rest	use with nonfinancial matters (The rest of the work can be done next week.)
each other	use with only two (The two assistants helped each other.)
one another	use with three or more (The three assistants helped one another.)
fewer	use with things that can be counted (The typist made fewer errors on this page than on the preceding page.
less	Use with things that cannot be counted. (The superintendent said there is less water in this lake than in any of the others.)
good	an adjective (The assistant does good work.)
well	an adverb (The assistant works well with others.)
hanged	past and past participle of *hang* when referring to taking a life (The man was hanged for the crime.)
hung	past and past participle of *hang* when referring to an object (She hung the pictures last week.)
healthful	serving to promote health (Cheese is a healthful food.)
healthy	being in a state of good health (Rebecca is a healthy child.)
in	position, used after a verb to indicate movement within an area (My uncle works in a large factory.)
into	to enter, used after a verb to indicate movement from one place to another (When the executive walked into his office, he noticed that a window had been broken.)
majority	use with things that can be counted (A majority of the employees preferred the new plan.)

portion	use with things that cannot be counted (Only a small portion of the work has been completed.)
neither	use with only two (Neither the typist nor the stenographer was in the office when I called.)
none	use with three or more (None of the six clerks understood the plan.)
percent	use after a figure (Almost 8 percent of the office employees attended the meeting.)
percentage	use without figures (Only a small percentage of the office employees have adequate life insurance.)

Stationery

The white 8½ by 11-inch stationery that is described in Chapter 3 is by far the most popular stationery for business letters. Other types that are appropriate for business use are described in this reference section.

SIZE

Some of the advantages of using stationery that is 8½ by 11 inches are these: (1) The letters fit nicely in the standard-size file folders and file cabinets. (2) Stationery of this standard size is inexpensive. (3) The letter can be folded well for mailing in any of the standard–size envelopes. (4) Because the typist uses more stationery of this size than of any other size, she can easily space the message properly on the page. (5) Readers of business messages are familiar with this size and therefore tend to like it.

Some top–level executives of an organization like to use smaller stationery for letters that are short and that will probably not be filed. This type of stationery has the advantage of attracting attention and of making a favorable impression. The attractiveness of a short letter on smaller-than-standard stationery appeals to many readers.

The dimensions of some of the popular sizes of small stationery are 7¼ by 10½ inches, 5½ by 8½ inches, and 8 by 10½ inches.

COLOR

Although white is by far the most popular color, some pastel colors are also appropriate for business stationery. Colored stationery is especially good for sales letters. Letters that are written on colored stationery get attention.

WEIGHT AND QUALITY

The 20-pound stationery is strong enough to be handled easily and to make a good appearance, yet it is thin enough to permit the typist to make clear carbon copies.

The stationery that is composed of 25 percent rag content makes a good appearance, and it is durable. Erasures can be made quite satisfactorily on this type of paper. Other paper that is somewhat lighter and that contains less rag content, or no rag content at all, can also be used for business letters and reports.

LETTERHEADS

In addition to the three essential elements of a letterhead—the name of the organization, the address, and something to indicate the type of organization—other elements may be included. Some of these popular items are department designation, telephone number, names of officers, slogans, and drawings or photographs.

Avoid including so much detail that the letterhead becomes cluttered, thus detracting from its attractive appearance. The following examples seem appropriate:

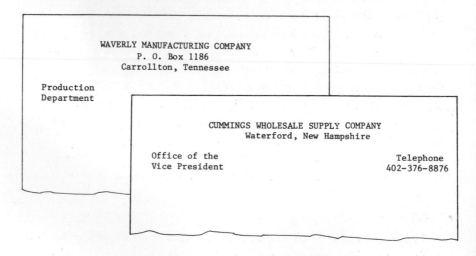

The letterhead style and content as well as the quality of the stationery should be appropriate for the type of organization and the product or service it provides. For example, the stationery for a nonprofit organization or for a small business should be simple in design and of conservative quality. Large organizations that stress quality and prestige should use more elaborate stationery. A resort hotel is an example of an organization that may appropriately use a high-quality stationery (perhaps a linen finish) with a colorful, yet dignified letterhead design. Simplicity in design can be combined with expensive materials to provide stationery of the highest quality.

A sporting goods business, a chewing gum company, or some other organization that handles products that are used in informal situations would wisely choose an informal design for its letterhead.

Letter formats

As was stated in Chapter 3, only one letter format was presented in the text so that more attention could be devoted to letter content, organization, and writing style. The letter format —modified block without paragraph indentions—that was described in Chapter 3 is as popular as any other format. Other formats, however, merit illustration in this reference section.

These four formats are illustrated on pages 447–450: (1) modified block with paragraph indentions, (2) full block, (3) AMS simplified, and (4) hanging indentions.

MODIFIED BLOCK WITH PARAGRAPH INDENTIONS

For the modified block format with paragraph indentions, the return address (when no letterhead is used), the date, and the closing lines begin at the horizontal center. All other lines begin at the left margin, except the first line of each paragraph, which is indented 5 spaces.

FULL BLOCK

When you use the full block format, you must begin each line (date, inside address, closing lines, and so on) at the left margin.

This format, which enables the typist to save the time that is required for indenting lines when using some other formats, is increasing in popularity.

AMS SIMPLIFIED

In addition to beginning each line at the left margin, further simplification is evident in the AMS simplified format by the omission of the conventional salutation and the complimentary closing. Even though this format enables the typist to save much time, its use has not become widespread because some readers object to the omission of the salutation and the complimentary closing.

When you do use this format, include a subject line and plan the contents of your letter so that you use the receiver's name in the opening sentence.

HANGING INDENTIONS

The use of the hanging indention format is usually reserved for attention-getting messages such as sales letters. This format obviously requires more work of the typist than is required by the other formats illustrated in this section. This unusual arrangement does, however, attract attention.

Multiple-page Letters

The second page of a multiple–page letter should contain these three items of information: the addressee's name, the page number, and the date. These items should begin about seven spaces from the top and should be followed by a triple space before the body of the letter is continued. These three items may be arranged vertically, as in the illustration on page 453 or horizontally, as on page 454. Either arrangement is acceptable for the formats that have indented opening and closing lines. The vertical arrangement (see page 453) would obviously be more appropriate for the full block or the AMS simplified formats.

These three items should also be shown at the top of the third and each succeeding page for the *rare* letters that are longer than two pages.

LINCOLN UNIVERSITY
Harrodsburg, Kentucky

April 12, 1973

Mr. Herbert T. Raines
Professor of Marketing
Canyon State College
Canyon Park, Arizona

Dear Mr. Raines:

Subject: Printing Services

After you and I talked on the telephone yesterday morning,
one of my former students, Michael R. Taylor, came by my office
for a short visit. He told me that he and his brother opened a
print shop in Phoenix last month. He worked part time in a
print shop while he was in college.

Mike is very much interested in talking with you about the
brochure that you are planning to prepare to publicize your new
marketing program. He will be in Canyon Park next week and will
call you for an appointment and will bring some samples of the
printing he has done.

I believe that you will be favorably impressed by his work.

Cordially yours,

John M. Walters

John M. Walters
Assistant Professor

/cjc

Modified block style
with paragraph indentions

A REGION OF THE

Southern Business Education Association

April 23, 1973

Miss Rubye Nell Blair
Willard Manufacturing Company
234 South Central Avenue
Holiday, NY 10521

Dear Miss Blair:

We should be very glad to have you exhibit your materials at
the annual convention of the Southern Business Education Association. That convention will be held during the Thanksgiving
holidays at the Regency-Hyatt House in Atlanta, Georgia.

For the details on arranging exhibit space, please write to
Dr. Basil O. Sweatt, Treasurer, Southern Business Education
Association, Southeastern Louisiana College, Hammond, LA 70401.

Cordially yours,

William H. Bonner

William H. Bonner
President

dbf

President . . . . William H. Bonner, Tennessee Technological University, Cookeville, TN 38501
President-Elect . . . . Lois Frazier, Meredith College, Raleigh, NC 27602
Vice-President . . . . Margarett Huggins, Belhaven College, Jackson, MS 39202
Secretary . . . . Juanita B. Parker, West Virginia Wesleyan College, Buckhannon, WV 26201
Treasurer . . . . Basil O. Sweatt, Southeastern Louisiana College, Hammond, LA 70401
Membership Director . . . . Nancy Langley, Ahrens Trade High School, Louisville, KY 40202
Editor . . . . Max R. Carrington, Florence State University, Florence, AL 35630
Past-President . . . . Wilson Ashby, University of Alabama, University, AL 35486

Officers

Full block

LINCOLN UNIVERSITY
Harrodsburg, Kentucky

April 12, 1973

Mrs. Mary B. Reece
Assistant Personnel Director
Dobbs Manufacturing Company
P. O. Box 8417
Bloomington, Virginia

SAMPLE OFFICE FORMS

I thank you, Mrs. Reece, for sending me sample copies of the
forms that you use in your office. They will be excellent illustrations of some of the points that I shall cover in the unit on
forms design.

Our two seniors, Margaret Holford and Shirley Harris, whom you
interviewed yesterday for stenographic jobs are very enthusiastic
about the possibilities of working for you. As I mentioned when
you were here last week, they are two of our best students this
year.

Please come by to visit with us again the next time you are in
this section of the state.

Samuel E. Rogers
SAMUEL E. ROGERS

gsk

AMS simplified

THE FURNITURE STORE
1346 Market Street
Purdy, Missouri 65734

April 12, 1973

Mrs. Herbert L. Milton
Apartment 415
Crystal Towers
Columbus, Missouri

Dear Mrs. Milton:

Do you need a new chair? table? or some other piece of furni-
    ture for your home? We're having a special sale that
    will begin on June 10 and will continue through June 20.

The prices for all of our chairs, tables, and lamps have been
    reduced at least 15 percent. The price reductions for
    some of the sofas, bedroom suites, and dining room suites
    have been reduced as much as 20 percent.

We have a large variety of styles and colors from which you can
    choose, and any of our salesclerks will be happy to help
    you in any way that they can to make your selections.

Come in any day between 9 a.m. and 6 p.m.

                        Cordially yours,

                        Robert L. Knowlton
                        Robert L. Knowlton

tso

Hanging indentions
(Used primarily for sales letters)

N B E A

A REGION OF THE

Southern Business Education Association

Organized 1922

April 12, 1972

Dr. Robert B. Comer
Director of Educational Relations
Radford Research Institute
126 Frederick Street
New York, NY 10031

Dear Dr. Comer:

Here are the answers to the questions you asked in your letter of April 10 concerning the leadership development seminar for the Southern Business Education Association.

1. You can choose the hours for beginning and ending the seminar. Beginning registration at 8:30 and the seminar at 9:00 has worked well in the past; and as you suggested these times in your letter, perhaps they are the best we could use.

   As you will notice when you look at the enclosed copies of the previous programs, the closing time has varied. Please feel free to close at any time that is most appropriate for what you want to cover. We do not want to shortchange you on time; neither do we want to overburden you with an excessive amount of time.

2. For each of the two earlier seminars, we have had 36 official participants (3 from each of the 12 states in this region); and the members of the executive board and a few visitors have also attended. The total last year was about 55. I suspect we will have about the same number this year.

3. I hope to know by the end of September the names of the 36 official participants, and of course I already know the names of the executive board members who will probably attend. In the past we have not known the names of some of the participants until the day of the seminar. That could be the situation for some of the people again this year.

President .... Dr. Lois Frazier, Meredith College, Raleigh, NC 27611
President-Elect .... Mrs. Margarett Huggins, Belhaven College, Jackson MS 39202
Vice-President .... Dr. Basil O. Sweatt, Southeastern Louisiana College, Hammond, LA 70401
Secretary .... Mrs. Juanita B. Parker, West Virginia Wesleyan College, Buckhannon, WV 26201
Treasurer .... Dr. Max R. Carrington, Florence State University, Florence, AL 35630
Membership Director .... Dr. Jean Voyles, Georgia State University, Atlanta, GA 30303
Editor .... Dr. Sara Anderson, Marshall University, Huntington, WV 25701
Past-President .... Dr. William H. Bonner, Tennessee Technological University, Cookeville, TN 38501

Officers
1972

Punctuation styles

Use conventional punctuation for the body of any business message. The opening and the closing lines of the letter may be punctuated according to two styles, *open* and *mixed*. Because of its popularity, the *mixed* punctuation style has been used in each illustration in this book. For this style a colon follows the salutation, and a comma follows the complimentary closing.

For the *open* punctuation style, no punctuation mark follows the salutation *or* the complimentary closing.

A third punctuation style, *closed,* is used so infrequently that it is not explained in this book.

Special notations

Occasionally, a letter should bear some special notation such as CONFIDENTIAL. Any notation of this type may be placed in any conspicious position. You should, however, place it so that it does not detract from the good appearance of the letter.

A postscript is sometimes added to a letter. The original use of the postscript was the inclusion of ideas that had been inadvertently omitted from the body of the letter or an idea that occurred to the writer after the letter had been dictated. The postscript is still used for these reasons, and it is used also to highlight an idea. Because it is short and in a position that causes it to stand out from the rest of the message, it gets special attention from the readers.

The postscript abbreviation (P.S.) may or may not be used. Two ways of presenting a postscript are illustrated on pages 453 and 454.

Dr. Robert B. Comer
Page 2
April 12, 1973

You have complete freedom in planning this seminar. I am enclosing
copies of the previous programs merely to let you know what has been
done earlier. I believe no two seminars should be alike.

Please send me one of your photographs for use in the convention PROGRAM.
The SBEA president would like to have the PROGRAM materials ready to send
to the printer by May 15. Can you send me the photograph before that
time? I will forward it to her.

I'll help you in any way that I can in conducting this seminar.

                    Cordially yours,

                    William H. Bonner
                    William H. Bonner
                    Past-President

dbf

Enclosures 2

P.S. A single room has been reserved for you at the Ridgeway Hotel for
Tuesday and Wednesday nights, November 21 and 22.

Dr. Robert B. Comer   2   April 12, 1973

You have complete freedom in planning this seminar. I am enclosing
copies of the previous programs merely to let you know what has been
done earlier. I believe no two seminars should be alike.

Please send me one of your photographs for use in the convention PROGRAM.
The SBEA president would like to have the PROGRAM materials ready to send
to the printer by May 15. Can you send me the photograph before that
time? I will forward it to her.

I'll help you in any way that I can in conducting this seminar.

                          Cordially yours,

                          William H. Bonner
                          William H. Bonner
                          Past-President

dbf

Enclosures 2

A single room has been reserved for you at the Ridgeway Hotel for Tuesday
and Wednesday nights, November 21 and 22.

On some occasions you may wish to send a carbon copy of your letter to an interested person. Usually, you would like the person to whom you are writing the letter to know that you are sending a carbon copy to the other person. In that case you should typewrite two spaces below the last notation on the page the letters *cc* followed by the name of the person who is to receive the carbon copy. This technique is illustrated as follows:

```
                                 Cordially yours,

                                 Ralph M. Turner
                                 Ralph M. Turner

        bfr

        Enclosures 4

        cc  Mr. Aaron B. Kemp
```

In some instances you may prefer that the person to whom you are writing the letter not know that you are sending a carbon copy to another person. In such a case you would omit the carbon copy notation from the original, but would typewrite the letters *bcc* (meaning blind carbon copy) on the carbon copies only. This technique is illustrated as follows:

```
                                 Cordially yours,

                                 Ralph M. Turner
                                 Ralph M. Turner

        bfr

        Enclosures 4

        bcc  Mr. Aaron B. Kemp
```

Folding letters

The most frequently used methods of folding letters are described in Chapter 3. Two other methods (overlap and back fold) are described here for folding letters to be mailed in No. 10 envelopes.

OVERLAP

Only *two* creases are needed for folding a letter by this method. *First,* place the letter "face up" on the desk and bring the bottom edge of the letter up toward the top edge so that slightly more than one third of the page is left uncovered, as in the following illustration.

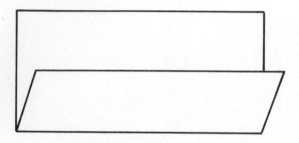

Crease the letter at this point. *Second,* bring the top edge of the letter down over the bottom one third of the letter that has already been creased. The top edge should overlap the first crease by about one quarter of an inch. Hold the top edge in this position as you make the second and final crease in the letter, as in the following illustration.

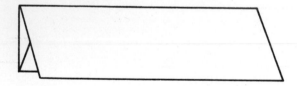

The folded letter is now slightly smaller than a No. 10 envelope and can, therefore, be easily placed into the envelope.

BACK FOLD

Only *two* creases are needed for folding a letter by this method. *First,* place the letter "face up" on the desk and bring the bottom edge of the letter up toward the top edge so that approximately one third of the page is left uncovered, as in this illustration.

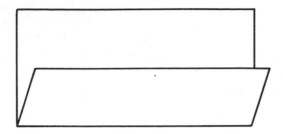

Crease the letter at this point. *Second,* turn the top edge of the letter backward so that this edge touches the crease that you have already made. Hold the top edge in this position as you make the second and final crease in the letter, as in this illustration.

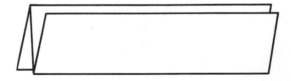

The folded letter is now slightly smaller than a No. 10 envelope and can, therefore, be easily placed into the envelope. This method of folding may be used when mailing a letter in any type of No. 10 envelope; it is the required folding style for mailing in a window envelope unless an address slip is also inserted into the envelope.

Memorandum formats

Several formats can be used for memorandums. A popular, easy–to–typewrite format is illustrated in Chapter 14 and two other formats are illustrated on the following page. Any of these formats may be used for this informal interoffice communication medium.

MEMORANDUM

TO: Mr. Byron E. Lloyd, Sales Manager

FROM: Larry M. Wainwright *Lm.w.*

DATE: April 18, 1973

SUBJECT: Meeting for Sales Representatives

        Please call a meeting of our sales representatives for 3 p.m.
on Friday, May 1. That date is the earliest time that I can meet with
the group to discuss the two new products that you asked me to discuss
with them.

        Let's meet in the Executive Conference Room.

/lbd

Memorandum

To: Mrs. Elizabeth J. Woodall

From: Barry C. White *Bew.*

Date: April 18, 1973

Subject: Reorganization of Stenographic Pool

Go ahead with the plans you outlined in your memorandum of April 17 for
reorganizing the stenographic pool. Mr. Hill has assured me that all of
the new equipment will be installed before June 1.

/kjd

Interview suggestions

When your job application letter and your résumé impress the reader enough to cause him to invite you to go for an interview, you can consider your initial job-getting step—preparing the letter and the résumé—as being successful. To obtain the job you are seeking, you must continue to put your best foot forward. The impression you make in the personal interview will carry a great deal of weight in determining whether or not you obtain the job for which you are applying.

No two job interviews are identical, yet all of them have some similar characteristics. Although no set of instructions can be written that will prepare you for every situation that may arise, some suggestions can be made. You may wish to use the suggestions that follow:

1. Dress appropriately. A man should wear a coat and a tie. A woman should wear whatever attire seems appropriate for work in an office. All clothing must be clean and well pressed. Your shoes must be polished, and they should have heels that are in good condition. Your hair style must be appropriate. Good grooming is essential for a successful job interview.

2. Learn all you can about the organization before you go for the interview. This knowledge will help you to relax and to develop self–confidence as well as to answer some of the questions that may be asked.

3. Take a pen with you so that you will be prepared to fill out an application form if you are asked to do so. Know your social security number. Be sure to give the proper date of your birth. Many applicants inadvertently give the current year instead of the year of birth. Making such an error is easily understood, but it does not supply the needed information.

4. If you expect to be asked to take a test, take the materials with you that you will need for the test. For example, an applicant for a stenographic or a secretarial job should take a pen, a notebook, a typewriting eraser, and a pocket dictionary.

5. Always go alone to the interview unless you are requested to bring your wife or husband with you. Many prospective employers ask applicants to bring their wives with them. The wife will not be expected to remain throughout the interview; some

activity will be planned for her while the husband continues with the interview.

6. Arrive at the interviewer's office about five or ten minutes before time for the interview. Arriving more than ten minutes early may cause the interviewer to believe that you are nervous; arriving late would certainly create a poor impression.

7. When you introduce yourself to the receptionist, tell her the name of the person you have come to see and identify the job for which you are to be interviewed.

8. As you wait in the reception area, you may read the company publications that are provided there; or you may write notes on cards or paper that you have taken with you. By engaging in some such appropriate activity, you appear to feel at ease.

9. Shake hands with the interviewer. A firm handshake is impressive. You can shake his hand firmly without squeezing it so hard that you cause him to believe that you are nervous. Prospective employers often choose to shake hands with a woman applicant even though she may not have offered her hand first.

10. Stand until the interviewer invites you to sit down. He will probably indicate the place for you to sit if there are more than two chairs (his and a guest's) in the office.

11. Relax and show self–confidence without appearing to be overconfident. Some anxious feeling is to be expected. To relax so that your anxiousness is not obvious, take a few deep breaths before entering the interviewer's office. Being well groomed and knowing a good deal about the organization to which you are applying for a job will also help you to relax and feel self–confident.

12. Wait about smoking until the interviewer has invited you to smoke. If you smoke, be sure to use the ash tray rather than let the ashes fall elsewhere.

13. Use good posture. Good posture will help you to feel more at ease, and it will help you to create a favorable impression.

14. Look at the interviewer. Although you will not be expected to look directly into his eyes throughout the interview, your doing that part of the time will indicate good character.

15. Let the interviewer guide the interview, but do more talking than giving simple "yes" and "no" answers to his questions. He will want to hear you talk.

16. The interviewer's desk is for *his* use. Your placing something on it unless you are asked to do so would be a breach of business etiquette.

17. Remain cool about any controversial points that may be mentioned during your interview.

18. Negative comments about former employers, teachers, or colleagues would probably cause the interviewer to form a poor opinion of you. Omit such comments.

19. Be prepared to answer questions concerning your ambitions, your reasons for desiring to work for the particular organization to which you are applying, and the salary you expect to receive if you are employed. Before the interview study the local conditions so that you will know what to expect for various types of expenses. Also, learn as much as you can about salaries that are paid by other groups for the kind of work you would do, and learn as much as you can about local salaries for jobs that are comparable to the one for which you are applying.

20. When you have questions that have not been answered, ask them near the end of the interview. Usually, the interviewer asks if you have questions.

21. Leave when the interviewer indicates through comments or gestures that he is ready to terminate the interview. Shake hands with him and thank him for interviewing you.

Index

This text has been set in 11 and 10 point Baskerville, leaded two points. Chapter numbers are 30 point Scotch Roman italic, and chapter titles are 18 point Scotch Roman italic. The size of the type page is 26 x 43½ picas.